TRAL AND THE CHURCH

"Faith then cometh by hearing; and hearing by the word of Christ."

—Romans 10:17

TRADITION
AND
THE CHURCH

By

Msgr. George Agius, D.D., J.C.D.

"But there are also many other things which Jesus did; which, if they were written every one, the world itself, I think, would not be able to contain the books that should be written." —John 21:25

TAN BOOKS AND PUBLISHERS, INC.
Rockford, Illinois 61105

Nihil Obstat: Rev. Paul Waldron
Censor

Imprimatur: ✠ Francis J. Beckman, D.D.
Bishop of Lincoln
March 28, 1928

Copyright © 1928 by The Stratford Company, Boston. Re-typeset and republished, with minor revisions (primarily punctuation) for clarity, by TAN Books and Publishers, Inc., in 2005. Revisions copyright © 2005 by Thomas A. Nelson.

ISBN 0-89555-821-1

Cover image of a statue of St. Peter seated and holding the Keys typical of similar statues placed at the front of the Catholic cathedral church buildings: By arrangement with www.AgnusImages.com.

Printed and bound in the United States of America.

TAN BOOKS AND PUBLISHERS, INC.
P.O. Box 424
Rockford, Illinois 61105

2005

"Therefore, brethren, stand fast; and hold the traditions which you have learned, whether by word, or by our epistle."

—*2 Thessalonians* 2:14

Foreword
To the Second Edition

MONSIGNOR George Agius was born on January 10, 1873 on the island of Gozo—a 40-square mile island with 30,000 inhabitants in the central Mediterranean Sea about three and one-half miles off shore to the northwest of the island of Malta.[1] He studied at the Jesuit Seminary on Gozo and was ordained in 1895 by Bishop Camilleri for that diocese. In 1897, he entered the Gregorian University in Rome and by 1901, Father Agius had earned two doctorates—one in Theology and the other in Canon Law.

One of his classmates at the Gregorian University was Father Eugenio Pacelli, who later became Pope Pius XII (1938-1958). Fr. Agius observed, "While I was a student at the Pontifical University, I never thought I was sitting on the same bench with a future successor to Saint Peter." Shortly after Father Agius completed his doctoral studies in Canon Law, he received a letter from Bishop Thomas A. Bonacum, the first bishop of Lincoln, Nebraska, offering him the position of secretary and chancellor for the Diocese of Lincoln. Having accepted this offer, Fr. George Agius arrived in Lincoln in September of 1902 and imme-

1. Biographical information was taken from *A Priest Forever* (Sr. Loretta Gosen, C.PP.S. The Catholic Chancery Press, Lincoln, Nebraska, 1988) and "A Glimpse of Our Heritage" (as found in the *Southern Nebraska Register,* by Sr. Loretta Gosen, June 2, 1995 through July 28, 1995).

diately assumed his duties as Secretary and Chancellor for the Diocese.

Father Agius continued to serve as Secretary and Chancellor for the Diocese of Lincoln for ten years. In addition to his administrative responsibilities, he had several pastoral responsibilities which included, among others, the assignment by Bishop J. Henry Tihen as resident pastor in Seward, which is the town in which the modern-day seminary, St. Gregory the Great, is located. After being pastor at Seward, Fr. Agius was transferred to Geneva, Nebraska in 1916, where he was able to devote time to study and research, in addition to caring for the spiritual needs of his parishioners. The purpose of his study was to define and then help meet some of the challenges that confronted the Church in the 1920's. He observed that the authority of the Church was being rejected, some of her doctrines were being "thrown to the wind," and some people were denying the divinity of Christ. It was during this time that Fr. Agius wrote *Tradition and the Church,* which was originally published in 1928. Testimonies on the depth of thinking demonstrated in this book were numerous. These praises came from the hierarchy, as well as from editors of newspapers and periodicals. Bishop Beckman wrote: "Dr. Agius takes a place alongside other leaders in the realm of Catholic thought and joins them in the noble effort of presenting the claims of the Catholic Church to a generation that can be saved by nothing else."

After serving for more than 18 years in the Diocese of Lincoln, Father Agius decided to seek permanent status as a priest of that diocese. Accordingly, he requested his *exeat* (official release) from his native Diocese of Gozo and was incardinated into the Diocese of Lincoln in 1921. In 1937, Fr. Agius was given the title of Monsignor. He was later the official representative of the Lincoln Diocese at the proclamation of the dogma of the Assumption of the Blessed Virgin Mary on November 1, 1950.

As a former classmate of Pope Pius XII, he enjoyed the privilege of a special place near the throne of the Holy Father. After serving as a priest for 67 years, Msgr. Agius died on March 6, 1962 and was buried on the island of Malta, in the same year which saw the beginning of Vatican Council II.

This book is one of the best texts written in English on Tradition, even though originally it did not enjoy a large circulation. It is understandable to the average layman, yet it provides a solid historical and doctrinal coverage of the basics of the theology of Tradition. The publishing of this book by TAN comes at an important time in the life of the Church when many are seeking a greater understanding of the entire subject of the Catholic Church. Those seeking a basic understanding of the Tradition of the Church—unencumbered by the influences of Modernism—would be well served to read this book. It is, therefore, my hope that *Tradition and the Church* will become widely circulated and known everywhere by the Faithful.

Fr. Chad A. Ripperger, F.S.S.P., Ph.D.
Our Lady of Guadalupe Seminary
Denton, Nebraska—September 3, 2005

Publisher's Preface
About This Book

CATHOLICS have all heard that the sources of our Faith are Scripture and Tradition. It is pretty easy to know what Scripture is, but Tradition is another story. Most Catholics have had only a vague idea of what Catholic Tradition really means and exactly what all is included in this concept. *Tradition and the Church*, however, will cure this problem, answering most of the questions that might arise regarding the nature of Catholic Tradition and how it works on a practical level. Before reading this book, most readers might think Tradition is a completely *oral* transmission of those truths we hold which are not specifically included in the Bible. This is partly true, but there is a whole lot more involved.

In this book, Msgr. George Agius has centered his discussion largely around what the Fathers of the Church have written about the faith of the Catholic Church in the early centuries of Christianity. Their writings, compiled into one edition, amount to a very large encyclopedia-sized set of volumes—perhaps somewhat larger than the biggest set of encyclopedia books in print today. And yet the Fathers of the Church have not recorded in writing *every* aspect and phase of Catholic faith. What they *have* recorded, however, is of inestimable value to the Church and to posterity, for they wrote against the early adversaries of the Catholic Church, starting already in the First Century. When problems or disputes arose as to what is proper Christian teaching on any given point, various eminent Catholic writers would refute these errors with their writings. Those men have come to be known as the Fathers of the Church, and their written testimony is invaluable because they witness to the exact teaching of the Catholic Church right from its earliest beginning and on down into the Fifth and Sixth Centuries. These writings are still referred to by the present-day Church authorities—for example, when it comes time for the Pope to make a solemn definition of doctrine or for an ecumenical Church council to settle a disputed question. In other words, there is a large body of *written* testimony about the Tradition of the Church, dating from the earliest centuries of Christianity, that records exactly the same beliefs as the Church holds today.

But even more interesting—and bordering on the miraculous—is the fact that the enormous body of truths included in the Catholic Faith has remained intact and uncorrupted for nearly 20 centuries, among people of all nations, spread throughout the entire world, so that the Catholic people in South America, North America, Europe, Asia, Africa, Australia, the Middle East and the many Island Nations all learn, practice and retain exactly the same faith and morals. Moreover, as the author points out, these truths continue to be passed on even in our time—and really without the aid of Scripture as a guide. The author repeatedly demonstrates that Tradition actually came before Scripture *historically* and precedes it *theologically*. Even when a Catholic considers the source of his own personal Catholic belief, he has to admit that his instruction in the Faith basically all came from the Tradition of the Church that has been codified into catechisms and other instructional texts, and that relatively little to none of what he was originally taught came directly from Scripture. This admission may horrify Protestants, who base their belief (they say) strictly on "the Bible alone"—*sola Scriptura* (though the author shows that they too follow *many* traditions that are not biblically based). None the less, the fact remains that the basic beliefs of Catholics, even today, come almost entirely from our Tradition, and almost nothing straight out of the Bible—exemplifying exactly the point the author makes about the relationship of Scripture to Tradition.

The New Testament itself is the product of Catholic Tradition. Our Lord did not commission the Apostles to go forth and *write*, but to go forth and *teach* all nations. The New Testament was produced by our Tradition, incrementally, *after* the Apostles had been preaching and working for a number of years to establish the Church, and here we are some 20 centuries later, and that Tradition is still working, still teaching, still informing, still permeating the entire Church of God. However, one must almost perforce be a Catholic to be able to recognize the amazing operation of Tradition and how it has been steadily working in the Church and even how it has formed one's own religious life. The New Testament, then—like the rest of the Bible—is really a Catholic book, and a person really needs to be a Catholic to have the background necessary to understand it, because it was produced by the Church to help explain her Tradition to the converts in the first century of Christianity. If a person does not know what that full Tradition of Faith teaches, he is basically blind and lost when it comes to understanding many of the meanings of the New Testament.

The author shows that even the creation of the Old Testament came out of the living *oral* Tradition that goes back to Adam and Eve. For many centuries of the Patriarchal era had passed away before the Tradition dating from Creation was written down by Moses, to form the first books of the Bible (*The Pentateuch*). The Bible, as the author points out, is really, therefore, a superb gift from God to His people, sort of like icing on the cake of Tradition. It would not be necessary, absolutely speaking, for the Catholic Church to have Scripture—Tradition, under the guidance of the Holy Spirit, being sufficient unto itself to teach the people. But Scripture is a grand and glorious adjunct to our Tradition that enlightens it, that helps us understand it better, and that gives us deeper penetration into the mysteries of God—*if* we know the Faith to begin with, and thereby possess the "blueprint" of Revelation in our minds in order to be able to understand what the New Testament is saying.

The only book in English we know of that discusses the nature of Tradition, *Tradition and the Church* covers most aspects of the nature of Catholic Tradition, and will be a font of tremendous understanding about the sources of our Faith for all those who are lucky enough to read it.

We are calling this publication of *Tradition and the Church* the "Second Edition," not because the book has undergone substantial additions or deletions, but rather because it has been thoroughly retypeset, repunctuated and copy-edited to reflect current English usage—in an effort to make the book easier to read. *Tradition and the Church* was obviously written by a very intelligent, well-educated and highly competent person, but he was also one who did not speak English natively and who did not have complete command of some of the English expressions he used. These problems have mostly been corrected in this edition, as has his tremendous overuse of punctuation. However, the author alternately refers to "*the* Scriptures" and "Scripture," as well as to "the Deposit of *the* Faith" and "the Deposit of Faith." I have chosen to leave both modes of expression in his book, though the second usage in both cases is the more common one in English. Also, stylistically, many of the author's original sentences were awkward; this problem was very easily solved simply by rearranging the selfsame words of many sentences into a different order for easier reading. The result of all these changes, it is hoped, is a book that now reads far more fluently and will cost the reader a great deal less labor to read than the original edition. In all other respects, nothing of the original book has been left out, and nothing has been added, save a few footnotes, some bracketed additions (which I have supplied) and here and there a word or two to help clarify an otherwise difficult sentence. Where parentheses occur within Scripture quotes or other quotations, these are the original additions of the author.

And finally, when the author refers to the Churches that were set up by the Apostles and their disciples, the reader must understand that these "Churches" (spelled with a capital "C") were not centers of disparate Christian faiths, not various non-Catholic sects or denominations, but rather what the Catholic Church today refers to as dioceses governed by bishops, but more likely archdioceses (metropolitan sees—or seats), which are now ruled over by archbishops or cardinals. Sometimes these principal bishops were, and occasionally still are, called "Metropolitans." Some of them are also called "Patriarchs," that is, if they governed Rome, Antioch, Jerusalem or Alexandria (and later Constantinople). Sometimes they are called "Primates"—if they govern the Catholic Church in an entire country or region. The reader must realize that discussion of the Catholic Church involves reference to an enormous worldwide religious organization governed by the Pope in Rome, but also including many major divisions of Church government united to Rome. These divisions in the first centuries and in the New Testament are often referred to as "Churches" (spelled here with a captial "C"), which usage we have retained to distinguish them from non-Catholic Christian churches (spelled with a lower-case "c").

A special acknowledgement must be made to Elizabeth Moors for her typesetting of the book and her *painstaking* correction of the initial typescript of this Second Edition, and also to Maureen McDevitt, who carefully checked the entire book word-for-word (!) to insure that nothing was omitted or copied incorrectly and then who also *painstakingly* checked all the many corrections and offered helpful advice on improved modes of expression where problems of understanding occurred in the original. All these measures were necessary, in my opinion, because *Tradition and the Church* is an extremely important book, yet bore the hallmarks of a text that had come directly from the pen of the author without having passed under the eye of a competent Catholic editor. I have tried to fulfill the normal function of an editor for this book, despite the lapse of time since the first edition appeared in 1928 and in the obvious absence of the author to approve all the minor changes to his text that routinely occurs in book publishing. All this has been done in the interest of providing readers with a far easier and more intelligible learning experience from a perusal of this landmark book.

Thomas A. Nelson
Publisher, December 12, 2005
Our Lady of Guadalupe

Author's Preface

IN the history of mankind there are two events which are paramount to all others. The first is the Incarnation of Christ. The second, almost equal to it, is the institution of the Church by Christ and the descent of the Holy Ghost upon her first priests. Both facts are well established in the Scriptures. The final aim of both is the salvation of mankind. But, while all Christians recognize the first fact, not all are in agreement about what the second is and means. The consequence is that Christianity is divided and subdivided into hundreds of Churches. Each claims to be the Bride of Christ, sanctified by the Holy Ghost on the Day of Pentecost. How then can we distinguish the True Church? The wheat from the cockle? Through Scripture? That is what we were told when almost the whole of Northern Europe tore itself away from Rome. Her authority was rejected. Her doctrines were thrown to the wind. The result was and is a fearful chasm that has separated brethren from brethren—Christians from Christians. Now infidelity is rampant everywhere. The Divinity of Christ and of the Church is denied through the length and breadth of the land. Worse still is such a denial by many of the clergy, who call themselves ministers of Christ.

It is evident, then, that man has gone too far. It is time for him to come back again. And the only way is to return to that "Divine Tradition" which Christ left among us and which is sustained and guided by God the Holy Ghost—the grand Old Mother Church. The bridge that can span the chasm produced in Christianity is only a full recognition of a Divine Tradition. *Such is the task undertaken in this work.* Scripture, being the Word of God, forms the base of our reasoning. But our reasoning must not be in conflict with the testimonies of the first Christians. The existence of Tradition is too evident for that. The doctrines of the Apostles and of the first Christians must be accepted, wherever we can find them, whether in the Scriptures or out of the Scriptures. They must not be added to, diminished or adulterated, but neither rejected if they are the truth. That they are substantially incorrupt today, as they were two thousand years ago, is due to the fact that a government for the Church and of the Church was established by the Apostles. The government of the Church of today must not then be different from the government of the Church of the Apostles. It must be homogeneous. Hence, such government is not only necessary, but it must not be transferred from the successors of the Apostles to the people. All this may be seen through innumerable testimonies, but especially, from the writings of the Fathers of the Church. The descent of the Holy Ghost gave the Church an "Intellect" which is constantly enlightened, sustained and directed to govern the Faithful in an unmistakable way. He taught the "all truth," which may be developed, not in itself, but rather, in ourselves; that is, the more we study the truth, the more we see its extent and beauty. That also means that new doctrines are never introduced in the Church. Hence, no other revelation is to be expected.

I do not expect this work to be perfect. This is something new and out of the ordinary. As far as I know, there is little of its kind in any modern language.

Whatever is herewith stated imperfectly, or not clearly enough, I wish to be understood according to the views of the Apostolic See, of which I profess to be a humble, but faithful child.

Contents

General Introduction

EVERY question of Christian Doctrine touches Tradition. The controversies of the centuries have been fought around it. Time only gives it an added importance. And now it is more important than ever; it takes deeper root as the centuries past.

What is Tradition and of what does it consist?

On the answers to these questions largely rests, under God and His grace, the return of our Separated Brethren. Were the principles of Tradition once more understood and its teachings accepted, the happy day of unity for which Jesus Christ prayed would be for many honest souls not far distant. "That they may be one, as Thou, Father, in me, and I in Thee, that they also may be one in us." (*John* 17:21). That day shall certainly come, because Christ's prayer cannot but be effectual. "Father, I give Thee thanks that thou hast heard Me. And I know that Thou hearest Me always." (*John* 11:41-42).

God has spoken to man. He has revealed Himself in and through Christ. He has given man certain commandments to observe doctrines to believe, institutions to make use of, and so save his soul. But how do we know that God has spoken? And what has He said? And where the revealed truths are to be found—in their fullness and not merely in part? These are questions that require an answer. Two answers are given.

For the Protestant, Scripture alone constitutes the Rule of Faith, to the exclusion of all other authority. For the

Catholic, the Church, combined with Scripture, forms his Rule of Faith.

"We believe the only rule and way, according to which all articles of Faith . . . must be judged, is no other than the prophetic and apostolic writings both of the Old as well as of the New Testament."[1] "Holy Scripture contains whatever is necessary to salvation. Whatever is not read therein, nor can be proved thereby, is not to be required of any man, that it should be believed as an article of faith or be thought necessary to salvation."[2]

Catholics answer with St. Irenæus: "We must not seek the truth from others, when we can easily acquire it from the Church. The Apostles, in the fullness of their riches, brought into it, as into a depository, all that belongs to the truth. He who wishes may take from it the cup of life. This is the entrance into life: all others are thieves and burglars. For this reason, we must avoid them, love diligently what belongs to the Church, and learn the Tradition of truth."[3]

Every Catholic who knows his Religion declares with St. Augustine: "I would not believe the Gospel were it not that I am moved to do so by the authority of the Catholic Church."[4] Hence the Council of Trent solemnly declares: "All truth and discipline are contained in the written books and in the non-written Traditions, which, being received by the Apostles from the mouth of Christ Himself, or under the inspiration of the Holy Ghost, being delivered to us, as it were, by hand, came to us."[5]

And Tertullian, in the Second Century: "To whom

---

1. *Lutheran Formula of Concord.*
2. "Sixth Article of the Anglican Church."
3. *Book III against heretics,* C. IV.
4. "Ep. Fund," C. V.
5. Session IV.

belongs the Faith itself? Whose are the Scriptures? By whom and through whom and when and to whom was the authority to teach delivered, by which men are made Christians. For where the true Christian discipline and doctrine are shown to be, there will also be the truth of the Scriptures, and of their interpretation and of all Christian Traditions."[6]

Christianity is, therefore, divided. According to all the Protestant denominations there is no other authentic way to know the word of God but from Scripture. Scripture is *the only Rule and the only Judge!* No living visible authority has any right to pass judgment on an article of Faith. To expect that Christians should abide by such judgment is an imposition. Each individual has the right to his own private interpretation of Scripture. "The seventh office of the Christians (who are all ministers), is to judge and to declare on the Articles of Faith . . . every one taking care of his salvation must be sure of what he believes and follows; he must be the free judge of all that teach him, being taught interiorly only by God."[7]

Some of the more prominent denominations among Protestants, especially the Episcopalians, have indeed approved of and adopted the Symbols of Faith [the creeds] and the definitions of the first four General Councils of the Church, which, considered in themselves, are Traditions. These creeds and definitions, however, are accepted, not as traditional truths—such would be against their fundamental principle—but because and in so far as they are conformable to the Scriptures.

The characteristic note of Protestantism, then, is the negation of authority outside of the Scriptures. Catholic

6. "Prescriptions," C. XIX.

7. Luther's *Institution of the Ministry of the Church,* Vol. III, p. 584.

Faith, on the other hand, declares that both the Church and the Scriptures are *the Rule of Faith.* Whereas the Protestant claims he is the only judge, the Catholic believes the Church is the Judge. She it is that proclaims what doctrines are to be believed and what practices are to be observed and whether such doctrines and practices are found in the Scriptures or not.

All Protestants, in order to justify their separation from the Catholic Church, deny that Christ ever established such a living authority besides the Scriptures. But in so doing, they have committed so many errors, they have denied so many Christian principles, they have fallen into so many contradictions that, if Martin Luther and the other so-called reformers of the 16th Century could ever come to life again, they would hardly recognize their work. The leaders of Protestantism—past and present—know too well that the admission of the general principle of Tradition would carry them to that very same Divine Tradition which was rejected in the 16th Century. That Divine Tradition is nothing else than the Apostolic succession of an ever-living, indefectible and infallible Church. If they admit to a living Tradition, they must also confess their mistake and culpable rebellion.

Here is the issue: Has Christ established, besides the Scriptures, any other agency or authority to preserve, explain and propagate His doctrines? We propose to prove that He has; that there is a way, by which divinely revealed doctrine is propagated and preserved in its integrity. That way is Tradition.

TRADITION AND THE CHURCH

"But you, my dearly beloved, be mindful of the words which have been spoken before by the apostles of our Lord Jesus Christ."
—Jude 1:17

1

General Notions of Tradition

1

Tradition Means Whatever is Delivered, as well As the Way and Means by Which the Object Delivered Came to Us.

THE proper source of Revelation is the word of God, which is both written and unwritten. The written is contained in Scripture; the unwritten in Tradition.

When we speak of the unwritten word of God, we do not mean that it has never been written, but that it was never written by the man to whom God revealed it. It was committed to writing *afterwards* by his disciples, or by others who heard it from his lips.

The word *Tradition,* considered in *its object,* means whatever is delivered or transmitted; in this sense it is called *objective Tradition*. If we consider, however, *the act,* or the *way and the means* by which an object is propagated and transmitted, this is called *active Tradition.* This active Tradition includes of necessity the object delivered to us. Likewise, the object of Tradition supposes an active Tradition, without which it could not have reached us.

We must always, therefore, take Tradition in its *composite* sense, that is, as made up of two parts—the act of transmission and the thing being transmitted. A tradition considered in its object loses its value without the Active

Tradition that delivers it. We can neither explain nor understand a tradition without knowing the source, the act, the way and the means through which it has reached us.

In the following pages, therefore, Tradition must always be understood to mean not only the doctrine accepted, or the custom that prevailed in Apostolic times, but also the way or the means by which that doctrine or custom has come down to us.

To give an instance, Scripture does not state on what day Jesus Christ was born. But an old Tradition tells us that the Son of God, as man, was born on the 25th of December. Behold the object of a tradition. The Church accepted and set that date for its celebration. Christians—in obedience to the Church—have observed it every year since Christ ascended into Heaven. Behold the active Tradition. These are the two elements: The belief that Christ was born December 25; the teaching Church that set that date for its celebration.

The observance of Lent, the Friday abstinence, the celebration of Sunday instead of Saturday . . . on these Scripture is for the most part silent. But Tradition tells us they were observed in Apostolic times. The Church approved of them and transmitted them from generation to generation to the present day. The Apostles did not write of them. Why should they? They were taken as a matter of course. Some of the early Christians, disciples of the Apostles, or in turn, of their disciples, wrote of them to inculcate in the Christians of their day what the Apostles had taught and preached. The same applies to other disciplines and doctrines that had not been written, but were believed and practiced.

Therefore, whenever we speak of Tradition in general, we always mean this "Complex Tradition"—the object with its manner of transmission, namely, the Church, which gives it value and authority. They both go together, as philosophers say, like matter and form. It is in this sense that the Council of Trent understood and considered Tradition. It solemnly declared: "All revealed doctrine and discipline is also contained in the unwritten Traditions, which, having been received by the Apostles from the mouth of Christ Himself, or through the dictation of the Holy Ghost by the same Apostles, reached us as if they were handed to us" . . . "the same Traditions, which belong to the Faith and discipline, *kept by a continued succession in the Church,* we accept and venerate with a likewise affection and reverence."[1]

2

Traditions, Not Being All of the Same Kind Have a Different Value and Authority.

Traditions are not all of the same kind; hence, they cannot have the same value or authority. We distinguish them, first of all, by the manner in which they are transmitted. Some of them had been originally written; others came to us orally, from father to son; or in a practical way, as through the ceremonies of the Church for instance. For this reason, Traditions are either *written, oral or practical.* Some Traditions are called *Written Traditions* because the word *Tradition* may be taken in its widest signification, to include *whatever has been delivered to us.* In this sense, even the Scriptures may be called Traditions. This point, however, will be further discussed later on.

Secondly, Traditions are distinguished by the objects they convey, *dogmatic* or *disciplinary,* according to whether they refer to a fundamental doctrine of the Church, or to

1. *Council of Trent,* Session IV.

some rule or law to be observed by Christians. The doctrines of the Immaculate Conception and of the Assumption of the Blessed Virgin Mary into Heaven are Dogmatic Traditions. That Mary was conceived without Original Sin, in view of the merits of her Divine Son has always been believed by the Faithful, even before its solemn proclamation [in 1854] by the Church. So, too, the doctrine of the Assumption. We hope that the time is fast approaching when this touching tradition about the Mother of God will be solemnly declared and proclaimed as a Dogma of the Infallible Church.*

Some of the *Disciplinary* Traditions are so old that we have no record whatever of the time when they were first introduced. Such are Lent, the mixing of water with wine in the Eucharistic celebration, and the Baptism of infants.

Traditions are also characterized by their *duration*—some have remained in vigor to the present day. Others were short-lived. They did not stand the test of time. The belief in the Millennium is a case in point.

Certain traditions *are found everywhere,* whereas others are only in *certain localities.* For this reason, some are *universal,* and others *local.* It is evident that the Universal Tradition is more important than the local. Universality is a mark of truth.

There are Traditions which impose *obligations,* as for instance, abstinence. Others are simply *counsels* or *recommendations,* as for instance, the vow of poverty. Hence the distinction of *preceptive* or *advisory* traditions.

Traditions may be either *constitutive* or *inhesive.* The former [Constitutive Tradition] constitutes a doctrine by

---

* The reader is reminded that this book was originally published in 1928 and that the belief in the Assumption was in fact officially proclaimed a dogma of the Catholic Church by Pope Pius XII in 1950.

—*Publisher,* 2005

itself, which is nowhere found in Scripture; the latter [Inhesive Tradition] speaks of a doctrine that is found in Scripture. It is well-known that the Holy Eucharist is clearly described in Scripture. Still, the same Sacrament is also very well-illustrated in other traditions, especially, in *The Doctrine of the Twelve Apostles* [the *Didache,* also called *The Teaching of the Twelve Apostles*], a work which scholars do not place later than the year 80 A.D. Such tradition is called *inhesive.*

Finally, Traditions are either *divine* or *ecclesiastical.* As this distinction is particularly important, we shall discuss it now.

3

Traditions are Either Divine or Ecclesiastical.

Traditions are *Divine* or *Ecclesiastical,* as they originate either from God or from the Church.

I. *Divine traditions* belong generally to the Faith; *Ecclesiastical,* to discipline. Divine Traditions have God as their immediate cause and author. In the New Testament, the first visible promulgator was God Himself, in the person of Jesus Christ, or the Holy Ghost, who spoke through the Apostles. These Traditions are called *Dominical*—from the Latin word *Dominus,* or Lord—if they were first revealed by Christ Himself; they are called *Divine-Apostolic,* if revealed by the Holy Ghost through the Apostles. They all consist of dogmatic truths, commandments and institutions which God directly revealed or instituted for man.

This distinction evidently supposes that not all Revelation was completed by Christ while He dwelt among us, but that it found its completion with the death of the Apostles. After Christ's Ascension into Heaven, the Holy

Ghost came down upon the Apostles, instructed and taught them, not only whatever Christ had said to them, but also all those truths which they neither heard nor knew before, nor could they understand while they lived with Christ. "But the Paraclete, the Holy Ghost, whom the Father will send in my name, he will teach you all things and bring all things to your mind, whatsoever I shall have said to you." (*John* 14:26). "I have yet many things to say to you, but you cannot bear them now. But when he, the Spirit of Truth, is come, he will teach you all truth. For he shall not speak of himself; but what things soever he shall hear, he shall speak; and the things that are to come, he shall show you." (*John* 16:12-13).

This distinction between *Divine* and *Divine-Apostolic Traditions* the [First] Vatican Council [1869-1870] indicates in the Constitution *Dei Filius.* "This supernatural revelation, according to the Faith of the Universal Church, declared by the Council of Trent, is contained in the written books and in the non-written Traditions, which, *being received by the Apostles from the mouth of Christ, or through the dictation of the Holy Ghost,* as if delivered by hand, came to us."[2] As far as their origin is concerned, there is practically no difference between a *Divine* and a *Divine-Apostolic Tradition.* They all came directly from God.

II. *Ecclesiastical Traditions* are those that were introduced by the Apostles themselves, or in post-Apostolic times. Hence, some are called *Simply-Apostolic;* others *Ecclesiastical.*

To understand the difference, one must bear in mind the double office of the Apostles. The Apostles were first of all Apostles, in the strict sense of the word—promul-

---

2. *[First] Vatican Council,* C. II.

gators of the truths and institutions revealed to them by God Himself. But they were also rectors and pastors of the Churches they founded. As promulgators, they wrote a part of those revelations made to them. They wrote as events and circumstances here and there induced them to write—to certain persons, or to the Churches which they had founded. They wrote occasionally. For their principal duty was to administer the Sacraments and "preach the Gospel," according to Christ's command. What they wrote forms part of the Scriptures.

That part of Revelation which as Apostles they preached only and did not write, and which was retained by their disciples, forms the *Dominical* or *Divine-Apostolic Traditions.*

But, as rectors and pastors of the Churches, they also established certain laws and rules which they deemed necessary or useful for the sanctification of the Faithful. "For to the rest, I speak, not the Lord." (*1 Cor.* 7:12). In this manner the Apostles must be considered as the first legislators of the Church, and such rules, laws and institutions which are not all to be found in the Scriptures comprise the *Simply-Apostolic Traditions.*

The Apostles, therefore, as Apostles and ambassadors of God, preached "the Gospel to every creature." (*Mark* 16:15). They all preached, but only *some* of them wrote. The others preached and did not write, but what they preached was subsequently retained by their hearers. This is what forms, as we have said, the *Divine-Apostolic Traditions.* Afterwards, having established here and there many Christian congregations, they made for them certain rules and laws and enacted certain precepts and institutions for their sanctification. Thus, they became the first legislators. These laws and institutions constitute the *Simply-Apostolic Traditions.*

When a tradition contains a doctrine that *belongs to the Faith* and it is proved to be of Apostolic origin, it must be considered as a *Divine Tradition—Dominical* or *Divine-Apostolic*—because it could have only God for its author. Only God could have made it possible. The *Apostolicity* of a certain doctrine and its *divine* origin was always considered by the Church as the same thing. On the other hand, if an Apostolic Tradition that concerns the Faith is *not divine,* then it is no tradition at all. It is *not authentic* and is not to be believed. The Church cannot think out and propose a new doctrine about the Faith. Hence, the doctrines of the Immaculate Conception and the Assumption of the Blessed Virgin Mary are Divine Traditions, because only God could have made them possible. Such are also the Sacraments, which are institutions that give grace, because God alone is the Giver of grace. These doctrines and institutions, if they are to be found everywhere and are approved by the Church, are certainly Divine Traditions. Consequently, they must be believed and observed by the whole Church. *Divine truths and divine institutions cannot be different in different places.*

But Simply-Apostolic Traditions may be different in different places. They are not more than ecclesiastical traditions. For instance, if a tradition is believed and practiced as an Apostolic Tradition—but only in certain places and not everywhere—that tradition cannot be Dominical or Divine-Apostolic. It is simply Apostolic, introduced by some one of the Apostles—not *as* an *Apostle,* but as a *legislator* of the Church, namely, as rector and pastor. As such, that tradition comes under the jurisdiction of the successor of St. Peter, is subject to revision, dispensation, or if circumstances are changed, to abrogation or annulment. Such was the observance of Easter in certain

Apostolic Churches in the first centuries of the Church. Some of the Apostolic Churches in the East did not observe Easter at the same time as some of the Apostolic Churches in the West. The Eastern Churches appealed to an ancient Apostolic Tradition, but so also did the Western Apostolic Churches. That ancient Tradition affected "discipline," not Faith. Consequently, it was a Simply-Apostolic Tradition, subject to the jurisdiction of the successor of St. Peter, the head of the Church.

The best rule, by which to distinguish Dominical or Divine-Apostolic from Simply-Apostolic Traditions is the practice and judgment of the Church. If the Church never dared to change a Tradition, or to dispense with it, that Tradition must be considered a Divine Tradition. Such is the Tradition of the Sunday observance. Such is also the mixture of water with wine in the celebration of the Sacrifice of the Mass.

Finally, concerning precepts and institutions which of their own nature do not necessarily require a divine origin, but which might have originated by Apostolic or Church authority, apply the golden rule of St. Augustine: "What the universal Church maintains, what was never instituted by the Councils, but was always retained in the Church, must be rightly believed to have been transmitted by no other than by Apostolic authority."[3]

To sum up: Traditions are either Divine or Ecclesiastical. *Divine* Traditions are either *Dominical* or *Divine-Apostolic. Ecclesiastical* Traditions are Simply-Apostolic or Simply-Ecclesiastical. Simply-Apostolic if they began with the Apostles, but only in their offices as pastors of the Churches. Simply-Ecclesiastical if they arose in post-Apostolic times.

3. *Bapt.* IV, 24

4

As a General Rule Tradition Must Be Considered In its Strict Sense.

It is a common mistake among those outside the Catholic Church to believe that Tradition can mean only doctrine or discipline not found in Scripture. They suppose, although not without foundation, that Tradition is simply an oral report, transmitted by word of mouth from father to son and from one generation to another. They may even admit that certain doctrines and rules of the Catholic Church have been consigned to writing, not by the Apostles, but perhaps by their disciples, or by others in the course of time. All this they call Tradition and nothing else. This notion is inadequate.

Tradition has more than one meaning. We must accept the signification which is generally found in Scripture. In its *broad* sense, Tradition means what has been handed on to us in any way, by writing or otherwise. In this sense, it includes Holy Scripture. In the *strict* sense it means what has been delivered *orally* or *practically.* When we say *orally,* we exclude the writings of the inspired authors. The rest of Divine Revelation, then, and most of the discipline of the Church, which have come to us, not through the writings of the Apostles, but simply through their preaching or the administration of their Churches, we call, strictly speaking, "Tradition."[4]

We say *practically,* because many laws, rules, rites, customs and institutions came to us through the practice of the Church. They are simply traditions—not that they have never been written, but the Apostles themselves never

4. From the Latin "tradere"—to deliver—as distinguished from "scripta," writing.

wrote them. The Apostles simply preached them as the word of God, if they belonged to the Faith; or imposed them on the Faithful, if they intended them to be the laws or discipline of the Church.

All these divine truths, laws, precepts and institutions were afterwards written by the disciples of the Apostles or by others who heard them or saw them practiced in the first centuries of the Church. They wrote them for no other purpose than to be better preserved and safely transmitted from generation to generation.

Nor has the Church arbitrarily accepted the term "Tradition" as a means of transmission different from the Scriptures. She accepted it because it is *generally* inculcated in the same Scriptures. We say *generally* because there is one exception. In his Epistle to the Thessalonians, the Apostle uses the word to signify both the written and the unwritten word of God. "Hold the traditions which you have learned, whether by word, or by our epistle." (*2 Thess.* 2:14).

There are at least nine other texts where, unquestionably, the word "tradition" or "deliver" means something distinct from the Scriptures themselves. They are the following: *Matt.* 15:2, 3, 6; *Mark* 7:3, 5, 8, 9, 13; *Luke* 1:2; *Acts* 16:4; *1 Cor.* 11:2, 23; 15:3; *1 Ptr.* 1:18; *2 Ptr.* 2:21. Two more texts are doubtful: *Gal.* 1:14 and *Acts* 6:14.

It is on account of this multiplicity of texts that Catholic writers have adopted the word "Tradition" and all that it means.

5

All Traditions Approved by the Church Should be Respected and Believed.

All Traditions which are approved by the Church—whether they are Divine or Divine-Apostolic, Simply-Apostolic or Ecclesiastical—command our respect and veneration. It is true that only the Divine or Divine-Apostolic Traditions contain in themselves the revealed word of God and constitute the object of our Faith, but it is not less true that all Simply-Apostolic and Ecclesiastical Traditions are based on a supernatural power and authority. *This supernatural authority or power is itself a revealed truth.* It must therefore be obeyed. "He that heareth you, heareth me, and he that despiseth you despiseth me." (*Luke* 10:16).

Hence, if a Divine or a Divine-Apostolic Tradition is defined and solemnly accepted by the Church, that Tradition must be upheld as sacred and true, because the voice of the Church is the word of God among us. If anyone rejects it, he rejects at the same time the infallibility of the Church, which is a revealed truth.

A man who rejects a Simply-Apostolic or Ecclesiastical tradition—for instance, the ceremonies in the administration of the Sacraments, the Signing of the Cross, holy water or other traditions, already approved by the Church—denies at the same time her revealed authority. He therefore violates the Faith. That supernatural authority was given to the Apostles and the Church by Christ Himself. He promised her the Holy Ghost, the Spirit of Truth, who abides with her forever. The Holy Ghost abides with the Church for no other purpose than to preserve all Christian doctrines, to render her immune from error in all matters of faith and morals, and to guide her destiny till the End of Time.

This authority on which all Traditions rest is so important and necessary that some of the Fathers of the Church go even so far as to declare that all Apostolic and Ecclesiastical traditions are *Divine Traditions,* because God gave the Apostles and the Church a divine authority. Thus, the election of a bishop by the neighboring bishops of the same province in the presence of the people—certainly an Ecclesiastical or a Simply-Apostolic tradition—is called by Cyprian "a *Divine* Tradition and of Apostolic observance."[5]

For this reason, in the same Catholic profession of Faith, we read: "I firmly admit and accept the Apostolic and Ecclesiastical Traditions and all the other observances and constitutions of the Church. . . . I also accept and admit the received and approved rites of the Catholic Church in the solemn administration of all the Sacraments."

On the other hand the Divine or Divine-Apostolic Traditions are sometimes called by some of the Fathers *Apostolic* or *Ecclesiastical,* because the Apostles and the Church were entrusted with the deposit of the great treasure of Traditions, and are instrumental in their propagation throughout the world.

Therefore, all Traditions approved by the Church must be respected and believed.

5. *Cyprian,* Ep. 68.

2

The Constitution of the Church

1

An Outline of the Constitution of the Church Throughout the Centuries

THE Church is a necessary and supernatural society, instituted by Christ for the salvation of mankind. All men are bound to belong to the Church under pain of eternal damnation. Such necessity and divine institution evince the fact that not man, but God Himself gave His Church an internal and essential organization—that is, a Constitution—which no man has the right to change.

This Constitution we find in vigor in the Church throughout the whole world today, and this Constitution we find written in Scripture. This appears, not according to that conventional manner by which the peoples of the earth write and proclaim their constitutional laws—the fundamental laws of their Country—but in a truly Scriptural way, that is, in the instructions which the inspired authors of the New Testament here and there preached, explained and wrote to the Faithful. For, the Scriptures were not intended to be a code or a textbook for Christians. They were written as circumstances and motives induced the Apostles [and Old Testament writers] to explain certain matters to the Faithful.

This Constitution includes the following elements:

1) The Church is an unequal Society, composed of two classes—clergy and laity. 2) Whatever power and jurisdiction the Church has must reside in the clergy. 3) Power is granted to the clergy because the clergy is of divine right and origin—bishops, priests, and deacons. 4) The priesthood was made subordinate to the episcopacy by the Apostles, according to Christ's command; for Christ did not ordain priests other than those whom He consecrated bishops and Apostles. When Christ told the Apostles, "Do this for a commemoration of Me," (*Luke* 22:19), He gave them the power to consecrate and ordain.[1] 5) The Church and the Scriptures are the "Rule of Faith." 6) There is a double hierarchy, of *Order* and of *Jurisdiction.* The former is established by the special Sacramental character; hence, it can never be lost or cancelled. The latter [Jurisdiction] originates from and is given by legitimate commission; hence, it can be lost—in the Supreme Pontiff only by renunciation or death. 7) Priests have the proper power of Order, but not of Jurisdiction. This comes from above; *viz.,* they must be sent by the Bishop. 8) Supreme authority, that is, the primacy of jurisdiction, is vested in the Bishop of Rome [the Pope], by the fact that St. Peter (appointed by Christ Himself, the Head of the Church) established his office in Rome permanently until his glorious death. His authority is universal—independent of anybody else. His power is *ordinary;* it passes to his successors. The power of the other Apostles was universal, but not independent of Peter. Whomsoever they received into the Church they made subject to Peter. Whatever [regional] Church they founded [i.e., diocesan church or metropolitan seat] they made dependent on Peter, for the jurisdiction of Peter was also over the Apostles them-

1. *Cavagnis* II, C. I, N. 1.

selves. The Bishop of Rome was and is the Vicar of Christ, the center of unity and ecclesiastical communion, the source of jurisdiction in the whole Church. 9) The Apostles had the extraordinary mission of preaching the Gospel to the whole world, to found [regional] Churches everywhere, to organize them and dictate laws to them. Moreover, they had individually the prerogative of infallibility and the gift of tongues, which they proved in fact and by miracles. But not every Apostle had authority over the Universal Church. Hence, they could not make laws for the Universal Church, except in promulgating them by Divine Revelation. But then such laws were divine laws, not merely Apostolic. Personally, they were not the heads of the Churches they founded, except in their offices as Pastors, subordinate to Peter, whom they acknowledged as the Chief Pastor of themselves and of their Churches. If Peter made any law or precept for the Universal Church, they had the duty to observe it. If they made any law for their Churches, Peter had the right to annul it. This however could not happen unless the Apostles issued a law not merely as Apostles, but as legislators. Having been endowed with infallibility, they could not break the unity of the Church. An Apostle could also reorganize Churches founded by other Apostles, changing what had been established by them as he thought expedient in the Lord. The same can be said of the laws made by Peter, not as Head of the Church, but as a legislator. As a body, the Apostles could make laws for the Universal Church, but under Peter, the Prince of the Apostolic College.[2] 10) The See, or Capital, of Christendom, is Rome. Whoever is elected Bishop of Rome is at the same time the Head of the Universal Church. These, however, are not two powers—of

2. *Cavagnis* II, C. I, N. 3.

the Episcopate and of the Primacy—but one power. They are distinguished only in name (*vi termini*—"in the power of the term"), not in substance (*non in re ipsa*—"not in the thing itself"). When Peter appointed others as bishops in other parts of the world—particularly Evodius to succeed him in Antioch—they did not succeed him in his authority of the Apostolate and of the Primacy. Peter himself continued to rule these Churches, applying to them the supreme authority of the Apostolate and of the Primacy. The fact that Peter lived and died in Rome demonstrates that, as his authority must continue until the Consummation of the World, the Church must have a stable See. The whole Church would suffer from an uncertain and changeable Principal See. It has always been well impressed on the Catholic world that the Capital of Christendom could not be changed, even by the Church authorities. Its establishment was the transmitted and fundamental power of Peter, according to the instructions of the Lord. The whole of antiquity recognized without any controversy that the Successor of Peter in Rome, not only succeeded him in the Episcopate, but also in the Primacy. All Peter's contemporaries knew what he had in mind; they knew it without any Church decree. This is itself a Tradition, and one of first importance. The Churches [throughout the world] would never have acknowledged Peter's successor in the See of Rome as Head of the [Universal] Church without a previous declaration from the Prince of the Apostles on this vital point. The authority of the Bishop of Rome and the Ruler of the Universal Church was one and the same. It is this identity that secured and secures that whosoever succeeds Peter in Rome succeeds him also in the Primacy. 11) The bishops of the Church owe obedience to the Head of the [Universal] Church, by whom they are to govern determined Churches.

Individually, they are not infallible. As a body *(collegialiter)* under Peter, they are. Bishops do not inherit the Apostolic charisms of infallibility, miracles, revelation and inspiration, nor the authority to preach the Gospel and found churches all over the world. They do inherit episcopal authority and power, which are ordinary.

No one of the Apostles, as an Apostle, had a successor. St. James, Bishop of Jerusalem, had no successor in his Apostleship. His successor received only his ordinary power as Bishop of Jerusalem. The bishops, moreover, do succeed the Apostles in their collegiate power, because that is also an ordinary power *(collegialiter).* 12) The form of the Church government is monarchical. In the Pope alone is all power supreme, full and independent. Neither bishops nor people have the right to limit the power of the Supreme Pontiff. The bishops, however, help him, at his request and good will, in and out of the General Councils. The Sacred Roman Congregations, headed by Cardinals chosen by the Pope, represent the Supreme Pontiff in the discharge of the duties connected with the general administration of the affairs of the Church. This renders the Church government an absolute monarchy, helped by a hierarchy of bishops throughout the world, and tempered by the love which the Father of Christianity owes to and bears towards all his children.

Not all the above declarations are found *explicitly* stated in the Scriptures. They are, nevertheless, implicitly understood from and based on the same Scriptures. They follow from the very nature of things. These elements listed above are but a brief outline of the Constitution of that Church of which St. Augustine could write in the Fifth Century: "There are many things, which in all justice hold me in her bosom (the Catholic Church): the consent of peoples and races; the authority, born out of miracles, nourished by hope, augmented by charity, strengthened by antiquity; the succession of the Pontiffs on the See of the Apostle Peter . . . down to the present Episcopate; finally, the very same name *Catholic,* which not without reason, in the midst of so many heresies, only this Church could achieve. While all heretics wish to be called Catholics, no one of them, however, points out to his church or house when a stranger asks to be directed to the Catholic Church. These ties of the Christian name, so many and so dear, rightly hold the believer to the Catholic Church."[3]

2

The Constitution of the Church is Substantially Unalterable.

Up to the 16th Century, with the exception of the Greek Church and a few schismatic churches in the East, there existed in the world only one Christian Church—the Catholic Church.

That Church was ruled by one supreme visible head, the Bishop of Rome and Successor of St. Peter. There was then "one fold and one shepherd," (*John* 10:16), with "one Lord, one Faith and one Baptism," (*Ephes.* 4:5), when a great religious rebellion broke out in Northern Europe against all established Church authority. After 30 years of civil and religious wars, when brethren fought brethren, most of the northern nations of Europe, which had received from Christianity and with Christianity their civilization, refused [religious] obedience to their old common Mother, Rome, the great center of Christianity, the source of all ecclesiastical jurisdiction.

---

3. Augustine, *Contra Manich,* C. IV.

In the first years of their rebellion, the leaders of these peoples appealed to Rome: one to set aside his legitimate, living wife and to marry a woman for whom he lusted; another to declare the power of the keys limited absolutely to the spiritual; others to have their heretical doctrines approved by the Successor of Peter. They asked for the impossible: to "put asunder what God hath joined together," to adulterate the Deposit of Faith, to change the doctrine of Jesus Christ. The Church could not possibly grant their demands. She could not allow the gates of Hell to prevail against her. But Christ said, "Heaven and earth shall pass away, but my word shall not pass away." (*Mark* 13:31). These children of men, having become "more wise than it behoveth to be wise," (*Rom.* 12:3), and having seen that their demands were not granted by the Supreme Authority of the Church, protested and rebelled against the venerable Church of Rome.

They set up a new system, a new authority (which is no authority), as a substitute for the authority of the Church. "Scripture and nothing but Scripture" was their doctrine.

Such a substitution of authority is a totally radical change from the provision which Christ and the Apostles established. It is an extirpation—root and branch—of the Constitution of the Church.

Authority is a *necessary* part of the Christian Religion. What is *necessary* in a society cannot be changed without destroying that society. This is even more true in the Church of Christ than it is in a human institution. Men may sometimes change or destroy their own work. But neither man nor Angel has any right to change or destroy the work of God. (*Gal.* 1:8-9). Not even the Pope has any right to change or alter what Christ, the Son of God, has incorporated as a necessary part of His Church. It exists by Divine Charter. The form of government He gave it is its life. It is a fruit of the Redemption. To introduce another form is to change the Church itself. To set up the silent authority of the Scriptures for the living authority of the Church is to undo the work of Christ.

The Reformers forgot that Christ intended to have the Constitution of the Church always the same. They overlooked His promises to the Church, especially the promise of infallibility in teaching, keeping her doctrine free from corruption, and so saving both herself *and* the Scriptures.

Therefore, what Christ has instituted as vital and necessary must remain unchangeable. It cannot be abolished, changed or supplanted, in or by any other form.

A nation may reject the teachings of the Church, but the Universal Church remains indestructible, though it may cease to function within the realm of the apostate nation. It is the apostate nation alone that suffers.

This does not mean that the Scriptures are a dead letter. They are the Word of God, and the Church bases upon them its own constitution and authority *historically* and *dogmatically.* The Scriptures are written for all, learned and unlearned. But they are not the Government of the Church. Nor are they the only Rule of Faith. Rather they are the Rule of Faith in the hands of a living, infallible Church.

3

Before Founding the Church, Christ Proved His Divinity.

Only God could make the Christian Religion. To take millions of men who hate and fear and kill each other, to bring them to accept one Faith and to live under one law of love—this is to prove that Christ was God. His Church is Divine on its own merits. But there are other and greater reasons: The miracles and the prophecies of the Founder. No created agent can of himself perform *miracles*. They transcend the powers of nature and require the special intervention of God. For this reason, the Evangelist, St. John, having related some of the many miracles of Christ—culminating in the most glorious of them all, His Resurrection from the dead—concludes the Twentieth Chapter of his Gospel with this striking passage: "Many other signs also did Jesus in the sight of his disciples, which are not written in this book; but these are written, that you may believe that Jesus is the Christ, the Son of God: and that believing, you may have life in his name." (*John* 20:30-31). The Gospel of St. John was written to prove that Jesus is God.

Prophecies are possible only to God. To predict future free events without supernatural aid is outside the pale of a created intelligence. Prophecies are in themselves miracles. For this reason, Jesus made use of prophecies to assert His divinity. The most terrible of all His prophecies was fulfilled only thirty-seven years after the Crucifixion [i.e., the destruction of Jerusalem by the Romans under Titus in 70 A.D.]. And Jesus concludes it with these words: "Amen, I say to you, that this generation shall not pass, till all these things be done." (*Matt.* 24:34). For the awful truth that lay hidden in these words, read the history of Josephus on the fall of Jerusalem.

By His universal *knowledge of creation,* especially in the searching of hearts, Jesus showed that He was God. "Nathaniel saith to him: 'Whence knowest thou me?' Jesus answered and said to him: 'Before that Philip called thee, when thou wast under the fig tree, I saw thee.'" (*John* 1:48). "And because he needed not that any should give testimony of man: for he knew what was in man." (*John* 2:25).

Innumerable texts in the Scriptures bear testimony to the divinity of the Child Jesus. His coming will be preceded by a universal peace. (Cf. *Ps.* 71). "His name shall be called Wonderful, Counsellor, God the Mighty, the Father of the world to come, the Prince of Peace." (*Is.* 9:6). At His birth "there was with the Angel a multitude of the heavenly army, praising God and saying: 'Glory to God in the highest, and on earth peace to men of good will.'" (*Luke* 2:13-14).

The life of Jesus belonged more to Heaven than to earth. His doctrine manifests a perfection impossible to a mere man. There is nothing more sublime than the doctrine of Christ concerning God, man and the world; nothing more perfect than the moral law which He taught in His sermons. "All that heard him were astonished at his wisdom and his answers." (*Luke* 2:47).

Even the enemies of Christianity are compelled to admit that "the morality of Jesus Christ is the foundation of human civilization." (Strauss). Another unbeliever declares that "the moral teaching of Jesus is the most beautiful doctrine ever received: the Sermon on the Mount will never be surpassed." (Renan).

Christ's Passion and Death are worthy only of God made man. "For, let this mind be in you, which was also in Christ Jesus, Who, being in the form of God, thought it not robbery to be equal with God: but emptied Himself, taking the form of a servant, being made in the likeness of men, and in habit found as a man. He humbled Himself, becoming obedient unto death, even to the death of the Cross. For which cause God also hath exalted Him, and hath given Him a name which is above all names: that in the name of Jesus every knee should bow, of those that are in Heaven, on earth, and under the earth: and that every tongue should confess that the Lord Jesus Christ is in the glory of God the Father." (*Phil.* 2:5-11).

After His ignominious death, "The centurion and they that were with him, watching Jesus, having seen the earthquake and the things that were done, were sore afraid, saying: 'Indeed this was the Son of God.'" (*Matt.* 27:54).

Christ, however, had said: "Destroy this temple (that is my body), and in three days I will raise it up." (*John* 2:19). He meant His Resurrection, which was to be the fundamental condition for the proof of His divinity. "If Christ be not risen again, your faith is vain." (*1 Cor.* 15:17). But Christ "rose again the third day according to the Scriptures, and that he was seen by Cephas and after that by the eleven. Then was he seen by more than five hundred brethren at once: of whom many remain until this present, and some are fallen asleep . . . if Christ be not risen again, then is our preaching vain, and your faith is also vain." (*1 Cor.* 15:4-6, 14).

Thus, Christ's Resurrection is the crowning seal of His divinity. Had He not risen, all His works and His claims would have been buried with Him. But He had also said: "And I, if I be lifted up from the earth, will draw all things to myself." (*John* 12:32).

Christ forever impressed on His disciples that events should take their own course. These things were to prove that He was the Messias. "How then shall the Scriptures be fulfilled, that so it must be done?" (*Matt.* 26:54). "Then he said to them: O foolish, and slow of heart to believe in all things which the prophets have spoken. Ought not Christ to have suffered these things and so to enter into his glory? And beginning at Moses and all the Prophets, he expounded to them in all the Scriptures the things that were concerning him." (*Luke* 24:25-27).

Even His Heavenly Father gave visible testimony: "This is my beloved Son, in whom I am well pleased."

(*Matt.* 3:17). "He was transfigured before them. And his face did shine as the sun, and his garments became white as snow." (*Matt.* 17:2).

Nor did the earth fail to render homage to its Creator. At the moment of His death, "the veil of the temple was rent in two, from the top even to the bottom, and the earth quaked, and the rocks were rent. And the graves were opened, and many bodies of the saints that had slept arose, and coming out of the tombs after his resurrection, came into the holy city, and appeared to many." (*Matt.* 27:51, 53).

It was a terrible claim for a man to make: the claim to be God. But Christ made that claim and held to it till the end. And every incident in His life and death bears witness to its truth and justice.

4

Authority is Necessary in the Church.

Christ called unto Himself twelve men, His first disciples, the nucleus of His Church. They were not learned. We do not even know that they were literate. But they had higher gifts: Faith in and obedience to the Master. It was to secure and save these gifts that He worked His miracles. St. Augustine puts it well: "By His miracles He gained authority. By authority, He secured their Faith. By Faith, He drew the multitudes."[4] And conversely we might say: Without authority, there would be no obedience. Without obedience, there would be no Faith. Without Faith, there would be no Church.

Authority and obedience, then, were soul and body to the infant Church. Without them, she could not have been

---

4. August. *Utility of Belief,* XIV, 32.

born, much less lived and grown. She simply would never have existed at all. She would have been just one more school, with its scholars free to come and go at will. And its Master another Socrates or Plato, only much greater. But the Church is not a school. She is a Church. She does not teach only. She commands. Her doctrines are not opinions. They are revealed truths. Her members may not come and go. They must come and stay. If they leave, it is to their own ruin. And Christ is not another Socrates or Plato, but greater. Christ is God. If He were less than God, He would have failed. It is authority that makes the difference. He spoke as one having power. And that is why the Church will live forever. She has in her that which is Divine. Like her Founder, she speaks as one having power. Her voice is the voice of God.

God in His infinite wisdom and providence instituted the Church to last as long as there are men to be saved. To that Church He gave teachers and doctors, to whom He communicated His authority and the power of preaching and teaching. He chose in a special way a few, to whom He gave a special power not given to others; upon them He founded His Church; through them He spoke to the future generations. He did not write any book to perpetuate His doctrine, commandments and institutions. Alone, a written book is a dead thing. The dead cannot speak. Only the living can give life to what is dead.

Authority, then, is necessary for the life of the Church, because such is the order chosen by Christ. Such authority cannot be anything accidental or secondary. It is something substantial and essential in the life of that society, which the Son of God established upon earth. Without authority, there is no obedience; and without obedience, there is chaos, a religious confusion that spells the end of any society. That authority is God Himself.

5

Christ Communicates His Authority to the Apostles.

The authority in the Church is the authority of Christ Himself. He bequeathed it to the Apostles, and through them to their successors. "The book which Christ wrote was the Apostles, a book written not in ink, but with the Holy Ghost, who gave to the Apostles all authority, all power and jurisdiction in the Church. He appointed them to rule, to teach and to sanctify the faithful."[5]

During the three years of His public ministry, He spoke of the Church as something that was yet to come. But on the evening before His death, the hour was at hand, and He called it into existence. At the Last Supper, He instituted the two Sacraments which perpetuate the life of the Church itself and sustain it in its members—Holy Orders and the Blessed Eucharist. "And when the hour was come, he sat down, and the twelve Apostles with him. And taking bread, he gave thanks, and brake; and gave to them, saying: This is my body, which is given for you. Do this for a commemoration of me. In like manner the chalice also, after he had supped, saying: This is the chalice, the new testament in my blood, which shall be shed for you." (*Luke* 22:14, 19-20).

After His Resurrection, He completed the Sacraments, imparted His authority to the Apostles, conferred the Primacy on Peter, and crowned the work by a promise that He Himself would be with them until the End of the World. "And Jesus coming, spoke to them, saying: All power is given to me in heaven and in earth. Going therefore, teach ye all nations, baptizing them in the name of the Father, and of the Son, and of the Holy

5. Franzelin, *Script et Trad.,* Th. IV.

Ghost." (*Matt.* 28:18-19). "Peace be to you. As the Father hath sent me, I also send you. When he had said this, he breathed on them, and he said to them: Receive ye the Holy Ghost. Whose sins you shall forgive, they are forgiven them; and whose *sins* you shall retain, they are retained." (*John* 20:21-23).

The impossible has happened. The Son of God has given His almighty power to eleven weak men: to bind and to loose, to rule and to guide, until the End of Time.

The Apostles, then, are vested with the power and authority of Christ Himself. They are sustained in their great mission by the promise of Christ's assistance and of the coming upon them of the Holy Ghost, to teach them all truth and preserve them from error. "Teaching them to observe all things whatsoever I have commanded you: and behold, I am with you all days, even to the consummation of the world." (*Matt.* 28:20). "And I will ask the Father, and he shall give you another Paraclete, that he may abide with you for ever." (*John* 14:16). "But when he, the Spirit of truth, is come, he will teach you all truth . . . ; and the things that are to come, he shall show you." (*John* 16:13).

Hence, the Apostles are like Christ: they are to reveal truths like Christ, to preach and teach like Christ, and to rule the Church like Christ. "And you shall give testimony, because you are with me from the beginning." (*John* 15:27). "Preach the Gospel to every creature." (*Mark* 16:15). "Going therefore, teach ye all nations." (*Matt.* 28:19). Therefore, what they preach and teach is free from error because they are assisted by Christ, taught by the Holy Ghost and filled with the same spirit. Nay, more than that: they are to use their own authority, as free beings in the hands of God. "It hath seemed good to the *Holy Ghost* and *to us*." (*Acts* 15:28).

When Christ said to Peter and to Peter only, "Feed my lambs . . . feed my sheep," (*John* 21:15, 16, 17), He conferred on him the supreme power of ruling over the people, the priests and the bishops of the Church. He fulfilled what He promised him before: "I will give to thee the keys of the kingdom of heaven. And whatsoever thou shalt bind upon earth, it shall be bound also in heaven; and whatsoever thou shalt loose on earth, it shall be loosed also in heaven." (*Matt.* 16:19).

Behold, then, the Church of Christ—established by divine charter, endowed with divine life, sharing in divine immortality. Under the guidance of the Holy Ghost, with a guarantee that they cannot fail and will not err, and in the company of the Master, who will never leave them, the Apostles go forth to preach and to teach and to baptize. The Church Christ founded was a Church with a Living Authority and will remain so to the end. The writings of the New Testament would come later, a proof—as the writings of the Old Testament had been a prophecy—that God had made good His word. These inspired writings would testify to that which already existed and which would have existed and been divine and true and everlasting, even if the Apostles had never written a line.

Ultimately, the Church is what it is, not because Matthew, John, or Paul or any Apostle has written it, but because Christ commanded it. The Apostles had their authority and were using it, and the Church was doing its work, years before a word of the New Testament was written.

6

The Apostles Assert Their Full Authority.

Obedient to the command of Christ to continue the great work He had only begun, the Apostles "going forth preached everywhere, the Lord working withal and confirming the word with signs that followed." (*Mark* 16:20). They ruled the Church by that authority and jurisdiction which the Son of God communicated to them before He went to the Father.

The Apostles presented themselves to the world, first of all, as *other Christs,* according to the words of the Master. "He that heareth you, heareth me . . . and he that despiseth me, despiseth him that sent me." (*Luke* 10:16).

Secondly, they asserted themselves as Christ's ministers and dispensers: "Let a man so account of us as of the ministers of Christ and the dispensers of the mysteries of God." (*1 Cor.* 4:1).

Moreover, they claimed to be the co-workers of God. "For we are God's coadjutors; you are God's husbandry, you are God's building." (*1 Cor.* 3:9).

Finally, they declared themselves to be Christ's ambassadors: "For Christ, therefore, we are ambassadors, God as it were exhorting by us. For Christ, we beseech you, be reconciled to God." (*2 Cor.* 5:20).

These declarations the Apostles confirmed by their deeds. As Jesus Christ told the Jews, "Though you will not believe me, believe the works," (*John* 10:38), so also the Apostles sealed by miracles the claims of their mission. "My speech and my preaching was not in the persuasive words of human wisdom, but in showing of the Spirit and power." (*1 Cor.* 2:4). "Yet the signs of my apostleship have been wrought on you, in all patience, in signs and wonders, and mighty deeds." (*2 Cor.* 12:12). Hence they required the full consent and compliance on the part of the Faithful. St. Paul, then, writes: "By whom (Christ) we have received grace and apostleship for obedience to the faith, in all nations, for his name." (*Rom.* 1:5). For their doctrine is not their own, but of God. And as God is *one, one* also must be the Faith of the people, and *one* their public profession in the doctrine of Jesus Christ.

No wonder, therefore, that the Apostles were inexorable and uncompromising on what belongs to Christian truth. "But though we, or an angel from heaven, preach a gospel to you besides that which we have preached to you, let him be anathema; as we said before, so now I say again: If any one preach to you a gospel, besides that which you have received, let him be anathema." (*Gal.* 1:8-9).

Behold, therefore, how the Apostles, in continuing Christ's work upon earth, asserted their authority.

7

Obedience by the Faithful Was Due to the Apostles.

It is of no avail to elect or appoint to an office men vested with authority, and at the same time to exonerate from obedience those who are placed under their jurisdiction. It is a contradiction. Authority is co-ordinate with obedience. Both are inseparable. One supposes the other. They are not unlike the notion of *"father"* and *"son."* As the notion of father cannot be conceived without the notion of son, so also the power of *authority* cannot be thought of without the duty of *obedience.*

Now, the Apostles were given the authority of "binding" and of "loosing." To *bind* and to *loose* whom? The Faithful. The Faithful, therefore, must obey those whom Christ appointed to rule over them. And to make that obedience more effectual, Christ gave the command to the Apostles: "Go ye unto the whole world, and preach the gospel to every creature. He that believeth and is baptized shall be saved, but he that believeth not shall be condemned." (*Mark* 16:15-16).

Here, then, we have, on the one hand, the command

given to the Apostles to teach the world, and on the other, the command to all the people of the earth to learn of them. The Apostles are ordered to preach to every creature to make Christ known to all, and to bring to all the means of salvation. "Woe is unto me if I preach not the Gospel." (*1 Cor.* 9:16). If that is true, then all creatures are commanded to listen to them, under pain of eternal damnation: "But he that believeth not shall be condemned." (*Mark* 16:16).

All men, therefore, are subject to the Apostles in matters of salvation. If they refuse to hear them, they refuse to hear Christ; if they despise their authority, they despise the authority of Christ Himself. "When you had received of us the word of the hearing of God, you received it not as the word of men, but (as it is indeed) the word of God." (*1 Thess.* 2:13). This authority of God is first of all shared by His legates. It is only through them that He makes it known to all the world. *They are sent* by God Himself to every creature, to preach and teach in His name.

Obedience is due to these legates, because it is through them that the will and the word of God are made known to the world. Hence, the Apostle: "By whom (Christ Jesus) we have received grace and apostleship for obedience to the faith, in all nations, for his name." (*Rom.* 1:5). That obedience is not of a free nature. It is *necessary* obedience. It is as necessary as it is in any other well-ordered and constituted society. This is evident from the warning of Christ: "He that believeth and is baptized shall be saved, but he that believeth not shall be condemned." (*Mark* 16:16).

The same *necessity* appears from St. Paul's, "Destroying counsels and every height that exalteth itself against the knowledge of God, and bringing into captivity every understanding unto the obedience of Christ; and having in readiness to revenge all disobedience." (*2 Cor.* 10:4-6). To the converted Hebrews, the same Apostle writes: "Obey your prelates, and be subject to them. For they watch as being to render an account of your souls." (*Hebrews* 13:17).

Obedience, then, to the Apostles—and as we shall see later, to ecclesiastical authority—was always considered necessary in the Church. The Church did not exist without it, nor can it exist now without submission to those whom the Holy Ghost has placed "to rule the church of God." (*Acts* 20:28).

3

Establishment of Divine Tradition, That Is, of an Apostolic Succession: An Ever-Living and Official Body to Govern the Church

Introduction

AUTHORITY and obedience are two essential characteristics in the Church of Jesus Christ. If one is wanting, the other cannot exist, and the result can only be anarchy.

We rest this conclusion on the conditions of human nature and the constitution of the Church as it appears historically in the Scriptures. We shall now examine thoroughly the words of Our Lord addressed to the Apostles as the first heads and legislators of the Church, and then the manner in which the Apostles carried out His command.

We do not contend that Christ could not have given His Church another system than that which He was pleased to choose. We simply state that, since He established a certain form of government, that form must remain. It is essential for the life of the Church. If changed, the whole Church is changed.

Our task, therefore, is to show that in the institution of the Apostolate, Christ intended that there should be an ever-living body of men to continue His work to the End of Time. In other words, in choosing the twelve Apostles as the first propagators of His Divine Religion, He also established a *perpetual apostolic succession* with the authority of teaching in His name. To be plain, He intended that the Apostles should appoint and ordain others to succeed them in their office, who in turn would appoint and ordain others to preach the Gospel and rule the Church, and so to the End of the World.

The government of the Church, after the death of the Apostles, is to be *homogeneous* with the original one. Its progress will be perfectly *identical* with that of the Apostolic government. No substantial change or modification of government will be suffered in the future; no different economy, no differently established order.

1

Christ Established a Perpetual Apostolic Succession.

Jesus Christ constituted the Apostles *teachers* to all the nations for all time. "All power is given to me in heaven and in earth; going therefore, teach ye all nations . . . teaching them to observe all things whatsoever I have commanded you: and behold I am with you all days, even to the consummation of the world." (*Matt.* 28:18-20). The Greek text has it, "Make all nations your disciples." And in the *Acts of the Apostles,* we also read: "But you shall receive the power of the Holy Ghost coming upon you, and you shall be *witnesses* unto me in Jerusalem, and in all Judea, and Samaria, and even to the uttermost part of the earth." (*Acts* 1:8).

The Apostles, then, are not only teachers of nations, but also *witnesses* of Christ—*witnesses* until the End of Time; *witnesses* in every part of the world; *witnesses* not only in the knowledge He imparted to them, but also *wit-*

nesses with the power of the Holy Ghost, namely, *infallible and perpetual witnesses.*

The Apostles, therefore, are not to be *common witnesses*. Unlike all other men and women who saw the works of Christ, the Apostles are to be His *official witnesses*. They saw not only what others saw, but they were also taught by Christ Himself and commanded by Christ to *teach* "them [the Nations] to observe all things whatsoever I have commanded you." "Wherefore, of these men who have companied with us all the time that the Lord Jesus Christ came in and went out among us . . . one of these must be made a *witness with us* of his resurrection . . . to take the place of this ministry and apostleship, from which Judas hath by transgression fallen, that he might go to his own place. And they gave them lots, and the lot fell upon Matthias, and he was numbered with the eleven apostles." (*Acts* 1:21-22, 25-26).

In their testimony, they are never to fall into error, because "the Paraclete, the Holy Ghost, whom the Father will send in my name, he will teach you all things, and bring all things to your mind, whatsoever I shall have said to you." (*John* 14:26). "Behold I am with you all days, even to the consummation of the world." (*Matt.* 28:20).

The Apostles are, therefore, appointed by Christ Himself to be infallible teachers to the whole world and perpetual witnesses to Himself. But did not Peter and all the other Apostles go the way of the flesh centuries ago? "Because by reason of death they were not suffered to continue." (*Heb.* 7:23). How can they be *teachers or witnesses* forever? How can Christ be with them all days? *With them* teaching, *with them* baptizing, *with them* "until the consummation of the world?" In what "uttermost part of the world" is Christ to be found with them today?

Yet it is so. Christ is with the Apostles today, as He

was with them more than 1,900 years ago. He is with Peter and the other Apostles as represented by the Bishop of Rome on the Chair of Peter, and by all the Bishops of the Catholic world. He is with Peter and the other Apostles as perpetual Legates and Ambassadors to mankind, as long as there are souls to be saved. He is with them as *perpetual teachers* and rulers of His Church, as *perpetual witnesses,* wherever the Cross is planted, even "to the uttermost part of the earth."

Christ is with the Apostles in the persons *of their successors,* the bishops and priests of the Church. The words of Christ concern not only the first Twelve. To be effective, they must extend to all who come after them for all time. Hence, He is with them everywhere and forever in their *official capacity.*

The memorable words quoted above: "Behold I am with you all days even to the consummation of the world," and "He shall give you another Paraclete, that he may abide with you forever," and "you shall be witnesses unto me, even to the uttermost part of the earth," were addressed not only to the individual persons of the Apostles, but also to all those who were to succeed them in office.

The commission, therefore, of teaching and giving testimony was not simply personal. It was given to the teaching Church, to an Apostolic Succession until the End of Time.

Thus has Jesus Christ established a perpetual Apostolic Succession to govern the Church in His name.

2

A Closer Analysis of Christ's Words in *Matthew* 28 and in *John* 14 Shows a Perpetual Apostolic Succession.

One may easily see from what has been said that Christ instituted a perpetual Apostolic Succession for the conservation and propagation of the Church. We have come to this conclusion, in a general way, from the words of Christ in *Matthew* and *John,* and the provision made to that effect by the Apostles.

We shall now examine these words more in detail. "Teach ye all nations" is Christ's order to His Apostles, "teaching them to observe all things whatsoever I have commanded you: and behold I am with you all days, even to the consummation of the world." (*Matt.* 28:19-20). "And I will ask the Father, and he shall give you another Paraclete, that he may abide with you forever." (*John* 14:16).

In order to understand the full import of these divine words, we must consider the persons to whom they were directed, the power and prerogatives which they might have on other occasions obtained from the Master, and the time and circumstances when those words were delivered. For three things must be considered with regard to this matter. *First,* they were the recipients of a new Revelation which was to be completed by them and by nobody else. *Second,* each of the Apostles had authority over the Universal Church as pastors and guardians of the Faith. *Third,* their authority was subordinate to Peter and in communion *with* Peter.

First: That the Apostles were to know *all Revelation* which was to be completed by them is evident from *John:* "The Holy Ghost will teach you all things," (*John* 14:26); "When he, the Spirit of truth, is come, he will teach you all truth," (*John* 16:13); "Thou hast fully known my doctrine . . . continue thou in those things which thou hast learned, and which have been committed to thee: knowing of whom thou hast learned *them*." (*2 Tim.* 3:10-14).

Second: That the Apostles had authority over the whole Church can be deduced from the fact that they preached *everywhere, establishing new missions wherever* they were, regardless of territorial limits. Those limits, however, were to be respected by those, whom they ordained in every city. (*Titus* 1:5-7). Clement of Rome says, "The Apostles preaching the Gospel in regions and cities . . . constituted bishops of those who were to believe."[1] That these bishops, unlike the Apostles, ruled over only certain parts of the flock of Jesus Christ is evident from Scripture: "Feed the flock of God *which is among you,* taking care *of it*." (*1 Ptr.* 5:2). "Take heed to yourselves and to the whole flock *wherein* the Holy Ghost hath placed you bishops, to rule the Church of God." (*Acts* 20:28).

Third: The authority of the Apostles was subordinate to Peter. There is no reason why the words of Christ in *Matthew* 28 and *John* 14 *could not be addressed* to the Apostles, not only as Apostles, but also in so far as they constituted a separate body in union and communion with Peter and under Peter, to last until the End of Time.

For Christ's words in *John* 14, "He shall give you another Paraclete, that he may abide with you forever," were addressed to the Apostles after *the Primacy had already been promised to Peter,* namely, after Peter had been promised that, of all the Apostles, he was to be chosen as *the only rock* upon which Christ was to build His Church. On the other hand, the words of Christ in *Matthew* 28, commanding the Apostles *"to teach all*

1. Clement, Ep. I, ad *Cor.,* N. 42.

nations" and promising them His presence and assistance, *"even to the consummation of the world,"* were directed to the Apostles also—*after* the Primacy had been already conferred on Peter, constituting him the supreme pastor of all the sheep of Jesus Christ. "Feed my lambs . . . feed my sheep." (*John* 21).

Therefore, the command of Christ to the Apostles, *to teach* all nations, and the charism of truth necessarily connected with that teaching, as well as His promise to be with them forever, *can be understood* to be promised and conferred upon *the whole Apostolic body in union and communion with Peter and under Peter,* because Peter had already been promised and had already received from Christ Himself the Supreme Pastorship. Therefore, those words may have been addressed to each and every one of the Apostles, not independently of Peter, nor individually, but as to one body of men *with* Peter and *under* Peter, as head of the Church.

That it *really must be so understood* is evident, first of all, from the fact that the prerogative of universal teaching and the charism of individual infallibility were *not ordinary* in each and every one of the Apostles (except in the Primacy of Peter). They were *extraordinary* prerogatives of the Apostleship.

In the second place, the student of Scripture can see that Christ's words in *Matthew* 28 and in *John* 14, "teach all nations . . . behold I am with you," and "the spirit of truth will abide with you forever," did not promise and institute a ministry to proclaim new revelations, but rather an infallible and perpetual ministry for a Revelation already accomplished, although it had not been all communicated to the Apostles when those words were addressed to them.

For, when Christ Jesus Our Lord promised the Apostles that "When he, the Spirit of Truth is come, he will teach you all truth," (*John* 16:13), He not only did not promise *then* any assistance from Himself, but He expressly told them that, on account of their present personal weakness, "the many things" which He did have to say to them 'they could not bear them now.' (Cf. *John* 16:12). They were, namely, to receive the Holy Ghost in an extraordinary manner. Hence, the promise of proclaiming new Revelations concerned only the persons of the Apostles. For that reason, while the words of Christ in *Matthew* 28 and in *John* 14 constituted an *ordinary* Apostolic and perpetual succession, nevertheless, the charism of new Catholic revelations was not to pass to the Apostles' successors, because it was a personal and extraordinary prerogative of the Apostles that was to end with the Apostles' death.

Moreover, the prerogatives of infallibility and of promulgating new revelations were not of the same kind in the Apostles. For, if the latter [new revelations] was *extraordinary and personal,* as we have seen, the former [infallibility] was not *only ordinary, but also extraordinary:* that is, ordinary in the Apostolic College; extraordinary in every Apostle as Apostle. Only what is ordinary is inherent to the office and passes to the successors in office. *Ordinary infallibility,* therefore, belonged to the Apostolic College *in union* and *communion* with Peter and *subordinated to* Peter, because the Apostolic College represented juridically and in perpetuity the future episcopal body of the Catholic Church, teaching and preaching *with* and *under* Peter's successors—although the Apostles were also *personally infallible,* which is not the prerogative of each individual bishop. Infallibility was an extraordinary gift of each Apostle.

Likewise, by virtue of the Primacy, the prerogative of teaching the whole Church and the charism of teaching infallibly were *ordinary* in Peter, because he was not only an Apostle, but also the Head of the Universal Church. He was to be the Rock against which the gates of Hell could never prevail. He was to be forever the Bishop of Bishops, present and future. Hence, these two prerogatives of universal teaching and of infallibility are always to be inherent to his episcopal office until the End of Time. Hence, they are also to pass to his successors in office, the Bishops of Rome. Not so with the successors of the other Apostles. For, the prerogatives of teaching the Universal Church and of teaching infallibly belonged to each and every one of the Apostles by virtue of the Apostolate. They were *extraordinary* and could not pass to their successors. Only the prerogative of teaching and teaching infallibly was *ordinary* in the Apostolic College, as they represented the future Catholic Episcopal body *with* Peter and *under* Peter. It is for this reason that the Catholic Episcopate is infallible in union with Peter and under Peter. But a bishop individually is not infallible, because he is not an Apostle.

Finally, Peter's prerogative of teaching the Universal Church and of teaching infallibly must not be confused with the prerogative of *promulgating new revelations.* Revelation was completed by the Apostles. The Pope never promulgates a *new* revelation. Promulgation of Revelation was *personal* in Peter, as well as in the other Apostles. It was not inherent either in Peter's or in the other Apostles' office. Hence, it was not to pass to their successors. It was an extraordinary prerogative in each of the Apostles, as Apostles, but not as bishops of the Church.

3

The Apostles Chose and Instructed Their Successors in Office.

The manner in which the Apostles carried out the command of their Master to *teach* and to *testify* leaves no doubt as to the meaning of Christ's words.

Having established Christian worship in various places, the Apostles had nothing else in view but to perpetuate that government by which they ruled in the Lord. The Church grew rapidly. The Apostles knew that the time of their dissolution was at hand, and mindful of Christ's command to teach all nations "until the consummation of the world," they ordained and taught others to help them in their work and to succeed them in office. This they did with the explicit provision and instruction that they also should in the proper time appoint successors. "For which cause I admonish thee" writes the Apostle to Timothy, "that thou stir up the grace of God, which is in thee, by the imposition of my hands." (*2 Tim.* 1:6). And to his disciple Titus the same Apostle says: "For this cause I left thee in Crete, that thou shouldst set in order the things that are wanting, and shouldst ordain priests in every city, as I also appointed thee." (*Titus* 1:5). And again he warns Timothy: "And the things which thou hast heard of me by many witnesses, the same commend to faithful men, who shall be fit to teach others also." (*2 Tim.* 2:2).

Both Timothy and Titus were consecrated Bishops by the Apostle St. Paul. In like manner the other Apostles appointed others to continue their glorious work, in obedience to Christ's command. This is the Apostolic Succession which, according to Christ's promise, will carry its work indefectibly unto the End of Time.

In the consecration and appointment of the bishops, the

Apostles intended that they should also instruct the people in the rudiments of the Christian Religion and to minister to them. Addressing the ancients of the Church of Ephesus, the Apostle said to them: "Take heed to yourselves and to the whole flock, wherein the Holy Ghost hath placed you bishops, to rule the Church of God." (*Acts* 20:28). But, as the Apostles had received from Christ the command to *teach and preach* and to be His *witnesses* "unto the consummation of the world," they also gave the same command to those whom they appointed as their successors. Thus the Apostle, writing to his beloved disciple Timothy, says, "Keep the commandment without spot, blameless, *unto the coming of our Lord Jesus Christ,* which in his times he shall show, who is the Blessed and only Mighty, the King of kings, and Lord of lords." (*1 Tim.* 6:14-15). Hence Vincent of Lerin in his famous *Commonitory* exclaims: "O Timothy, guard the deposit. What is Timothy today, but either the *Universal Church* (as to her belief), if considered in a general way, or the *whole Body of the Bishops* (in teaching), if taken in a particular way?"[2]

Therefore, there must be a body of men to rule and teach the Church, not only those whom the Apostles themselves appointed as their immediate successors, but also others, who must succeed these immediate successors of the Apostles, because they must keep the commandment "unto the (second) coming of our Lord Jesus Christ," that is to say, "unto the consummation of the world." "And the things which thou hast heard of me," writes the Apostle to Timothy, "by many witnesses, the same commend to faithful men, who shall be fit to teach others also." (*2 Tim.* 2:2).

2. *Commonitory,* v. 17.

These instructors are the same "pastors and doctors" of the Church of which the Apostle speaks in his *Epistle to the Ephesians.* "He gave some Apostles . . . and other some, pastors and doctors . . . for the work of the ministry, for the edifying of the body of Christ, until we all meet into the unity of faith . . . unto the measure of the age of the fulness of Christ." (*Eph.* 4:11-13).

These "pastors and doctors" are the bishops and priests of the Church, who by their preaching will at last succeed in bringing a universal unity of Faith before the second advent of Our Lord Jesus Christ.

This Apostolic Succession, Clement, disciple and successor of Saint Peter, describes in his first letter to the *Corinthians:* "Christ is sent by God, and the Apostles by Christ. . . . For this reason, they went out announcing the advent of the Kingdom of God with the full inspiration of the Holy Ghost. Therefore, preaching the word of God in every city and country, after they were approved by the Holy Spirit, they constituted the first bishops and deacons for those who were to believe . . . and commanded them that after their death, other virtuous men must succeed them in the ministry."[3]

Such must be the Apostolic Succession until the End of Time. It is the command of Christ to the Apostles. It is the command of the Apostles to their successors. "Jesus Christ, yesterday, and today, and the same for ever and ever." (*Heb.* 13:8). Jesus said to the Apostles, and in the Apostles to their successors in office: "Teach ye all nations. . . . Behold I am with you all days, even to the consummation of the world." (*Matt.* 28:18-20).

3. Clement, *I Cor.,* N. 42-44.

4

Not All the Gifts, with Which Christ Enriched the Apostles, Passed to Their Successors in Office.

What Christ promised and gave to His Apostles also passed to their successors. But the words: "Behold I am with you all days, even to the consummation of the world" (*Matt.* 28:20) and "He shall give you another Paraclete, that he may abide with you forever" (*John* 14:16) must not be construed to mean that *all the gifts* with which God filled and adorned the Apostles are also to fill and adorn those who succeed them.

Many of these gifts concern only the persons of the Apostles. Such was the gift of new Revelations. This is evident from the fact that the Apostles themselves instructed and enjoined their successors not to teach otherwise. "Thou hast fully known my doctrine," writes the Apostle to Timothy, "but continue thou in those things which thou hast learned, and which have been committed to thee: knowing of whom thou hast learned them." (*2 Tim.* 3:10, 14).

That this gift of new revelations ended with the death of the Apostles is manifest from another fact. Their successors never claimed to have their own writings considered as inspired revelations. They never dared to add another word to Holy Scripture. Otherwise, Revelation would still have to be finished. Such an assumption on their part would contradict the exclusive role taken by the Apostles.

The proclamations of the Successor of Peter, the Bishop of Rome, made *ex cathedra*—"from the chair," are indeed infallible. But they are not *new* revelations.

The Apostles were adorned with other personal gifts: the gift of tongues, conferred on the day of Pentecost;

the prerogative of every Apostle to be pastor and doctor and guardian of the Faith for the whole Church; the power of working miracles.

These were imparted by Christ as *extraordinary* gifts. Hence, they could not possibly be communicated by the Apostles to their successors without a special divine intervention. Once the reason for these gifts had ceased, their discontinuance can be easily understood.

Different times require different men. Troublesome times with arduous problems require strong leaders. This is true in civil society, but more so in the Church, the greatest society in the world. In His infinite wisdom and Providence, God invests certain men with extraordinary talents and sanctity to achieve extraordinary results for the good of the Church. In its infancy, especially, the Church needed this extraordinary protection for its existence and propagation.

The establishment of the Church of Jesus Christ among men is a nobler work than the Creation of the Universe. It required the Blood of the Son of God. God invested the first workers with gifts and powers which enabled them to deal with the devil worship, idolatry and paganism of those days. The frightful condition of the world took all the powers of the new ambassadors of God. With the death of the Apostles, those extraordinary gifts and powers ceased to exist. They were no longer needed. The Church was established on a solid basis. It was a stable and recognized institution. The necessity for men endowed with preternatural and miraculous powers no longer existed.

Therefore, when the Apostles appointed others to take their places, they simply communicated to them their *ordinary power* and *jurisdiction* as priests and bishops, not the extraordinary or personal gifts which they had received from Christ. This ordinary power and jurisdiction belonged to their office as priests and bishops of the Church. The episcopal office, which is so exalted as to be a heavy burden even on the shoulders of Angels—as the Council of Trent teaches us—is none the less an *ordinary* and not an extraordinary office.

To sum up, the Apostles appointed others to succeed them—not as Apostles, but as *rulers and seniors* of the Church—to succeed them, not in the Apostleship, but in the Episcopacy.

Even the Primacy of Peter, which is the greatest office in the Church, is *ordinary.* It passes to his successors in office because the Pope succeeds Peter, not as an Apostle, but as Bishop of Rome.

5

The Apostolic Succession is not Impaired by the Absence of the Extraordinary Charisms.

It is the will of God that the Church of Christ will last until the End of Time. For this the Apostles, faithful to the command of the Master, appointed others to succeed them in office. But the power and authority of their successors must not be confused with the prerogatives and gifts which the Apostles had received through God's special intervention. Such were the gifts of *tongues* and of *new revelations,* of *infallibility,* and the prerogative to have *authority over the Universal Church,* which they received on the Great Day of Pentecost. For there was only one such Pentecost. That Great Day was the birth of the Church, the birth of the first spiritual Fathers who were to have such a long generation of spiritual children, until the End of Time.

The Apostles received their special charisms only *after* they had already been made priests and bishops by Christ

Himself. The Holy Ghost later completed the work of Christ, elevating them to loftier heights, which to all other mortals were inaccessible.

Some contend that neither Christ nor the Apostles left a perpetual Apostolic Succession. If they had, then those successors should be endowed with all the gifts and prerogatives of the Apostles themselves. To be more explicit [these critics say]: There is not and there should not be any Apostolic Succession to rule the Church. No human authority whatever [should exist] in the Church—no bishops and consequently no Pope of Rome. The words of Christ affect in their full meaning all those to whom they are addressed. Therefore, if by the words, "Teach all nations. . . . Behold I am with you all days, even to the consummation of the world," and "I will ask the Father and he shall give you another Paraclete, that he may abide with you forever," Christ intended to establish an Apostolic Succession to rule the Church until the End of Time, then all the Apostolic successors would also be gifted, like the Apostles, with the inspiration of *new revelations,* with the *gift of tongues* and with the power of *working miracles,* with the prerogative in every single bishop of *infallibility* and of *authority* over the whole Church. However, as there are no such men [the critics' argument goes], the conclusion must be that Christ never intended to establish an Apostolic Succession. His words were intended for all the Faithful. What power there may be in the Church must ultimately come from the faithful [so their argument goes].

The answer to all this is easy—if we bear in mind that the Apostles received *ordinary,* as well as *extraordinary* or *personal powers.*

The Apostles were not only Apostles, but also the first bishops of the Church, while the bishops of the Church today are simply bishops and not Apostles. The Apostles, before they were Apostles, were made priests by Christ Himself. He gave them, first of all, the power of changing bread into His Body and the power of forgiving sins. "This is my body, which is given for you. Do this for a commemoration of me." (*Luke* 22:19). "As the Father hath sent me, I also send you. When he had said this, he breathed on them, and he said to them, Receive ye the Holy Ghost. Whose sins you shall forgive, they are forgiven them; and whose *sins* you shall retain, they are retained." (*John* 20:21-23).

This power of changing bread and wine into the Body and Blood of Christ and the power of forgiving sins are ordinary powers in every priest of God. After His Ascension into Heaven, Christ was to ask the Father to send upon the Apostles the Holy Ghost as *another Paraclete,* (*John* 14:16), to bestow upon them His seven-fold gifts with all the plenitude of grace. The Apostles received such gifts on the Day of Pentecost. The Apostles, therefore, from priests or bishops, were elevated to the plenitude of grace through *the second coming upon them of the Paraclete,* namely, they received *extraordinary* gifts and prerogatives. Both *ordinary and extraordinary* gifts can be found in the same person, but that can only happen through God's special intervention and Providence, as on the Day of Pentecost.

4

Necessity of an Apostolic Succession

Introduction

WITHOUT an ever-living Apostolic Succession, that is, without a living Magisterium to govern the Church, Faith can be neither *universal* nor *one.*

In the Christian Religion, there are two elements which cannot exist without a living constituted authority. They are the *Universality* and the *Unity* of Faith.

Universality of Faith is the presenting of the same Revelation to all men in all ages and places, according to their intelligence. It is only in this way that they all may believe without error what God has revealed.

Unity of Faith is that uniformity of belief and profession which is identical in every member of the Church, in the Negro of darkest Africa, as well as in the Head of Christendom. The intelligence of Christian truth may not exist in the same depth or degree in every individual, but it must be implicitly the same in all the Faithful. The Apostle insists on this in his Epistle to the Ephesians "One Lord, one faith, one baptism." (*Eph.* 4:5).

As there can be but "One Lord and Father of all," so also there can be but *one Faith,* not faiths: *one* without change, *one* in its entirety, *one* in the present time, to the End of the World.

Universality and Unity of Faith are so necessary in the Church of Jesus Christ that, without them, there would be not one Church, but *churches,* as the history of Protestantism and the vicissitudes of human nature demonstrate.

1

The Last Word of the Church on Religious Unity.

When Christ wished to institute something great and indispensable in His Church, He promised it first and conferred it afterwards. Such was the institution of the Primacy of Peter and of His Church. But He not only established a Church. That is not too difficult a task. Men have also established churches. They may be counted by the hundred. Many are gone, many more exist, and others will follow. They are all founded on the sand of human frailty; hence not durable. God only can make His Church everlasting because He is with her "unto the consummation of the world," and because He founded it on the rock. That rock is Peter. "Thou art Peter (rock), and upon this rock I will build my church, and the gates of hell shall not prevail against it." (*Matt.* 16:18). According to these words, Christ was not only to establish a Church, but to establish it on rock. That rock is to be so strong, so great, so durable that it is indestructible. "The gates of hell shall not prevail against it."

And what He promised before His death, He conferred after His Resurrection. He told Peter, and only to Peter: "Feed my lambs," (*John* 21:15-16), that is, the Faithful; "Feed my sheep," (*John* 21:17), that is, "the mothers of lambs," that is, again, the priests and bishops of the Church. To Peter only, Christ also said: "Confirm thy brethren." (*Luke* 22:32).

The above words of Christ Jesus Our Lord, brief as

they are, contain the whole history of Religion—past, present and future. It is the history of the establishment of the grandest institution upon earth, the Catholic Church—the work of God, not of men. It is the history of numberless vicissitudes and of man's ingratitude towards the Creator. But it is also a history of triumphs throughout the ages over Hell and heresy. The rock on which Christ founded His Church shall be beaten for all time by the waves of error and of human depravity, but it shall stand glorious forevermore, "to the consummation of the world." (*Matt.* 28:20).

Every century has brought forth its peculiar error against the Church. So today, under the cloak of religious unity, heresy demands a back door entrance into the Catholic Church.

Pope Pius XI, happily reigning on the Chair of Peter, issued an Encyclical Letter to all the Bishops of the world, warning them of the approaching danger. [This book was first published in 1928, during the reign of Pope Pius XI.] He writes: "In the consciousness of Our Apostolic Office not to let the flock of the Lord be led astray by error, we invoke your zeal to ward off this evil. Nothing is more hallowed to Mother Church than the recall and the return of her wandering children to her bosom. Yet beneath the coaxing words (the appeal of non-Catholics for reunion with the Catholic Church), there is concealed an error so great that it would result in destroying utterly the foundation of the Catholic Faith."[1]

The Encyclical is a document of the first ecclesiastical importance to all Christianity. It is one of the landmarks in the long road of the heretics' return to Mother

1. Pope Pius XI, *On the Promotion of True Religious Unity,* (issued and proclaimed Jan. 6, 1928). Translation made for the N. C. W. C.

Church. It is so adamantine that no doctrinal compromise is possible. "Heaven and earth shall pass away," (*Luke* 21:33), but the Pope's attitude on Dogmatic Truths shall not pass away. It shall stand forever. One denial, one reverse, one compromise on Dogmatic Truths asserted by former Popes, or by the present Pope, is the end of the Catholic Church. Such a possibility is against the promises of Christ; "The gates of hell shall not prevail against it."

The Holy Father first sets forth what non-Catholics ask of him. He then gives the reasons why he cannot comply with their demands. Finally, as a good father, he invites them to their father's house.

Having declared that, "Not all who profess themselves Christians are in agreement," he says, "The authors of the plan for the confederation of all Christian churches believe that Christ's words, *'one fold and one shepherd,'* only express a desire and a prayer of Christ Jesus that has been thus far unanswered. They contend that the unity of faith and government, which is the sign of the true and only Church of Christ, has almost never existed up to this time, and does not exist today; it can be desired, and perhaps in the future it can be obtained through general good will, but meanwhile, it must be considered a fiction. They say, moreover, that the Church, by its very nature, is divided into parts, that it consists of many churches, or particular communities, which are separated among themselves; and although they have certain points of doctrine in common, they differ in others; that each enjoys the same rights; that at most, the [Catholic] Church was the one and only Church between the Apostolic era and the First Ecumenical Councils. . . . There are some among them who assume and grant that Protestantism has rejected inadvisedly certain articles of Faith and certain external rites of worship, which are fully acceptable and useful, and which the Roman Church still preserves. But they add immediately that the Church has corrupted the early religion by adding to it and by proposing for belief certain doctrines that are not only foreign to, but are opposed to the Gospel, among which they bring forward, chiefly, that of the primacy of jurisdiction assigned to Peter and his successors of the Roman See. . . . On such conditions it is clear that the Apostolic See *cannot in any way participate in the reunions,* and that Catholics cannot in any way adhere or grant aid to such efforts. If that would happen, it would give authority to a false Christian religion, completely foreign to the one Church of Christ. Could we tolerate an iniquitous attempt to drag the truth, and indeed the divinely revealed truth, to the level of bargains? For it is the safeguarding of revealed truth now that is being considered."

The Encyclical goes on and says that, if Jesus Christ sent the Holy Ghost upon the Apostles, that they may be taught all truth, "could this doctrine of the Apostles disappear or even be darkened in a Church of which God Himself is the ruler and guardian? And if Our Redeemer openly said that His Gospel cared not only for the apostolic period, but also for all future generations, could it be that the content of the Faith would become, in the passing of time, so obscure and uncertain as to permit today the acceptance of opposed opinions? If that were true, one must likewise say that the coming of the Holy Ghost upon the Apostles and the permanence of the Holy Ghost in the Church, and even the teaching of Jesus Christ, have for these many centuries lost all efficacy and usefulness. To affirm this is blasphemy."

The Holy Father then proceeds to illustrate in a masterly way the incompatibility of Christian societies based on private judgment with the Catholic Church founded on authority. "How could a Christian Society," he says, "be even considered, whose members in matters of faith could each retain his own way of thinking and judging, although it were contrary to the belief of others? Through what agreement could men of opposed opinions become one and the same society of the Faithful? How, for example, can they who affirm that Sacred Tradition is a true source of Divine Revelation and they who deny it become members of one Church? They who hold that an ecclesiastical authority formed of bishops, priests and ministers is divinely constituted, and they who assert that little by little it has been introduced through conditions of time and events? They who adore Christ really present in the Most Holy Eucharist by that wonderful change of bread and wine called transubstantiation, and they who say that the Body of Christ is present there only through the sign and the virtue of the Sacrament? They who hold that in the Eucharist there is a Sacrifice and a Sacrament, and they who say that it is only a remembrance or commemoration of the suffering of Our Lord? They who believe it good and useful to pray to the Saints reigning with Christ, and above all to Mary, the Virgin Mother of God, and to venerate their images; and they who pretend that such a form of worship is wrong, because it draws from the honor due Jesus Christ, the Mediator of God and men? (Cf. *1 Tim.* 2:5). In such differences of opinions, we do not know how a road may be paved to the unity of the Church save alone through one teaching authority, one sole law of belief, and one sole Faith among Christians."

To those who claim that the Church of Jesus Christ is made out of many branches, the Roman-Catholic branch, the Anglo-Catholic branch, the Greek-Catholic branch, etc., the Holy Father answers: "Since the Mystical Body of Christ, that is to say, the Church, is like the physical body, a unity (*1 Cor.* 12:12), a compact thing, closely joined together, (*Eph.* 4:16), it would be false and foolish to say that Christ's Mystical Body could be composed of disjointed and separated members. Whoever, therefore, is not united with it is not a member of it, nor does he communicate with its head, who is Christ. (Cf. *Eph.* 1:22; 4:15). In the one Church of Christ, no one is found and no one perseveres unless he recognizes and accepts obediently the supreme authority of Saint Peter and his legitimate successors. Did not the very ancestors of those who were confused by the error of Photius [of the schismatic Greek church] and the Protestants obey the Roman Bishop as the high shepherd of souls? Children did, alas, abandon their father's house, but the house did not, therefore, fall into ruins, supported as it was by the unceasing help of God."

Finally, the Holy Father makes a touching appeal to all non-Catholics to "return to the common father of all"; he has forgotten the unjust wrongs inflicted against the Holy See and will receive them most lovingly. "If, as they repeat, they desire to be united with Us and with Ours, why do they not hasten to return to the Church, 'the Mother and mistress of all the followers of Christ?'[2] Let these separated children return to the Apostolic See, established in Rome, which the Princes of the Apostles, Peter and Paul, consecrated with their blood; to this See, 'the root and matrix of the Catholic Church,'[3] not indeed with the idea or hope that 'the Church of the living God, the pillar and ground of the truth,' (*1 Tim.* 3:15), will abandon the integrity of the faith and bear their errors, but to subject themselves to its teaching authority and rule. Would that what has not been granted to our predecessors would

---

2. *Council* Later. IV. C. V.
3. *St. Cypr.,* Ep. 48, ad Cornelium, 3.

be granted to Us, to embrace with the heart of a father the children over whom We mourn in their separation from Us by evil discord."

Needless to say, an infinity of different comments, of keen resentments, and we may also add, of impertinent insults, followed the issue of this Encyclical Letter. This is unfortunate. But the Holy Father's attitude, on a Scriptural basis, is the only possible one. All men have an obligation to belong to the Church, and Christ's true Church is the Catholic, Apostolic, Roman Church. To her only the Divine promises have been made. They are unchangeable. The Holy Father, as the custodian of the Revelation, holds it impossible to conceive of a Christian Church where everyone is free to believe as he chooses. However desirable a reunion of all churches might appear, there can be no surrender of revealed truths. There can be no compromise, no independence, no disjunction from the rock on which Christ built His Church. Unity of Faith proceeds only from that rock. That rock is Peter and his legitimate successors.

2

Universality of Faith Cannot be Attained Through The Scriptures Only.

God in His infinite mercy wants all men to share in the fruit of the Redemption. For this reason our Divine Lord charged His first priests, the Apostles, and in their persons all their successors in office to *teach* and *preach* the Gospel to all mankind: "Teach all nations." (*Matt* 28:19). "Preach the Gospel to every creature." (*Mark* 16:15).

However, when God orders His legates to make His message known, He intends them so to propose it that men may believe without error. On such knowledge and belief depends salvation or damnation. "He that believeth and is baptized shall be saved, but he that believeth not shall be condemned." (*Mark* 16:16).

Now, Revelation is not an earthly knowledge—scientific or philosophical—which one is free to admit or reject. It is a knowledge and belief upon which depends eternal happiness. Hence, that knowledge and belief must be based on absolute truth and without danger of error. But how can man acquire truth without error? By reading the Scriptures, some will say. And if we further ask them: Are all God's truths contained in the Scriptures? Yes, they will insist. We must not believe whatever is *not* found in the Scriptures: "Search the Scriptures." (*John* 5:39). But does the mere reading of the Scriptures lead us to the true knowledge of Faith? Comparatively speaking, typography is only a "modern" invention, and not all men can read or write. In the first 1500 years of Christianity, reading and writing was a blessing confined to only a few. Even today there are millions who are illiterate. How are they to be saved?

Granted, however, that all men and women could read, how many of them would have time and leisure to read and study? Even if they had, how could they learn and judge of all Christian truths without responsible teachers and without danger of error? And when they would disagree about the most fundamental truths of the Christian Religion, who would be able to settle their controversies—and settle them without error once and for all? St. Augustine remarks: "If one wants to learn a trade, no matter how low and easy, he must have a master and a teacher. What is more arrogant than to refuse to know the books of the divine sacraments [sacred things] and their interpreters and to condemn what they know nothing about?"[4]

---

4. St. August., *Utility of Belief*, N. 35.

But some will claim that the true knowledge of Faith is attained through the reading of the Scriptures accompanied by *internal illustrations* and *inspirations* of the Holy Ghost. There is nothing to warrant such a claim. Experience teaches that one's inspirations are subject to ridiculous illusions. What one person affirms, another denies. How can the Holy Ghost enlighten the mind of the Faithful on the same subject in opposite directions? Can the Spirit of Truth show the same thing as *black* to one and *white* to another? Granted that all God's truths were to be found in the Scriptures, can we know them well from that source alone? Some passages are very hard to understand, whatever Protestants may say to the contrary.

Who, then, is to solve these problems for us and solve them without error? Preachers, or those who make a special study of Religion? Behold, how some Christians blindly contradict themselves. They separated themselves from the Church and rejected its authority on the grounds that the Bible and the Bible only is the Rule of Faith, without any other outside authority. Private judgment, according to them, is the supreme authority on all matters of Religion. And still they are forced to admit that they need the help of preachers or of others well versed in the Bible—but never of the Church! What does that mean? Nothing, except that a great blunder has been committed in the past. One precipice leads to another. Whole nations rebelled against the *living voice* of the *Infallible* Church, only to have recourse to other *living but fallible voices.* Is it any wonder that those same nations are now giving up Bible, preachers *and* Religion?

The Catholic Church has always taught the Scriptures. She saved them from destruction in the ravages of time and explained them to the people. This is a fact and not a presumption nor usurpation on the part of the Church.

She bases her authority of teaching and preaching on the commission given to her by Christ Himself. Without her authority of teaching and direction, there would be a complete chaos as to what man must know and believe in order to be saved.

It is not enough to "search the Scriptures" (*John* 7:52) for acquiring the right knowledge of the Faith.

3

Universality of Faith Cannot be Effected by Immediate Revelation or Scientific Demonstration, But Only by the Living Authority of the Church.

The theory that Universality of Faith can be reached through the Scriptures must be abandoned. But there are two more conceivable ways: *Immediate revelation* and *scientific demonstration.*

Immediate revelation is made to single individuals. Scientific demonstration is the manner in which one may be convinced by arguments of the truths of the Christian Religion.

Both lack *generality* or *universality*. They cannot reach the great mass of the faithful. They are therefore of no avail to the great bulk of humanity.

We do not deny that *immediate revelation* can be and has been granted by God to some favored souls. But we emphatically declare that such cases have been rare. We are even ready to admit that, absolutely speaking, God could make such immediate revelation to every man, woman and child. But we cannot concede that such order of revelation has ever been promised by God. Nor has it ever existed in the Christian Religion.

Scientific demonstration should comprise not only the possibility and the fact of Revelation, but also all the truths, precepts and institutions of the Religion of Christ, as well as the true and infallible sense of the Scriptures. All these things should be shown to every man and woman, not through the authority of the Church, but through human reason, persuasion and conviction. This would be the scientific method. But how many could be able through this scientific method to grasp the truth? How many could be reached with this method? And who can ever think that such has been the case with the vast majority of mankind? All men are to a certain extent, according to St. Augustine, "foolish before they receive the Faith."[5]

The authority of man is always human and must be fallible. Who then can depend, especially in matters of religion, on human authority? Where are those *learned* men who—in the sphere of Revelation, but without much sanctity—have reached the summit of Science so safely and to such a degree that no one can doubt their sincerity or decision? We know too well from history and experience that in *abstract matters,* considering the nature and difficulties of the truths of Faith, learned men—even great Saints—have disagreed. How then can the uneducated ever be induced through scientific demonstrations to accept so blindly the conclusions of *learned men?* As a rule, the more *learned* men are, the more they disagree among themselves. And that too about current questions of the day.

Why then should these *learned men* supplant the Church authorities, constituted by Christ to teach and preach on matters of Faith? Was not this human factor the very reason why so many peoples rejected the authority of the Church? They did not want any human authority. This is a pitiful contradiction. There is nothing else to solve the

5. August., *Utility of Belief.*

problem of arriving at truth, then, but an infallible authority. This Authority can make no mistakes in matters of Faith. It has been constituted by Christ as the Official Teacher of mankind—to the End of Time. "Behold I am with you all days, even to the consummation of the world." (*Matt.* 28:20).

Without the authority and direction of that Infallible Teaching Body, Universality of Faith is impossible.

4

Without Church Authority There can be No Unity of Faith.

There are many reasons which show the necessity for an authoritative tribunal if the words of the Apostle, "One Lord, one faith," (*Eph.* 4:5), are to be realized in every age, and in the uttermost parts of the world.

Human nature is and always will be the same. Man is inclined to be independent in his views and tries to force his ideas on others, until he is shown to be evidently wrong. Nor does he sometimes stop even then. He persists in his error and resists the known truth, thus sinning against the Holy Ghost.

There will always be scandals in the Church, but Christ said, "Woe to the world because of scandals. For it must needs be that scandals come, but nevertheless, woe to that man by whom the scandal cometh." (*Matt.* 18:7). God, however, permits this evil, that the faith of the elect may be strengthened. "Power is made perfect in infirmity." (*2 Cor.* 12:9).

This is especially true of our own times. All manner of literature floods the world. There are too many people who consider themselves the judges of everyone and of everything. Teachers of all kinds raise their chair of pestilence in every corner of our cities and villages. Perhaps the grand old Church is still there, or it has just made its appearance. Its doors are open. But most people pass by and go to hear those who suit their passions and inclinations. New fads are the order of the day. Wind and pride are sown in their hearts. Very little is left of the old and eternal truths, which Christ and the Apostles proclaimed to the world. "For there shall be a time, when they will not endure sound doctrine; but, according to their own desires, they will heap to themselves teachers, having itching ears, and will indeed turn away their hearing from the truth, but will be turned unto fables." (*2 Tim.* 4:3-4).

Thus is Christianity divided and subdivided. The books of Revelation are made the anvil of centuries, on which every Christian is allowed to pound at his own pleasure. Confusion and deafening sounds are heard where peace should be announced "to men of good will." Should not such a condition of things open the eyes of all Christians and make them realize the necessity of a living tribunal, to which Christ has committed the sacred right and duty of keeping intact, at any cost, the Deposit of Faith? "Preach the word, be instant, in season, out of season: reprove, entreat, rebuke, in all patience and doctrine." (*2 Tim.* 4:2).

But the world does not want Christ. Nations and societies are governed by their own laws. Living judges are appointed to interpret a dead-letter code of laws or by-laws, and their decisions are final and binding. The same treatment is not accorded the Church by those same children of the world. Are not perhaps the Scriptures and the laws made by man equally a dead letter in themselves? The Scriptures are indeed the Word of God. But at the same time, they need living interpreters. If the laws of man, made by man and for man, need living and authoritative interpreters for their enforcement, how much more does the Word of God need interpreters, to explain it without error and enforce it with authority?

If the Scriptures are clear to understand, why did Martin Luther and his imitators make new catechisms of Christian doctrine? Why do they fill the libraries with innumerable books of interpretations, explanations and commentaries? Above all, why have they *any* churches, where the Scriptures are explained, if the Scriptures are sufficient? And if there should be a church, why so many churches, of so many denominations, in every city and in every town?

If there is a clear statement in the Scriptures which all Christians should endeavor to put into execution, it is certainly the desire which Christ expressed in His prayer to the Eternal Father on the eve of His Passion and Death, "That they all may be one, as thou, Father, in me, and I in thee; that they also may be one in us." (*John* 17:21). What else do such words mean than that all Christ's followers should first of all have the same faith?—"One Lord, one faith, one baptism." (*Eph.* 4:5).

But unfortunately, there are too many controversies which agitate and divide Christianity. How are they to be settled? If there must be a judge, can it be the Scriptures? Can the Scriptures speak and pronounce the sentence in such unmistakable terms that both litigants know who is right and who is wrong? Well did the old Roman wisdom proclaim more than 2000 years ago: *No one is judge in his own case.* Hence, it was not to the Scriptures, but to Peter and his successors that Christ said, "confirm thy brethren." (*Luke* 22:32). Tertullian declared in the Second Century that "Religious controversies should not and cannot be settled only by the Scriptures because, not only does the Apostle forbid such disputes among Christians, but also because they bear no fruit. 'Avoid foolish questions,' says the Apostle (*Titus* 3:9) 'and genealogies, and contentions, and strivings about the law. For they are unprofitable and vain.' "[6] "What good will it do," the great apologist continues, most expert in the Scriptures, "if what you will defend shall be denied; or on the contrary, what you will deny shall be defended? You will certainly lose nothing but your voice in the contention; you will gain nothing but bile from the blasphemy."[7] And he comes to the following unanswerable conclusion: "We must not have recourse to, nor constitute a fight on the Scriptures, in which victory is uncertain or none at all," but "the order of things required to be first proposed, [and] what is now only to be disputed: To whom belongs the Faith itself, whose are the Scriptures? By whom, and through whom, and when, and to whom was the authority to teach delivered, by which men are made Christians? For where the true Christian discipline and doctrine are shown to be, there will also be the truth of the Scriptures and of their interpretation and of all Christian Tradition."[8]

A living, infallible tribunal is therefore essential and necessary to keep intact, not only the Deposit of Faith and to propose it without error, but also to keep everywhere and at all times the Unity of the Faith, which is so essential in the Religion of Christ.

5

Universality and Unity of Faith Have Been Lost by All the Oldest Denominations of Protestantism.

All that we have been saying is fully confirmed by the history of Protestantism. Having rejected the authority of

6. Tertull. "Prescript," C. XV.
7. Tertull. C. XVII.
8. Tertull. C. XIX.

the Church, the first so-called Reformers substituted the private judgment of the faithful. Individual judgment takes the place of all Church authority. Every man, they said, who hears or reads the Scriptures, is enlightened and inspired by the Holy Ghost to such a degree that the Scriptures become clear to him and the soul is filled with inspiration and good will. That illumination and inspiration renders any outside authority useless and of no avail. Each one is sufficient to himself. Hence, Universality and Unity of Faith must of necessity follow, as the Holy Ghost, the Spirit of Truth, is one and cannot contradict Himself.

Beautiful theory indeed, but not supported by facts! If the pagan poet Horace had once tried that theory, as he had more than once tasted the wines of ancient Rome, he would have once more exclaimed: "The laboring mountain brings forth a ridiculous mouse."

The theory is nothing but illusion and deception. First of all, if the Holy Ghost illuminates and inspires in the same way everyone in the reading or hearing of the Scriptures, then there could not be but one Christian Church, and that Church could not be other than the Catholic Church. She was the first one that came out of the hands of the Son of God. Only with her did the Holy Ghost promise to abide forever.

Suppose, however, for the sake of argument, that the Catholic Church should be excluded from the illumination and inspiration of the Holy Ghost, then there should be but *one* great Protestant Church. For the Protestant principle is the same, namely, that everyone who reads or hears the Scriptures is enlightened and inspired by the Holy Ghost. That illumination and inspiration must have the same conclusion in everyone. It is the same spirit, who illumines and inspires each. This principle, however, instead of being a bond of union, has proved to be a terrible cleaver, splitting Protestantism into divisions and subdivisions. Every Protestant can be a church in himself and unto himself.

Instead of establishing one Religion that could command the respect of the world, this alleged illumination and inspiration has created so many Protestant sects that we can hardly determine their correct number. The history of Protestantism is nothing but a history of variations, as Fenelon calls it. Not even the first Reformers could agree among themselves. Is it then any wonder that their followers devastated for many years with sword and fire great parts of Germany, Switzerland, France, Scotland and England? Many of them escaped persecution and death by settling in America.

Recognizing the fallacy of this principle, Luther himself, writing to Zwingli, declared: "If the world will last much longer, on account of the different interpretations of the Scriptures that now exist, in order to keep the Unity of Faith, it will be again necessary to receive the decrees of Councils and to have recourse to them."[9]

Fair-minded Protestants are obliged to recognize two Luthers; one before the year 1525, or before the great rebellion in Germany; the other after the year 1525. The first Luther, by breaking with the authority of the Church, told the people that every Christian is "taught of God." (*John* 6:45). The second Luther, seeing the great divisions which began to spread within his own ranks, in order to keep some unity and coherency among his followers, declared that "the ecclesiastical teaching body, having been instituted by God, has for its source Christ Himself, as well as His mandate and institution."[10]

9. Luther, *About the Eucharist.*
10. In Jörg., T. I, p. 386.

"The first Luther," writes the Protestant Schwartz, "with a seditious audacity appealed to the conscience of the people against ecclesiastical hierarchy (namely, the Church authorities); the second Luther wavered nervously between the unlimited liberty of the spirit and the severe authority of an authentic teaching ministry."[11] Hence it is that the same Martin Luther, the head of the revolt against the authority of Rome, he who in the beginning of his rebellion claimed to be "taught of God," illuminated and inspired by the Holy Ghost, gave at different times different judgments on the revealed truths, as if the Holy Ghost could reverse Himself to suit Luther and his political intriguers.

The majority of the Protestant denominations afterward declared that Unity of Faith—consequently, Universality of Faith also—are not necessary. Such admission, although wrong, is however, more conformable to the principle of private judgment.

6

Universality and Unity of Faith Do Not Exist in the Protestant Denominations of Today.

If neither Universality nor Unity of Faith could be found in the older Protestant denominations, the Protestantism of today does not fare any better.

All the Protestant denominations of today, although each differs from the others, may belong broadly to two classes: those who have retained the fundamental principle of private judgment; and those who, seeing the pernicious consequences of private judgment, have set up an authority.

To the first class belong all those who carry the prin-

11. In Jörg., T. I. pp. 416-419.

ciple of private judgment to its furthest end. They are the *genuine Protestants* and by far the more numerous, especially among the intelligent classes. They practically deny that the Scriptures are really the only Rule of Faith. On the contrary, they affirm that one is perfectly free to follow the Scriptures, or only a part of them, according to his own view, and always in the way he understands it to be true.

These are the Rationalists, who are, strictly speaking, Christian only in name. For, as the Atheist Hartmann remarks: "The Reformers did not realize that their faith, by which they believe in the infallible canonicity of the Scriptures, is based entirely on the faith which teaches *the infallible testimony of the Church and of the Ecclesiastical Tradition.* By protesting against the infallibility of the Church and of Tradition, they destroyed the foundation itself. The keystone of the firm hierarchical building, once broken, the ruin of the whole edifice had by degrees to follow."[12]

Thus has the principle of private judgment slowly but surely paved the way to unbelief. It is the Father of Atheism. With this class of Protestants are connected all those who believe that, to be a Christian, it is enough to profess a certain faith in Christ as Saviour, or a certain *general* faith in Christ and in the Scriptures, as a certain *public testimonial* of the Christian Religion. Many do not believe in the virgin birth of Christ, and still they believe they are good Presbyterians, good Episcopalians, good Methodists, good Congregationalists. They have established their own creeds and revise them periodically. But neither the elders nor their bishops dare but seldom to bring to trial their preachers accused of heresy. These men

12. Hartmann, *Internal Dissolution of Christianity.*

know too well that such teachers have the sympathy of a good part of the brethren. Should action be taken, the denomination is disrupted, and thus another denomination comes into existence. It is a fact that a great number of Protestants, among them preachers and bishops, do not, practically speaking, believe in any dogma.

They are now distinguished as *Modernists* and *Fundamentalists.* The Modernists follow the dictates of their private judgment, enlightened, as they claim, and inspired by the Holy Ghost. The fundamentalists believe in and are bound by their "Creed," based on the Scriptures.

All Protestant denominations, from the Reformers down to our present day, try to justify their break with the Catholic Church on account of authority. Hence, they substituted the private judgment of the faithful. If such is the case, then the Protestant Modernist principle, wrong as it is, is more consistent with the Protestant principle of private judgment, because, as they say, "no Christian is obliged to be bound by any human authority in matters of faith."

Fundamentalists, while they apparently are right, because they uphold the Scriptures and authority, are in open contradiction with themselves, because their "Creeds" are made by their own ministry—a human, self-constituted authority. Was it not on account of *authority* that they broke with the Church of Rome? Who gave them the *authority* to impose *authority* on others?

To the *second class* described above belong all those who, preferring *unity of faith* to *private judgment,* want an ecclesiastical authority firmly established upon the faithful and obeyed by all. To this class, strictly speaking, belong the *Fundamentalists,* as we have already seen, but more especially the Lutherans of the old faith and the Reformed Lutherans or Evangelicals. The old Lutherans follow the authority of the first Reformers, together with the Symbolic Books and those traditions which in this way crept in since the 16th Century.

When the old Lutherans defend themselves against *indifferentism and rationalism,* or *too much independence* in matters of faith, they deny that there should be in matters of faith any *principle of independence,* but rather the *principle of authority.* But they forget that it was through that same principle of independence that they came into existence as a religious body, separating themselves from the Church of Rome. At the same time, when they insist on the principle of authority, they overlook the fact that they were the first who rejected authority, by rejecting the authority of the Catholic Church. For the Divine Tradition of the Catholic Church—that is, for an Apostolic Succession—they substituted another tradition, the origin of which was the negation of the same principle of Tradition.

The Reformed Lutherans do not admit the authority of the first Reformers. They approve and defend the authority of their church. It was given to her—they say— by Christ and the Apostles. But in the same breath they approve the rebellion of the 16th Century. They admit that there must be authority in the Church, but as authority did not really exist in the Church in the time of the great religious Reformation, so they say it came to them through their apostasy from the Catholic Church.

One contradiction upon another! It is no wonder that many Protestants who do not belong to the old or the Reformed Lutherans have many times declared that "they would rather follow a more holy Tradition and a more Spiritual Pontiff of the Catholic Church than those tables of stones which do not have their origin from Mount Sinai."[13] The Protestant D. Shenkel, writing to the Protes-

13. In Jörg., T. I., pp. 122-130.

tant D. Stahl, says: "If I had to recognize any authority in the Church, logic itself convinces me to turn to the Catholic Church."[14]

The same argument could be used against the High Episcopalians, Latter Day Saints, Adventists and others.

Therefore, all denominations which at the beginning of their rebellion rejected the authority of the Catholic Church cut themselves off from the Tree of Life. They became dead branches. For, rejecting the authority of the Catholic Church, they severed their connection with Peter, to whom Christ said, "Feed my lambs . . . feed my sheep." (*John* 21:15, 16, 17). And when they saw the deadly consequences of their rebellion and decided that they must be governed by some authority, not by the authority of the Catholic Church, but by an authority established by themselves, they became guilty of the greatest crime in the history of Christianity. They had no right to substitute their own traditions nor their own authority for the Traditions and Authority of the Catholic Church. Only to the Apostles and their successors in office Christ said: "As the Father hath sent me, I also send you." (*John* 20:21). Christ did not send them, nor did the Church.

7

The Successors of the Apostles Are the Infallible Guardians of the Deposit of Faith.

When Our Lord gave the commission to the Apostles to go and teach all nations, He also accompanied His command with the consoling and encouraging words,"Behold I am with you all days, even to the consummation of the world." (*Matt.* 28:20). As long then as

---

14. In Jörg., p. 135.

the Apostles were to teach all nations, *viz.,* all humanity, of all ages and places "to observe all things whatsoever" He had commanded them, He was also to be with them even unto the End of the World. (Cf. *Matt.* 28:20). Christ will guide, protect and assist the Church forever, that she may live and prosper and teach nothing but the truth. Therefore, according to the command of Christ, we have on the one hand the Apostles who must teach the whole world—all generations in every place—in order that they may "observe all things whatsoever I have commanded you," (*Matt.* 28:20); and on the other hand, we have the assurance of the same Lord Jesus Christ that He will be with them forever—with them preaching, with them teaching, with them ruling the Church of God. This is God's will, that all humanity may be saved. As the Son of God has redeemed all, even the last man who will ever be born of woman, "all truth" that belongs to man's eternal salvation must also be taught in *all generations* by the Apostles in every part of the world. This, however, the Apostles could not possibly do of themselves. Like all other mortals, they had to go the way of the flesh. This work they did throughout the ages, are doing now, and will do "even unto the consummation of the world," *through their successors in office.* Therefore, the command given to the Apostles to "teach all nations . . . teaching them to observe all things whatsoever I have commanded you," (*Matt.* 28:19-20), is binding not only on the college of the Apostles, but also upon their successors in office; for Christ's command is an ordinary one. It did not concern only the persons of the Apostles, but the Apostles as teachers, namely, the teaching body of the Church, which is to endure as long as there are souls to be saved.

If the solemn office and duty of the Apostles was to promulgate "all truth" to all nations, without corrupting or adding to it, the duty of their successors is consequently to keep without corruption all the truth which the Apostles promulgated to the world. They must keep intact the Deposit of the Faith entrusted to them, without mutilation, corruption or addition. Hence the Apostle writes: "Hold the form of sound words which thou hast heard of me in faith, and in the love which is in Christ Jesus"; and "keep the good thing committed to thy trust by the Holy Ghost, who dwelleth in us." (*2 Tim.* 1:13-14). "And the things which thou hast heard of me by many witnesses, the same commend to faithful men, who shall be fit to teach others also." (*2 Tim.* 2:2). "Continue thou in those things which thou hast learned and which have been committed to thee, knowing of whom thou hast learned *them*." (*2 Tim.* 3:14). Likewise, the Faithful are commanded, under pain of excommunication, not to accept any other Gospel besides the one which they have received and was preached to them. (*Gal.* 1:8-9). "Contend earnestly for the faith once delivered to the saints," (*Jude* 1:3), and "Confirmed in the faith, as also you have learned . . . beware lest any man cheat you by philosophy and vain deceit; according to the tradition of men, according to the elements of the world, and not according to Christ." (*Col.* 2:7-8).

The successors of the Apostles are therefore the guardians of the Deposit [of the Faith]. They are the only ones. The Faithful must simply accept from them the Deposit and the doctrines contained therein. What else does this mean but that the successors of the Apostles are the sole and infallible guardians of the Deposit?

We also know, as proved in another part of this work, how the successors of the Apostles throughout all ages, obeyed the above mentioned Apostolic warning. This they could only accomplish because Christ is with the Church, "even unto the consummation of the world" and because He is "full of grace and truth." (*John* 1:14).

8

Those Who are Charged with the Infallible Guardianship of the Deposit of Faith are Also its Infallible Teachers.

It is a fact that even intelligent men do not always agree, even on elementary subjects that belong to this world. No wonder, therefore, that certain human beings, brought forth in sorrow by their earthly mother into this world, cause so much grief to their Spiritual Mother, the Church. They seem to live a life of constant disputes, altercations and discussions—kept too long by pride and heated by the inspiration of the devil. They do not or cannot perceive the abstruse and profound truths of religion.

When we observe the controversies which so often arise among the members of the Church, when we reflect upon the abomination of desolation of so many national churches, when we consider that the Church has suffered so much from the rebellion of her children, we cannot but behold the necessity of Divine Tradition.

It is a mistake, however, to entertain the idea of "Tradition" as consisting in the conversation of a certain aggregate of the formularies of the Faith. That may be the object—the material object—of the things to be believed. *The essential principle of Divine Tradition is the perpetual and infallible keeping of the true sense and of the true understanding of the Deposit of Faith by an ever living Apostolic Succession.* We must never lose sight of this most important point.

If controversies arose in the past and are still going on at present, we may be sure that some of them will survive and others will spring up in the future. What then could settle a religious question definitely? Not the material object of Tradition, that is, not the dead letter, but the Spirit; not the Bible, but the living voice of those whom "the Holy Ghost has placed . . . to rule the church of God." (*Acts* 20:28).

It is absolutely essential that the true sense of the doctrine, as well as the integrity of the Deposit of Faith, be maintained in the Church. For if it is useful that what is implicitly contained in other revealed truths be explicitly declared, it is also expedient that what is doubtful or ambiguous be authoritatively explained and settled. More so, it is necessary that what is injurious, pernicious or destructive to the Faith be peremptorily repelled. But all this cannot be accomplished unless the guardians of the Faith are not only learned and holy, but also infallible. If the Faith is to be kept intact, whole and pure, it is necessary that the guardians—the infallible guardians of the Deposit—be also its infallible teachers and defenders.

For we cannot conceive of an infallible guardianship of the material Deposit of Faith without its being also infallible in its declarations, explanations and defense. Evidently, an infallible guardianship involves and contains a double office. These offices may be distinguished, but cannot be separated; they must go together.

The words of the Apostle, "And he (Christ) gave some apostles, and some prophets, and some evangelists, and other some pastors and doctors," (*Eph.* 4:11), evidently distinguish and separate the persons having a different duty to perform, that is, of Apostles or of prophets, etc.; but when the Apostle designates the same persons with a different title through the conjunction *and*, that is, of pastors *and* doctors, he plainly indicates the *same persons* having the *double duty* of pastorship and doctorship.

This unity of pastorship and doctorship in the same person, according to the Apostle, is confirmed by the teaching of the Fathers. Thus St. Augustine: "The pastors and doctors whom you wanted me above all to distinguish, I believe, are those same ones which you yourself have thought, namely, that we must not think that *some ones* are the pastors and *some others* are the doctors; but rather, having mentioned first the *pastors,* he (the Apostle) subjoined *doctors,* in order that pastors may understand that it belongs to their office to teach. For, he does not say *some are pastors* and *some are doctors,* in the same manner of speaking above, saying that He [Christ] gave *some* Apostles, and *some* prophets, and *some* evangelists; but He comprises and designates two names somewhat as one: *other some* pastors and doctors."[15]

Likewise, St. Jerome declares: "From what the Apostle said about the three above mentioned offices, namely, that some are Apostles, others are prophets, and others are evangelists, must not be understood that there must also be different offices to pastors and to doctors. For he does not say *other some are pastors and other some are doctors,* but *other some are pastors and doctors,* in order that he who is pastor must be also doctor."[16]

This is so true that the same Apostle, writing to Timothy, joins together the duty of the pastorship with that of the doctorship, that is to say, the duty of keeping whatever was entrusted and delivered to him with the duty of teaching. After he warns him, "But continue thou in those things which thou hast learned, and which have been committed to thee, knowing of whom thou hast learned them," (*2 Tim.* 3:14)—behold the duty of the pastorship—he rec-

---

15. August., *Epist.* 149, N. 11, ad Paulinum.
16. St. Jerome's *Commentaries.*

ommends to him the Scriptures as a means to salvation for himself (*2 Tim.* 3:15) and as an instrument to teach others: "All Scripture, inspired of God, is profitable to teach, to reprove, to correct, to instruct in justice." (*2 Tim.* 3:16). Behold the duty of teaching.

Moreover, as the Apostle enjoins Timothy to teach the right doctrine, "O Timothy, keep that which is committed to thy trust, avoiding the profane novelties of words, and oppositions of knowledge falsely so called," (*1 Tim.* 6:20); he also commands him to keep the Deposit of Faith: "Hold the form of sound words which thou hast heard of me in faith . . . keep the good thing committed to thy trust by the Holy Ghost, who dwelleth in us." (*2 Tim.* 1:13-14).

In other words, the Apostle wants Timothy—and in the person of Timothy, all the bishops of the Church—to teach the doctrine of Christ, because it is to them that God has entrusted the guardianship of the Deposit of Faith.

Therefore, these two offices of pastorship and of doctorship can be distinguished, but not separated in the same person. The "pastor" is also "doctor." He is pastor "by keeping the good thing committed to thy trust by the Holy Ghost"; he is doctor "by holding the form of sound words which thou hast heard of me in faith." There is a union, a personal union, in the double office of pastorship and doctorship: neither one can be legitimately and truly conceived or exercised without the other.

Hence, if as we have already proved the pastors of the Church are infallible in the guardianship of the Deposit, how much more so they must also be in its teaching? For the same principle which confers infallibility for the integral keeping of the Deposit of the Faith confers also infallibility in its teaching.

Whatever proves the tutelage of Christ and the assistance of the Holy Ghost promised by Christ Himself to the pastors of the Church, at the same time proves that that same tutelage and the assistance of the Holy Ghost are the *efficient cause* by which the same pastors of the Church are also infallible in its explanation, declaration and defense. *For no other reason are the pastors infallible in the keeping of the Deposit of Faith than for rendering its true sense to the people.* What good can the infallibility of the keeping of the Deposit of Faith afford the Church if the same pastors who are charged with such infallible guardianship could err in its teaching?

Hence, the Fathers of the Church, in explaining the promised tutelage of Christ (*Matt.* 28:20) and the promised assistance of the Holy Ghost (*John* 14:26), by which they prove the infallibility of the pastors of the Church in the guardianship of the Deposit of Faith, prove also in the meantime, the infallibility of the same pastors in its teaching.

Cardinal Franzelin writes, "The reason why it is heretical to reject the sense of the Scriptures given by the common consent of the Church is derived, according to Irenæus, 'from the *charismata* of the Lord, by which all those—among whom is the succession of the Church from the Apostles—explain to us the Scriptures without danger.'[17] The *efficient cause* by which 'the most diligent study does not go into error in the Universal Church,' according to Augustine, is 'the Lord, who dwells in the Church.'[18] The *cause of the infallibility* of dogmatic definitions, according to Cyril of Alexandria, 'is Christ, who presides,' and 'the Holy Ghost, who speaks through the councils.'[19] The *cause* for which 'Religion has always been

17. Iren. IV, 26, N. 5.
18. August., *In Ps.,* N. 12.
19. *Cyril Alex,* Tom. V, Part II, 175.

kept *immaculate* in the Apostolic See' is due to the fact that we cannot pass over the sentence of Our Lord Jesus Christ, who said: 'Thou art Peter, and upon this rock I will build My Church,' according to the Profession of the Orientals, subscribed under Pope Hormisdas. The *incontestable reason for the admirable consent* of the Fathers—scattered in all parts of the world and in all ages—is nowhere to be sought but in the 'special divine gift of the Holy Ghost which they received in the one and same spirit to teach,'[20] according to Theodoretus, and in 'the grace of the Holy Ghost, by whom they are taught, and in consent among themselves,'[21] according to Leontius Galland." Thus Cardinal Franzelin.[22]

Therefore, the pastors of the Church who are charged with the infallible custody of the Deposit of Faith are also at the same time its infallible teachers.

---

20. *Theodoretus,* T. IV, p. 33.
21. *Leontius Galland,* XII, p. 682.
22. *De Trad. et. Script,* Th. XXV, part II.

5

Testimony of the First Centuries

Introduction

THE principles and fundamentals of the Christian Religion were from the beginning not something theoretical, but something practical. They were substantially observed every day in the usages, practice and profession of the first Faithful, as they have always been in the Catholic Church. It was precisely the ministry established by Christ and the Apostles—namely, the Apostolic Succession—that kept ever alive those principles and fundamentals. It was that *living, teaching body* which trained the hearts of the first Christians in the Love of God, that Love which is cherished by the longings of Hope and nourished by the bread of Faith. This same living, authoritative ministry is as vital to the Christian Religion as food is to the body. It is such a necessary element in the life of the Church, such an indispensable foundation to the whole edifice which Christ built up by His Death and Resurrection, that it is impossible that it should go unnoticed or be ignored, even by those who do not belong to it. It shows itself in such a tangible manner in all ages and places that it inspires and thoroughly permeates, not only the daily actions of the Faithful, but to some extent, even of those who are outside the Church.

Such being the case, it was impossible that the Constitution which the Apostles established in the name of

Christ could have ever changed so suddenly and so substantially as to make place for another that is radically different.

Such is the change, the enemies of Tradition contend, that took place soon after the death of the Apostles. According to them, Tradition was entirely discarded and the Faithful had complete recourse to the Apostolic writings.

But how could this change ever happen when every church had its pastor appointed by the Apostles or by their immediate successors? Do the Scriptures sanction that change? Rather, were not the Faithful warned to *"hold the traditions* which you have learned, whether by word, or by our epistle?" (*2 Thess.* 2:14). Such claim is without foundation; it lacks good judgment and is a reflection on the power of Christ—as if He founded His Church upon the sand and not upon the rock. The impossibility of change is fully evident from all the monuments and testimonies of the early centuries. These testimonies are as numerous as the stars in the firmament and as clear as the light of the midday sun.

All the writers of the first centuries bear testimony to Tradition. These writers have been justly called "Fathers" of the Church because they have been the witnesses of that Faith which was professed and believed in the usages, practices and solemn professions in the first centuries of Christianity.

We shall at present confine ourselves to the first three centuries, which to a certain extent may be called the *Apostolic Period,* because of its venerable antiquity, being so closely connected with the time of the Apostles. For, Tertullian justly observes: "Christ sent the Apostles, who founded Churches in every city, from which the others have borrowed the traditions of the Faith and the seed of doctrine, and daily borrow in order to become Churches, so that they are also Apostolic in that they are the offspring of the Apostolic Churches."[1]

For this reason if among the first generations of Christians—beginning with the first down to the last generation of the Apostolic period—we find the Christian Churches governed by the principles of Tradition, namely, ruled by a continued succession of bishops in union and harmony among themselves in the doctrine of Christ, in communion with one another, especially with the successor of St. Peter in Rome, teaching, warning, commanding the Faithful to "hold the traditions which you have learned, whether by word, or by our epistle," (*2 Thess.* 2:14), without doubt Tradition *is and must be*—with the Scriptures—the Rule of Faith which Christ and the Apostles intended and in fact left in the Church for the government of the Faithful until the End of Time. *If this is proved to be the case in the first ages of Christianity, there is no reason why the same order of things should have been changed afterwards.* We must keep in mind the remarkable words of the Apostle: "But though we or an Angel from heaven, preach a gospel to you besides that which we have preached to you, let him be anathema." (*Gal.* 1:8).

1

The Apostolic Churches Were Ruled by Tradition, as Well as by the Scriptures.

Before we begin to discuss thoroughly this part of our subject, we must make our meaning clear. When Catholics resort to the testimonies and the doctrine of ancient Christianity, they do not appeal as to authentic, veritable or

---

1. Tertull., "Prescript," C. XX.

unadulterated truths of Divine Revelation. They simply appeal to the unanimous consent of antiquity as to an *historical testimony of the Faith,* which no reasonable man will reject. Such *historical testimony* shows *what the whole Christian antiquity thought of, what they believed, and how they professed always and everywhere the institution of Christ and the Apostles.*

From such testimony, however, students of Religion cannot fail to reach one conclusion: The principle of Tradition which all antiquity held—theoretically and practically—was always and everywhere the same as the Catholic Church holds today. This most important conclusion, however, is not reached on account of the supernatural authority of the witnesses, which authority Protestants rightly or wrongly deny. It is reached because of the historical impossibility of change and corruption, which, according to them, must have happened immediately after the death of the Apostles.

That this assertion is historically untrue is evident from the Apostolic Churches and writers. Although the Apostolic Period extends to the first centuries, strictly speaking, *Apostolic Churches* are only those particular Churches which were founded by the Apostles. On that account, they enjoyed a special dignity and were held in great esteem and importance. Tertullian sometimes calls them *"Mother Churches."* We intend here to speak only of those Churches. The time to which naturally belonged the first few generations of Christians extends to about the middle of the Second Century.

As those Churches are called "Apostolic," so also are called "Apostolic Fathers" those early writers of the Church who flourished in that limited time, as being either disciples of the Apostles, or men who had conversed with the Apostles' immediate disciples. While their writings do not, as a rule, exhibit much intellectual power or ability, they are of a value because they show how the first generations of Christians understood the work of Christ and the Apostles, what they believed, and what is most important, how the *Church was governed.*

These Apostolic Fathers most emphatically declare that the consent and testimony of the bishops and pastors in one uninterrupted succession and union in the Old Faith of the Apostles is the surest sign of the true doctrine of Jesus Christ. They believed that only in this way could the Deposit of the Faith always be kept intact and pure.

The Apostle had already warned the first Christians that after his departure, many false teachers would arise among them to pervert their Faith. In order to keep the Faith, he had therefore advised them most emphatically not to listen to false teachers. "As we said before, so now I say again: if anyone preach to you a gospel besides that which you have received, let him be anathema." (*Gal.* 1:9).

Hence, before their death, the Apostles disposed that others should succeed them in office. It is for this reason that the Apostolic Fathers, such as St. Clement of Rome, successor of Peter in Rome; St. Ignatius, Bishop of Antioch; St. Polycarp, Bishop of Smyrna; and after them in the first half of the Second Century, Hegesippus, testify, *in the first place,* that by command of Christ, the Apostles ordered that in the future they must be succeeded in their office by a perpetual series of bishops. *In the second place,* they declare that, in order to avoid heresy and keep the true doctrine, agreement with the bishops is necessary, who are to be followed as Christ Himself. Moreover, they declare that it is only in this way that Christ's doctrine may be preserved in its purity and entirety, as it had been received in the beginning, even in the most distant Churches.

Clement, who according to Tertullian,[2] was ordained by St. Peter, describing this succession, writes to the Corinthians: "Christ is sent by God, and the Apostles by Christ. Therefore, with the whole inspiration of the Holy Ghost, they went out proclaiming the coming of the Kingdom of God. Preaching in every town and village, they constituted the first converts under bishops and deacons—and then they ordered that after their death, other good men should succeed them in their office."[3] Commenting on these words, St. Irenæus, who flourished in the Second Century, says that "Clement restored the faith of the Corinthians and the Tradition which they had lately received from the Apostles."[4]

St. Ignatius, the successor of Peter in the See of Antioch and disciple of St. John the Evangelist, was more anxious of nothing else than that the Faithful should be in harmony and of one mind with their bishop. Writing a paternal letter to the Ephesians, he says: "I have already warned you to be of one mind in the word of God, because Jesus Christ, our inseparable life, is the Word of the Father, as also the bishops, scattered in every part of the earth, are in the doctrine of Jesus Christ."[5]

Eusebius, the historian of the Church, who wrote in the Fourth Century, commenting on this Epistle of St. Ignatius, says, "First of all, he admonished the Churches of every city that, most of all, they should avoid heresies, which already had begun to break out, and advised them to hold firmly to the *Traditions* of the Apostles."[6]

Another disciple of St. John the Apostle was St.

---

2. Tertull., "Prescript," C. XXXII.
3. Clement, Ep. I, NN. 42-44
4. Iren. III, C. III, N. 3.
5. Ignat. ad Ephes., N. 3.
6. *H. E.*, III, C. XXXVI.

Polycarp, Bishop of Smyrna. Writing to the Philippians, he gave them a good rule to enable them to avoid all heresies: "Leaving the vanity of many men and all false doctrines, let us turn to the doctrine which was handed to us from the beginning."[7]

Hegesippus, who wrote in the Second Century, informs us that he went to Rome and met many bishops, all holding the same doctrine. "While in Rome," he says, "I wrote the series of succession of the Pontiffs up to Anicetus, whose deacon was Eleutherus: to Anicetus succeeded Soter, who was succeeded by Eleutherus. Such is the order of things in every city, as it is required by the Law and the Prophets and the Lord Himself."[8]

The Apostolic Churches, therefore, according to the Apostolic writers, were ruled by Tradition and acted accordingly. These are facts of history. No student of religion can deny them. And as the Apostolic Churches were made up of Christians who belonged to the first few generations after Christ's Resurrection, it is evident that up to the middle of the Second Century, Tradition, in the full sense of the word, governed the Church.

2

Tradition and Scripture Ruled the Church In the Last Half of the Second Century and All of the Third Century.

We have seen how the Church was ruled by Tradition up to the middle of the Second Century. The same is true up to the end of the Third Century.

The history of the Church teaches us that Christianity was never free from heresy. Even before the last of the

7. Ep. ad Philipp., N. 7.
8. In *Euseb. H. E.,* IV, C. XXII.

Apostles, St. John, went to his reward, heresies, like poisonous weeds, began to appear here and there in the Lord's vineyard. But in Apostolic days, just as the disciples of the Apostles, Ignatius and Polycarp, warned their people against false doctrines, so also did the pastors and doctors who succeeded them put their flocks on guard against the wolves.

In the last half of the Second Century, St. Irenæus valiantly defended Tradition against the Gnostics and other heretics. The Gnostics claimed that Tradition was a secret and private doctrine, which had come down to them alone through consecutive generations. Irenæus, on the contrary, proved that Tradition is a public doctrine, which belongs to the Universal Church, ruled by the succession of bishops.

This controversy with the Gnostics shows but one plain conclusion, namely, that both parties appealed to Tradition, although in a different way.

St. Irenæus, born in Smyrna about 135-140, was a disciple of St. Polycarp. He became Bishop of Lyons, France and died in the year 202. Writing against the Gnostics, he says: "While they argue from the Scriptures, they make a poor exhibition of the Scriptures . . . because truth cannot be found by those who do not know Tradition, for not through writing, but by the living voice, Tradition was delivered."[9] "In every Church, all those who wish to see the truth can look at the Tradition of the Apostles, which is evident all over the world by enumerating those who were constituted Bishops in the Churches by the Apostles and their successors to the present time." . . . "What then," continues the same Father of the Church, "if even a little controversy comes up for discussion, must we not have recourse to the oldest Churches in which the Apos-

9. In *Euseb. Hist. Eccles.*, L. II, C. II.

tles spoke, and receive from them what is certain and evident with regard to the present question?"[10] "For that reason," he says, "in order to settle all religious controversies, obedience is due to the priests of the Church who are the successors of the Apostles . . . because they watch our faith in one God, the Creator of all things, and explain to us the Scriptures."[11]

When the heretics tried to prove that their doctrine was that of Christ, the same Irenæus exclaimed: "These dogmas are not in harmony with the Church . . . these dogmas were not delivered by the priests who lived before us and who were the disciples of the Apostles."[12]

After Irenæus, Tertullian, who wrote in the Second and Third Centuries, inveighs against the heretics of his time in his famous *Prescriptions*. In Roman law *prescriptions* meant the cutting short of a question by refusing to hear the adversary's arguments, on the grounds of a precedent point, thus cutting away the ground under his feet.

He writes: "Anyhow, if they claim to be connected with the Apostolic age, as if delivered by the Apostles, because they were under the Apostles, we may say to them: Let them therefore publish the origins of their Churches; let them unroll the Catalogue of their Bishops; following one another from the beginning, in such a continued succession that the first Bishop had as author and ancestor one of the Apostles, or some Apostolic man who had however persevered in the doctrine of the Apostles. For in such manner the Apostolic Churches report their Census. Such being the case, in order to get to the truth, whoever follows the rule which the Church received from the Apostles, the Apostles from Christ, Christ from God, will find

10. Iren. in *Euseb. Hist. Eccles.*, L. III, C. IV, N. 1.
11. Iren. in *Euseb. Hist. Eccles.*, L. IV, C. XXVI.
12. Iren. in *Euseb. Hist. Eccles.*, L. V, C. XX.

out what we intend to prove, namely, that heretics are not to bc allowed to discuss the Scriptures because, not being in possession of the Scriptures, they do not belong to the Scriptures."[13]

Hence, this same Father of the Church tells us that we must learn the truth from the Apostolic Churches. "What have the Apostles preached, what has Christ revealed to them, I herewith also prescribe that it should not otherwise be proved than through the same Churches, which the same Apostles founded by preaching to them by the living voice and afterwards by their epistles. Such being the case, then it is evident that any doctrine which agrees with the faith of the original Apostolic and Mother Churches is based on the truth; without doubt, holding what the Churches received from the Apostles, the Apostles from Christ, Christ from God. All other doctrines—which differ from those of the Churches and of the Apostles and of Christ and of God—must be branded as lies."[14] Then he declares most emphatically: "We have no right whatever to add to or choose anything arbitrarily from the Scriptures. The authors are Our Lord's Apostles, who even themselves did not write anything of their own will, but faithfully assigned to the Nations the discipline which they received from the Lord."[15]

In the Third Century, we have Origen, the most voluminous writer the Church has ever had and the greatest theologian of those times. "As there are many," he writes, "who claim to know what belongs to Christ, and some of them do not agree with others about many things, let everyone keep the Church preaching (Tradition), which was delivered to us by the Apostles, by order of succes-

13. Tertull., "Prescript," CC. XXXII, XXXVII.
14. Tertull., "Prescript," C. XXI.
15. Tertull., "Prescript," C. VI.

sion and which continues to remain in the Churches up to the present day. The only truths that must be believed are those which do not differ in anything from the Ecclesiastical and Apostolic Tradition."[16]

For this reason, the Christians of the first three centuries always acted according to the rule: "Having been once revealed, nothing must be detracted from, nothing must be injected into, the heavenly dogma." That rule was nothing else than what Augustine proclaimed against the Pelagians one century later: "What they (the Pastors and Doctors) found in the Church, they kept; what they learned, they taught; what they received from the Fathers, they delivered to the children."[17]

Therefore, in the first three centuries of the Church, the Fathers and doctors, who either had charge of the flock assigned to them or who were present witnesses of the principles by which the Church was ruled in their time, repeat and insist that the principal duty and solicitude of the bishops is to maintain and deliver to the Faithful and to their successors the Deposit of Faith as they received it themselves from the older generations.

It is evident, therefore, that in the first three hundred years the Church was ruled by Tradition.

3

In the First Centuries of the Church the Practical Manner of Judging the Truth or Falsity of Doctrine was Based on the Fundamental Principle That all Revelation is Kept and Delivered in its Integrity only Through the Common Consent of the Pastors and Doctors.

16. Origen, *De Principiis,* praef. N. 2.
17. August., *Contra Jul.,* L. II, N. 34.

All Christian antiquity relied and based its fundamental belief, as upon an immovable rock, on the following unchangeable principle: "Revelation is kept and delivered to us in its entirety and purity by the common consent of the Pastors and Doctors."

By *Pastors and Doctors,* the Faithful always understood those ecclesiastics who taught and ruled them spiritually, in consent and union with the other successors of the Apostles, especially with the successors of Saint Peter.

As in the Old Law God preserved the hope in a future Redeemer through the Prophets, so also in the New Law, after Christ founded His Church upon the Apostles, He gave His Holy Spouse her *"Pastors and Doctors* for the perfecting of the Saints, for the work of the ministry, for the edifying of the body of Christ." (*Eph.* 4:11-12). The whole Church was always imbued with the belief that the consent of her Pastors and Doctors is a sure mark of that divine Tradition that came down to us from the Apostles.

For this reason, any doctrine, especially a new one that was repugnant to that general consent, was always branded as contrary to Revelation and to all Tradition. In the first centuries, just as in every other century, the Church always managed to guide herself by that principle . . . by the consent, namely, of her Pastors and Doctors. It was through that *principle* that the Church judged what is true and what is false.

It embraced two Golden Rules, which were openly adopted and solemnly proclaimed in the General Councils of the Church. The First Rule was: *"So believes the Catholic Church under Heaven, and all the Bishops consent with us."* It was declared against Paul of Samosata in the Council of Antioch in the Third Century. The same declaration is also found at the end of the Nicene Symbol [Creed]. The Second Rule was: *"We must follow antiq-*

uity, proved by Tradition: any new doctrine opposed to it must be rejected." The First Rule is so intimately connected with the Second one that it has in it the reason of its being. For the belief of the Church and the consent of the Bishops exist and are based on antiquity; they have their root, as it were, in the doctrine's antiquity.

In conformity with the First Rule, St. Vincent of Lerin, who wrote in the Fifth Century, relates that in the Council of Ephesus, held in the year 431, it was resolved by all the priests in attendance, "to place in the center of the assembly the writings of the Fathers, some of whom were either Martyrs or Confessors, or who remained Catholic to the end of their life. This was done in order solemnly and rightfully to confirm by their consent and decree the religion of the old dogma and to condemn the profane novelty as blasphemy."[18]

So also in the Fourth Century, St. Athanasius, writing to Epictetus and reprobating his doctrine, says: "These errors do not belong to the Catholic Church, nor are they the doctrine of the Fathers."[19]

Likewise, Origen writes in the Third Century: "As there are many who think that they know what belongs to Christ, and as some of them differ from others about many things, let them keep the ecclesiastical preaching which has been delivered by the Apostles through the order of succession and remains to the present time in the Churches. The only truth to be believed is that which does not differ in the least from the Ecclesiastical and Apostolic Tradition."[20] And addressing himself to one who is looking for the truth, the same Father says: "Search, therefore, [for] Jesus in the temple of God, search for

18. *Commonitorium,* C. XXVIII.
19. *Athanas.,* Ep. 3.
20. Origen, *De Principiis,* praef. N. 2.

Him in the Church; look for Him among the teachers who are in the Temple, and do not get out of it [i.e., do not leave the Temple (Church) till you find Him]. If thus you look for Him, you will find Him."[21]

Hence, in order to prove the orthodoxy of each bishop, or of some of the Faithful, appeal was made to the general consent of the bishops of the Catholic Church, or to the conformity of doctrine with the Apostolic Churches, especially with the Roman Church.

In the Sixth Century, the Oriental bishops adopted the profession of faith prescribed by Pope Hormisdas, containing the same rule.

With regard to the Second Rule, viz., *"We must follow antiquity, proved by Tradition; any new doctrine opposed to it must be rejected,"* we state that the Church adopted it because she always held that any doctrine of Faith was given by God to the Apostles, and by the Apostles to the Church; hence, the old doctrine must always be preferred to the new. When an old doctrine was attacked, appeal was soon made to its antiquity, and this requirement was proved by the consent of the late Fathers. For the same reason, when a new doctrine appeared in the Church, it was immediately condemned on account of its novelty and its repugnance to the Ancient Faith. Hence, the famous sentence of Tertullian: *"It is true what was first, and the first is what was from the beginning; it is from the beginning what is from the Apostles."*[22]

The illustrious sentence of Pope Stephen I (254-257), *"Nothing must be introduced but what has been delivered,"*[23] as well as the words of Pope Celestine I (422-432), *"Let nothing be allowed to novelty, because nothing*

21. Origen, Hom. 18.
22. Tertull., *Contra Marc.* IV, C. V.
23. *Apud Cypr.*, Ep. 74.

should be added to antiquity,"[24] are well known by all students of Religion.

In this way were the Gnostics and other ancient heretics condemned, according to the testimonies of Irenæus[25] and of Tertullian;[26] [as also] the Arians in the Council of Nicæa, according to Athanasius;[27] the Nestorians in the Council of Ephesus, according to Cyril;[28] and the Pelagians, according to Celestine.[29] In these and in all other Councils the same principle always prevailed; *"Antiquity is retained, novelty rejected."*

It is to be noted, however, that in the first centuries the Church appealed to the earlier *Doctors and Pastors,* not only to show *historically* that the doctrine in question was derived from the Apostles, but also to prove *theologically,* through that earlier consent, its true Apostolicity.

It was always a matter of certainty among Christians that the late Doctors and Pastors could never have agreed and delivered to their spiritual children except that which was delivered to them, nor could they fail to teach others what they themselves had learned from their predecessors.

This was so generally accepted by the Faithful that to prove the Apostolicity of a doctrine, they did not think it was even necessary to appeal to the testimony of the most ancient Fathers. The testimony of the latest Pastors and Doctors was enough. Thus, according to Vincent of Lerin,[30] in order to prove the Apostolicity of a doctrine, the Fathers of the Ephesian Council appealed to the Fathers of the Church, of which only two, Cyprian and Pope Felix,

24. Ep. 21, N. 2.
25. Iren. III, 4.
26. Tertull., "Prescript," 8-10.
27. Athan., *De Synod,* N. 4-9.
28. Cyril ad Clericos, N. 10.
29. Celestin, Ep. 21.
30. Vincent of Lerin, *Commonitorium,* N. 42.

belonged to the Third Century; all the others to the Fourth or the Fifth Century. Likewise, of 25 Fathers, cited by St. Augustine, only two, Cyprian and Irenæus, lived before the Fourth Century. So also the Lateran Council, held in the Seventh Century, mentioned 20 Fathers, as witnesses of Apostolic doctrines, but only three or four were more ancient than the Fourth Century, such as Justin, Hippolytus and Dionysius the Areopagite.

Therefore, the common consent of the Pastors and Doctors of the Church, in communion with one another, especially with the Head of the Church, was always considered as the fundamental principle that kept and delivered Divine Revelation, *pure and entire,* in the first centuries of the Church.

When the student of Religion reads the above testimonies, he cannot fail to observe that the same principles, which obtained in the ancient Church, may also be justly applied to the present *status* of the Catholic Church. This happens because the Two Rules mentioned above have been always in vigor—not only in the first centuries, but also in every century down to our own times.

4

The Church of the First Centuries Attributed the Bishops' and Pastors' Doctrinal Consent to the Assistance of the Holy Ghost.

The common consent of the "Pastors and Doctors" in communion with one another, especially with the Head of the Church, with regard to all doctrinal Traditions, was always, as it is today, the effect of the promise of Christ and the assistance of the Holy Ghost. This has been always and everywhere the belief of the Faithful, especially in the first centuries of the Church.

When we consider the immense material of Tradition, the intricate questions which must arise from abstruse doctrines, the inclination of men to disagree rather than to agree (even on minor questions), we must conclude that the consent of those whom "the Holy Ghost has placed . . . to rule the Church of God" (*Acts* 20:28) is not a simple human consent, but a consent formed by that same Holy Spirit who, according to Christ's promise, "will teach you all truth." (*John* 16:13).

The Fathers of the Church, even of the first centuries, were not slow to realize the fact that the efficient cause of such marvelous consent in matters which belong to the Faith is the Spirit of God, "the operation of the Spirit."[31] This is done "through the certain charism of truth,"[32] "through the Doctor of Truth, who does not let the Church otherwise believe."[33]

On this point Tertullian argues as follows: "Suppose that all the Churches have erred, that even the Apostle was deceived in giving testimony that the Holy Ghost did not care to lead the Church to the truth, although for that purpose He was sent by Christ and asked of the Father, letting the Churches understand one way and in the same time believe in a different manner than He preached through the Apostles, . . . how can it be credible that so many and such great Churches could ever err about the one and the same Faith?"[34]

Hear what Irenæus has to say on this point: "We must therefore obey the priests who are in the Church, those who have succeeded the Apostles, those who with the episcopal succession received the never-failing divine gift

---

31. Iren. III, C. XXIV, N. 1.
32. Iren. IV, C. XXVI, N. 2.
33. Tertull., "Prescript," C. XXVIII.
34. "Prescript," C. XXVIII.

of truth, according to the will of the Father."[35]

The reason "for which the Catholic Religion remains inviolate in the Apostolic See is that the words of Jesus Christ—who said, 'Thou art Peter [rock] and upon this rock I will build my Church'—cannot pass away." Thus did the Oriental Bishops subscribe to the Profession of Faith under Pope Hormisdas (498-514).

Therefore, the Council of Trent proclaims that "the same Holy Synod (is) taught by the Holy Ghost"[36] and that it followed "the judgment and custom of the Church itself."[37]

Here it is where our Protestant brethren make the great mistake of throwing to the winds all Traditions, on the grounds that Traditions may be easily corrupted. They forget the promise of Christ and the assistance of the Holy Ghost, "the Spirit of Truth," who will never allow the Church to fall into error. They forget that Christ promised the Apostles and their successors that He will be with them "even to the consummation of the world." (*Matt.* 28:20). They forget that the Holy Ghost abides with the Church for no other purpose than to instruct, guide and direct the Church in her deliberations until the End of Time. They should listen, rather, to the remarkable words of Peter of Cluny, who belongs to the Eleventh Century: "Should we not therefore believe the testimonies of the Church, with which Christ invisibly lives unto the consummation of the world? Should we not believe the testimonies of the Church, who is one with the Father and the Son, as the Father is in the Son, and the Son in the Father? To whom the Son of God gave that glory which He received from the Father? Therefore, how could the Church deceive and be deceived—that Church with whom

35. Iren. IV, 26.
36. Session XX, 1.
37. Session XXIII.

the Father, who is all truth, with whom the Son, who is the Truth, with whom the Spirit of Truth remained forever? *But as this is utterly impossible, it remains that a complete faith must be given to all her Traditions as truly Apostolic.*"[38]

Our separated brethren, unfortunately, always dream of an *oral Tradition* to be carried on from generation to generation, *only through the help of word of mouth!* They fail to realize that there are two elements which preclude such an inference: The *first element* is the promised assistance of God, whose words shall never fail; the second is that *human element,* which humanly speaking, renders the corruption of Tradition a moral impossibility. This we have already seen in another part of this work and one which we shall further develop later on, speaking of those auxiliary means by which Tradition is transmitted in its integrity, purity and truth [one of which means is the voluminous writings of the Fathers of the Church].

5

In the First Centuries of the Church, Social Intercourse and Consent in Doctrine of the Churches With the Church of Rome were Considered a Mark Of Truth and Apostolicity of Their Own Doctrine.

After the death of the Apostles, many Churches or parishes sprang up throughout the world. Their communion and consent with Apostolic Churches, namely, with those Churches which claimed a continued succession of bishops from the time of the Apostles, were considered as an essential mark of Apostolic truth. Those Apostolic Churches were justly regarded as deposits of the Faith.

---

38. *Migne,* 189, 739.

Among them all, there was one which was always looked upon as the greatest of them all, the most revered, the most powerful, the one that exacted the obedience of all the Faithful, the one whose last word was law. *That Church was, as it is today throughout the whole Christian world, the Church of Rome.*

At that time, just as in our own time, the Church of Rome was the source of truth and jurisdiction. Hence, the Church that agreed with Rome was considered a true Christian Church, while the one that rejected Rome's truth and jurisdiction separated itself from Christ.

The Christian world looked upon the Church of Rome as its head and leader against the works of darkness and the intrigue of imperial satellites. If it was from Rome that emanated the brutal decrees of Christian persecutions, it was also from Rome that were issued the directions for fidelity to the Faith. It was in Rome that the noblest acts of Christian virtue and heroism were made manifest to the world. For in His Divine Providence, God has so arranged the destinies of humanity that, no matter how great is man's malice, still greater is His divine assistance: *Ubi abundavit malitia, superabundavit et gratia, viz.,* "Where malice abounded, grace also did more abound."

The Emperors of Pagan Rome—Nero, Diocletian, Galerius and others—waged the fiercest persecutions against the Church, but the Bishops of Rome, the Successors of Peter and Vicars of Christ upon earth, were also there to strengthen the faith of the Christians. For Christ said to Peter: "Confirm thy brethren." (*Luke* 22:32). It was for that reason that the noblest men and women of those times shed their blood for Christ.

Happy art Thou then, O Christian Rome, because Thy Peter and Thy Paul, the greatest of the Apostles, fertilized Thy soil with their blood. Illustrious is Thy name,

O Christian Rome, because the glorious figures of Christian fortitude—Ignatius of Antioch, Polycarp of Smyrna, Thy own Lawrence and many others, too many to enumerate, were immolated on the altars of human malice. Noble art Thou, O Christian Rome, because in Thee and for Thee Thy own Agnes, Cecilia and an innumerable phalanx of virgins preferred a heavenly Spouse and sealed virginity with their blood. Great indeed wert Thou, O Pagan Rome, magnificent and most powerful: Thou didst rule the world as then known, for "Thou wert born to rule the nations of the world,"[39] but far greater art Thou now: Thou rulest the world, not by the force of arms, but by divine commission. "If Thou wert once the teacher of all errors, Thou art now the disciple of truth."[40] Thou art, according to the greatest of poets, "that Rome by which Christ is Roman."[41]

It is an historical fact that the Church of Rome was always considered the first, the most important, and the most powerful Church in Christendom. This was admitted in the first centuries and is so regarded today. She saved civilization and the Scriptures. Her children outnumber by far the members of all the other churches put together; and what is most important, they are bound in "One Faith," as there can be but "one Lord, one faith, one baptism." (*Eph.* 4:5).

This unity of Faith—derived from a strict conformity of doctrine in all the Churches—cannot be achieved except by their consent and communion with the Chair of Peter. It is for this reason that all the Churches of old claimed that such consent and intercourse with the Church of Rome is an evidence of their Apostolic doctrine. Irenæus,

39. Virgil, in the Sixth Book of the *Æneid.*
40. Pope St. Leo, *Sermo* I, in nat. SS. Petri et Pauli.
41. Dante *Allighieri. Purg.,* Canto XXXII.

writing in the Second Century, declares: "As it would be tedious to enumerate the whole list of successions, I shall confine myself to that of Rome, the greatest, most ancient and most illustrious Church, founded and constituted by the two most glorious Apostles, Peter and Paul; receiving from the Apostles that Tradition and Faith which was announced to all men and which, through the succession of her Bishops, has come down to us. Thus we confound all those who—through evil designs, vainglory or perversity—teach what they should not. For it is necessary on account of *her superior headship* that every other Church should have recourse to this Church, that is, the Faithful of all countries in which Church has always been preserved by those who are everywhere, *that Tradition* which comes [to us] from the Apostles."[42] And having enumerated the succession of the Roman Bishops on the Chair of Peter, the same Irenæus continues: "By this order and succession, *that Tradition* which is in the Church from the Apostles and *the preaching* of truth came even to us. This demonstration is most complete, the one and the same vivifying Faith, which is preserved and delivered in truth in the Church from the Apostles to the present day."[43]

Hence it is that St. Cyprian, Bishop of Carthage, who lived and died in the Third Century, calls the Church of Rome the "Chair of Peter and the Principal Church,"[44] while St. Augustine calls it, "the Roman Church in which always existed the Principality of the Apostolic Chair."[45]

It is evident, then, that in the first centuries the Church of Rome was considered the center of unity, and all other Churches were most anxious to conform their faith with

42. Iren., L. III, C. II.
43. Iren., L. III. C. II.
44. Cypr., Ep. 55.
45. August., Ep. 43.

the "Chair of Peter." But such conformity of all Churches with the Church of Rome could not be effected unless all the other Churches looked upon the Roman Church as the *formal cause* of their unity. For Peter was appointed by Christ to be the Head of the Universal Church, and it is that same Peter who, having established his See in Rome, lives in the person of his Roman successors.

It is for this reason that the Fathers of the first centuries—as in every other century—were most solicitous to demonstrate and enumerate the Apostolic Succession of the Roman See, because *"it is necessary on account of her superior headship that every other Church must have recourse"* to this Church. They were induced to disclose the perpetual succession of the Roman See, because they were so convinced that the Church of Rome was in possession of the Apostolic Tradition that, in proving their communion and consent with the same Church of Rome, they were at the same time proving that they also were in possession of the Apostolic Faith.

This Apostolic Succession on the "Chair of Peter" is therefore enumerated by several Fathers of the first few centuries, "on account of her superior headship." Principal among them are Irenæus,[46] Ephrem the Syrian, Optatus[47] and Epiphanius.[48] Irenæus enumerates the succession as follows: "Linus, Anacletus, Clement, Evaristus, Alexander, Sixtus, Telesphorus, Hyginus, Pius, Anicetus, Soter and Eleutherius, the twelfth from the Apostles, who now governs the Church. It is not from others that we should seek the truth, which may be so easily learned from this Church; for *to this Church, as a rich depository, the Apostles committed whatever is of divine truth;* all other teach-

46. Iren., L. III, C. III.
47. Optatus, L. II, N. 3.
48. *Epiph.,* C. XXVII, N. 6.

ers must be shunned as thieves and robbers."[49]

Truly, *the rock* upon which Christ built this Church, in order that "the gates of hell shall not prevail against it"—that is, *Peter,* in his perpetual succession (*Matt.* 16:18)—is the principle of that visible unity by which the Church is one in communion and in consent of Faith. Hence, the *Rock,* or *Peter,* placed by Christ as the foundation of His Church, is the *formal cause* of strength and unity, in order that the teaching Church may be one body, infallible in its definitions, to keep and explain the Deposit of Faith. The body of the teaching Church, however, is not infallible in itself, unless it is united with its *head,* that is, Peter and his successors in office, because only to Peter did Christ say: "Feed my lambs . . . feed my sheep." (*John* 21:15, 17). The *formal cause,* therefore, of the unity and consent in Faith is *the Head*—Peter, and in Peter, all his successors in office—constituting, as it were, *the form,* which molds and renders infallible the Body of the Church, through the assistance of the Holy Ghost and the protection of Christ as *the efficient* or *operative cause* of that infallible Head and Body.

The Christians of the first centuries understood well this point. For that reason they were most anxious to be in communion and consent with the Church of Rome, until the demon of heresy snatched them from that blessed unity.

Epiphanius, writing in the Fourth Century and having most accurately described all the names of the Roman Pontiffs, declared: "Let no one wonder that I have given every name with such diligence, *because by such names* the truth shall be manifest forever."[50]

Optatus, who in the same Fourth Century was the fore-

49. Iren., L. III, C. III.
50. Epiph. Heres. 27.

most opponent of Donatism, writing to the Donatist Parminian, says: "You cannot deny that you know very well it was through Peter that in the City of Rome was established the first episcopal Chair, in which sat the Head of all the Apostles, Peter, whence also he was called Cephas: *only in that one Chair can unity be preserved by all,* lest the other Apostles should each stand up for his own chair: so that now he would be a schismatic and a sinner who against this one chair would set up another." And mocking the recent succession of Donatist antipopes in Rome, he exclaims: "Tell us the origin of your chair, you who wish to claim the Holy Church for yourselves."[51]

In the same vein, Tertullian has written, "Christ sent His Apostles, who founded Churches in every city, from which the others have borrowed the Tradition of the Faith and the seed of doctrine, and daily borrow in order to become Churches, so that they also are Apostolic, in that they are the offspring of the Apostolic Churches. . . . All are that one Church that the Apostles founded, so long as peace and intercommunion are observed. What then the Apostles preached, namely, what Christ revealed to them, I herewith also prescribe, that they must not be proved than by those same Churches which the same Apostles founded, preaching in them first with their own voice and with their Epistles afterwards. If it is so, then all the *doctrine which is conformed with those Apostolic Mother Churches and originals of the Faith must be true; without doubt holding what the Church received from the Apostles, the Apostles from Christ, Christ from God. . . . We communicate with the Apostolic Churches, because we cannot admit a different doctrine: this is the testimony to the truth.*"[52]

---

51. Optatus, L. II, N. 3.
52. Tertull., "Prescript," C. XX, 21.

Naming some of the Apostolic Churches and pointing above all to Rome, the same Tertullian exclaims: "Happy Church, in which the Apostles poured out their whole teaching with their blood, where Peter suffered a death like his Master's, where Paul was crowned with an end like the Baptist's, where John was plunged into fiery oil without injury."[53]

Therefore, according to the testimony of the Fathers, the Churches of the first centuries were most anxious to be in communion and consent of doctrine with the Apostolic Churches, but especially with the Church of Rome, because they held and believed that such communion and consent were essential characters of the apostolicity and integrity of their own doctrine and belief.

6

In the First Centuries, When a New Doctrine Appeared Among the Faithful, the Feeling of the Church Was So Aroused, That She Used All Possible Ways to Put an End to it.

The promise of Jesus Christ that the Holy Ghost will abide with the Church until the End of Time shall never fail. It is the promise of God, who cannot deceive nor be deceived. The Spirit of Truth, having first spoken through the Prophets, and then through the Apostles, abides with the Church. He is with her in all her troubles and difficulties. He is with her by directing, assisting and guiding her in the great work of the salvation of souls.

However, as the Church is not by any means composed of Angels, but of men, both in her subjects, as well as in her government, the *human element* cannot be dispensed

53. Tertull., "Prescript," C. XXXVI.

with. It is this human element—especially the governmental element—which the Holy Spirit guides, assists and directs from falling into error, because as the Apostle declares, the Holy Ghost placed the bishops to rule the Church of God. For that reason, we shall now consider more distinctly the principles, the means and ways, which the successors of the Apostles employed to protect the Deposit of Faith. In this way, we shall thoroughly understand how the corruption of Tradition, especially in the first centuries of the Church, as claimed by Protestants, was a moral impossibility.

The Church of Jesus Christ always took care that no bishop should be elected without having first looked thoroughly into his private life and the sincerity of his faith, "in order that the unworthy may not invade the sacerdotal place."[54]

In the first centuries of the Church, it was customary after his election, for every bishop, especially of the most important sees, to give to his neighboring bishops and especially to the Roman Pontiff a clear profession of his faith. "An Apostolic and old Tradition in the holy Churches of God throughout the world held that all those who were promoted to the bishopric would sincerely expose to those who were placed in the highest sacerdotal places what they thought and how they stood in what belonged to the Faith—that they might not run in vain." Thus, wrote St. Sophronius, Bishop of Jerusalem, in a synodical epistle to Pope Honorius and to St. Sergius, Bishop of Constantinople, after making his profession of Faith.

The reason for such a custom is not only evident—when we consider the turmoil of those times and the interference of temporal princes for political reasons and selfish inter-

54. Cypr., Ep. 68.

ests in the affairs of the Church—but it was necessary.

St. Gregory the Great fittingly illustrates such institution: "While we transmit to one another the confession of our faith and show toward us our own charity, what else do we do in the Church of God but to coat with tar the Ark in order to keep out the waves of error?"[55]

Whenever one of the bishops was declared not in communion with the other bishops, his name was at once cancelled from the list of the Catholic bishops. Whoever was denied that communion (of faith and doctrine), according to Cyprian, "whoever he may be, he was not a Christian, because he was not in the Church."[56]

Moreover, as the bishops were very solicitous to appear in one communion of faith, so also they were very much concerned about the genuineness of the faith of their predecessors in office. Hence, in every diocese a list of the names of all the bishops of the same diocese was kept and described with great diligence, eliminating all those who had fallen from the Faith or were excluded from the communion of the Universal Church. This was considered so important that many strenuous and long controversies took place, as for instance, in reinstating the name of St. John Chrysostom in the list of Patriarchs of Constantinople and in cancelling the names of Acacius and of his successors from the list of that Patriarchal See.

Furthermore, whenever a new doctrine contrary to the long accepted Faith began to be introduced, the whole Church was in commotion. The Bishop of the place in which it had its origin not only condemned it, but also informed first of all the Roman Pontiff and then the neighboring Bishops. The new doctrine was considered as a

55. Greg., L. VII, Ep. 4.
56. Cypr., Ep. 51.

new danger that threatened them all: it was like a wound that afflicted the whole body.

Thus, for instance, in the Council of Antioch, the bishops accused Paul of Samosata to the Roman Pontiff and to Maximus, Bishop of Alexandria; St. Cyprian reported to the Roman Pontiff the schism of Felicissimus and Fortunatus; Alexander, Bishop of Alexandria, exposed Arius to all the Catholic bishops.

The bishops were ever so eager to maintain intact the old Faith that when some one of the clergy or of the laity passed from one diocese to another, his bishop gave him letters testifying to his faith. If such letters were lacking, he was looked upon with suspicion, and the Faithful were warned to avoid him."[57]

Finally, if all these means and precautions were not deemed sufficient to suppress the incipient heresy, the bishops came together to protect, maintain and more solemnly proclaim the old Faith. Such was the origin of the *Provincial* and *of the General Councils of the Church.*

History furnishes not only the names of the innovators or heretics, together with their new doctrines, but also the places and times of conflict. In every case the bishops of the Church upheld antiquity, condemned the new doctrine and excommunicated the innovators and their followers.

All this goes to show how vigilant were the "pastors and doctors" of the Church in watching over the flock which the Holy Ghost committed to their care, how careful they were in keeping their spiritual pastures free from obnoxious weeds.

---

57. *Apost. Const.,* L. II, C. LVIII.

7
The Church Has Always Been Ruled by Scripture and by Tradition.

Some Protestant theologians, like Twesten,[58] claim that the older Church appealed only *historically* to Tradition. This means that the early writers of the Church wished only to demonstrate that in the Apostolic Churches in which the Apostles themselves preached, the Faith which they left and delivered to them was not corrupted, but remained pure through the continued succession of bishops, until the Second and Third Centuries; later on, however, the Church asserted her authority, which she did not possess by any testimony of Tradition. In other words, they claim that the old Church got along only with the Bible for the first three centuries, but afterwards, she added to it her own authority.

Others, like Lessing and Delbrück, invert this order and maintain that until the Council of Nicæa in the Fourth Century, the Church was ruled by Tradition, but after that time, she was governed only by the inspired Scriptures as *her only source and Rule of Faith.*

Others, joining together these two views, claim that Scripture, down to the Seventh Century, was the only Rule of Faith, but after that time, *both Scripture and Tradition* became the two Rules of Faith. See Franzelin[59] and Perrone.[60]

That all these claims are unfounded is manifest from the evidence we have submitted in the foregoing parts of this work. However, for a clearer and more abundant vindication of the Catholic Dogma, we declare that the

58. Dogm. T. I, p. 117.
59. *Script. et Trad.,* C. X.
60. *De Trad.,* N. 381.

testimonies of both Ante-Nicene and Post-Nicene Fathers with regard to Tradition are identical. They all have the same voice, the same heart and the same sentiments. They all appeal to Tradition, and their appeal is prompted by the same motives and purposes and produced in the same way.

First of all, both series of Fathers appeal to Tradition that came down to them through the Bishops' succession. Thus, if the Apostolic Fathers and those of the Second and Third Centuries, like Irenæus[61] and Tertullian,[62] make reference to the doctrine, *"delivered from the beginning,"* so also the Fathers who lived after the Nicæan Council, like Athanasius, Epiphanius, Augustine and others, assert that "what they received from the Fathers, they also delivered to the children," as the same Augustine says.[63] Famous are the words of Athanasius on this point: "We teach how the Fathers delivered to the Fathers: you follow the Council."[64] On the other hand, if the Apostolic Fathers appeal to the Apostolic Succession in the Church, especially of the Roman Church on account of its "greater principality," as Irenæus says,[65] so also the Fathers who came after them appeal to the same Apostolic Succession and in a special way to the Roman See because, as Epiphanius says, "Through that succession the truth always appears evident,"[66] and as St. Augustine declares, "What holds me in the Church is the succession of priests from Peter to the present incumbent."[67]

In the second place, if the Fathers who came after the

61. Iren., L. III, 4.
62. Tertull., "Prescript," C. XXI.
63. August., L. II, *Contra Jul.,* N. 34.
64. *Athanas., on the Nicene Decree,* N. 27.
65. Iren., L. III, C. III, N. 2.
66. Epiph. Heres. XXVII.
67. August., *Ep. Fund.,* N. 5.

Nicæan Council—like Athanasius, Chrysostom, Augustine and Jerome—assert that the consent of the Bishops is the effect of the assistance of the Holy Ghost, and for that reason they appeal to the authority of the teaching Church; so also the most ancient Fathers—like Tertullian, Cyprian, Irenæus and Ignatius—while they insist that the reason for which no one should part from the teaching of the Church is that the truth came down *pure and entire* to us through the *common consent* and *orderly succession of Bishops;* at the same time they proclaim that that is due to the *authority given by Christ to the Apostles and by the Apostles to their successors.*

Thus, if after the Nicæan Council it had been well established that, as St. Vincent of Lerin declares, "In the Apostolic See the Catholic Church is kept inviolate,"[68]—for the reason that "we cannot set aside the sentence of Jesus Christ, saying, 'Thou art Peter and upon this Rock I will build my Church'"[69]—so also does Tertullian attribute the common consent of the bishops, long before the same Council: i.e., "through the Doctor of Truth, who does not let the Church otherwise think, otherwise believe,"[70] or as the disciple of the Apostles, Irenæus, says, "through the operation of the Holy Ghost."[71]

Therefore, according to all the Fathers of the Church, there is a double element in Tradition, the *visible* and the *invisible.* The *visible* consists in the legitimate succession and public consent of the bishops; the *invisible* is the direct assistance of God Himself.

These two elements are connected because the visible depends on the invisible, and in some manner it is formed

68. *Commonitorium.*
69. *The Oriental Bishops under Hormisdas.*
70. Tertull., "Prescript," C. XXVIII.
71. Iren., C. XXIV, N. 1.

by it. But they are distinct, and the Fathers consider them distinctly. Hence, both series of Fathers—Ante- and Post-Nicene Fathers—argue *historically, philosophically,* and *theologically.*

Historically, in reference to the *visible,* they point to the bishops' continued succession as the tested guardians of the Faith, whose names would not otherwise even be tolerated in the bishops' list. If the name of a bishop were not on the list, his doctrine, as they argued, was not Apostolic.

Philosophically, they argue in reference to the bishops' *consent and union in doctrine* of all the Churches, especially with the Roman See, the root and center of unity. Such consent and union are an argument of truth because, as Tertullian remarks, "If the churches had erred, their error would not be one, but many; what is found as *one* among many (Churches) is not erred, but delivered."[72]

Theologically, in reference to the *invisible,* the Fathers conclude that since there is a continued succession of bishops all in communion and consent with one another, especially with the Roman Pontiff, such communion and consent must be *attributed to the promise of Christ* and the *assistance of the Holy Ghost.*

Here lies the great Protestant mistake: There is no difference whatever among the most ancient and the more recent Fathers in the manner in which they consider Tradition and in their method of proving the integrity of the delivered doctrine. It is true, as we have said, that the two arguments, *historical* and *theological,* drawn up from the two elements as mentioned above, *visible* and *invisible,* are connected to each other, but they must not be confused and used indiscriminately, one for another. Those

72. Tertull., "Prescript," C. XXVIII.

who have inverted this method of arguing consider only the *historical* argumentation among the Ante-Nicene Fathers, neglecting the theological argumentation. Likewise, they chose the *theological part* of the Post-Nicene Fathers when the same Fathers appeal to the Church authority [that is] derived from the charism of truth, neglecting the Fathers' *philosophical and historical* argumentation.

It is on this account that both series of Fathers—*Ante-* and *Post-Nicene*—appeal to three elements: the continued succession of bishops, their consent and communion with one another, and the charism of the Holy Ghost. These elements represent that *visible* "column of truth" upon which the Fathers construct and enthrone, as it were, the *invisible* authority of Jesus Christ, who gave the commission to the Apostles and their successors to go and teach all nations. It is for this reason that St. Vincent of Lerin exclaims: "Whoever despises the Doctors and Pastors placed by God in the Church in every place and at all times, being all in harmony about all Dogmatic Doctrines, despises not man, but God."[73] The historical principle of the early Church, therefore, excogitated [invented] by Protestants in opposition to the principle attributed to the Church of a later period, is not based on truth or on facts.

The Church, according to the testimonies of the Fathers—Ante- and Post-Nicene—was ruled both by Scripture and by Tradition.

---

73. *Commonitorium,* C. XL.

8

The Explanation Offered by Protestants on the Testimonies of Tradition of the Early Church Cannot Be Accepted Because the First Christians Interpreted Scripture According to Tradition.

From their fundamental principle that Scripture is the only authority and Rule of Faith, Protestants proclaim that not even the testimony of the whole world can ever prove the trustworthiness of Divine Religion. In other words, all the faith, sentiments and attestations of the early writers and Fathers of Christianity are not competent authorities or trustworthy sources that enable us to judge the purity, essentials, requisites or truths of the Christian Religion because their beliefs did not constitute an authoritative statement. If their testimony, they [the Protestants] say, means anything, it only shows their individual faith and nothing else. It does not prove that our faith should be conformed or shaped according to their testimony; rather, such testimony must be examined and judged according to the only Rule of Faith—the Scriptures. If conformable to the Scriptures, it must be accepted; otherwise, it must be rejected.

Protestants tell us that the first so-called Fathers of Christianity appealed to the doctrines of the early Churches, especially to the Apostolic Churches, *because* and *in so far as* they saw that they were actually *conformed to the Scriptures;* hence, the demonstration of the Apostolic doctrines from the Scriptures was entirely independent of the consent or unity of the Churches; that is to say that that demonstration came *first* and was the only proper demonstration; the reference of those writers and their testimonies came afterwards.

Thus they explain that the appeal of the Fathers to the

Apostolic doctrines produced a certain confirmation of their apostolicity, not independently of the Scriptures, but by doing away entirely with the consent and union of the bishops, because the Scriptures came *first* as an absolute and essential foundation on which was based and to which was conformed the Faith of the early Christians. Hence, it was the Scriptures themselves, they say, that brought into existence the harmony and consent of the bishops, which harmony and consent came afterwards.

Such is the standpoint of the most advanced or *Progressive Protestants.*

Notwithstanding these statements, they feel the weight of the witnesses of the whole Christian Religion and leave no stone unturned to prove their contention. It is impossible. The testimonies of the old Christians are so strong, their statements are so clear, their condemnation of error is so powerful and so unmistakable, that they cannot be disposed of so easily. For the ancient writers of the Church appeal to the continued succession of bishops, to their common interpretation of the Scriptures, to their unity and consent in matters of Faith, and most of all, to their abhorrence of novelty in doctrine.

There is no greater unanimity and clearness among the early Christian writers than on the relation of the Church to the Scriptures. Ecclesiastical authority is the rule. On this depends the interpretation of the Scriptures, even their formation and existence.

Without the authority of the Church and her sanction, the books of the Bible have no life. Left to themselves, they cannot quicken. The number of books which today we accept as truly inspired, their interpretation, authenticity and genuineness, depended and depend entirely on the authority of the Church. The Scriptures *are* because —and *in so far as*—the Church has approved of them as containing the Divine Revelation. It was through Divine Providence that the Church, in the most critical times of the world, saved the Scriptures from complete oblivion and total loss, first to Christianity and then to civilization. The authority of the Church is the tribunal to which the Scriptures themselves—every book and every part, of which the Scriptures are composed—are brought for examination, retention or rejection, and infallible interpretation. This authority on the part of the Church does not mean that the Church is really superior to the Scriptures. Far from it. It simply means that the Church—and the Church only—has the right to tell us what is Scripture and what is not, and what is its true and infallible interpretation.

How many know that the Catholic Church herself compiled, gathered, and formed together the different books of Scripture as they existed centuries ago and as they exist today? Not a few believe that Martin Luther discovered or rediscovered the Bible. That is ridiculous.

We shall show that the Scriptures are the object and Rule of Faith—only *after* they are approved and interpreted by the Church! The statements of the early Christians prove this. Tradition was neither drawn from nor determined by the Scriptures. Quite the reverse. Then, as now, Tradition itself was the Rule. It was the authority according to which the Scriptures were declared genuine, authentic and inspired. From this they received—then as today—their infallible interpretation.

In his *Commentaries on Matthew,* Origen writes: "Whenever they—the heretics—bring before us the Scriptures, which every Christian approves and believes, they seem to say: 'Behold the words of truth in your homes,' (*Matt.* 24:26), but we must not believe them, *nor do away* with *the first* and *Ecclesiastical Tradition,* nor believe otherwise than what has been handed over by succession to the Church of God."[74] Does it not seem that this same Father of the Church, Origen, who belonged to the Third Century, is equally rebuking with these words those in error today? Our separated brethren claim that the Bible is sufficient, and for that reason it should be found in every house, being the only authority in matters of faith and morals. They regard it as the only revealed word of God and "do away with the first and Ecclesiastical Tradition." But "we must not believe otherwise than what has been handed over by succession to the Church of God." For Origen the Scriptures do not come first and Tradition afterwards.

The Book of Recognitions, written at the beginning of the Third Century and attributed by some to Clement the Roman, contains the following admonition of St. Peter: "I see that some clever men find in what they read many likelihoods; and *yet it must be diligently observed that in reading the law of God, we must not read it according to the intelligence of our own mind.* For there are many words in the Divine Scriptures which can be taken in whatsoever sense which every one of us may like or presume to give them. This should not be done. For you must not bring in a strange and inappropriate sentence which you try to confirm by the Scriptures; but you must get the true interpretation from the same Scriptures; hence, one must *learn the knowledge of the Scriptures from him who acquired it from the ancients, according to the truth delivered to them.*"[75]

It is evident from this ancient testimony that the Scriptures do not come first, but they are subject to the doc-

---

74. Origen, *Comment.,* N. 46.
75. *Book of Recognitions,* B. 10, N. 42.

trine *acquired from the ancients,* that is, to Tradition.

According to Tertullian, *no one should even use the Scriptures without belonging to the Catholic Church, because she is the only one who knows how to give a proper interpretation of them.* "Therefore, we should not have recourse to the Scriptures, nor dispute about them. The order of things requires to propose, in the first place, to whom belongs the Faith itself? Whose are the Scriptures? By whom, and through whom, and when, and to whom was the authority to teach delivered by whom men are made Christians? For where the true Christian discipline and doctrine are shown to be, there will also be the truth of the Scriptures, and of their interpretation, and of all Christian Traditions."[76]

But where is the Doctrine of Faith to be found? The same Tertullian answers: "In the succession of the Bishops."[77] Hence, St. Irenæus, who lived even before Tertullian, warns us in these solemn words: "Where the charisms of the Lord are, there also we must learn the truth, because it is through them that the Apostolic Succession is found in the Church. They (the priests) watch our Faith and explain to us the Scriptures without error."[78]

Thus, Tertullian and Irenæus place the authority of the Church over the Scriptures, not as if the Church is superior to the Word of God, but as giving it the right explanation and interpretation, "without error."

We shall conclude this point with an appropriate argument of St. Vincent of Lerin. St. Vincent knew very well that all the Fathers of the Church, beginning with the Apostolic down to those of his own time, admitted and professed two Rules of Faith. He says: "Everyone must

76. Tertull., "Prescript," C. XXIX.
77. Tertull., "Prescript." C. XX.
78. Iren., L. IV, C. XXIV, N. 5.

safeguard his faith by two Rules, first, by the authority of Divine Law; secondly, by the Tradition of the Catholic Church."

The reason why the authority of the Church must be added to the books of Scripture is given by St. Vincent: "because not all accept Sacred Scripture in the same sense, on account of its loftiness; but this one and that give the sayings of Scripture so many different significations that there are almost as many minds as there are men. Novatianus explains Scripture differently from Sabellius, [and] Donatus from Arius, Photinus from Apollinaris, and so forth. . . . Consequently, it is absolutely necessary that on account of so many errors, the line of prophetic and apostolic interpretation must be drawn according to the direction of the Ecclesiastical and Catholic sense."[79] If we change only the names of Novatianus, Arius, Donatus, Apollinaris and so forth, into the names of Methodists, Baptists, Congregationalists, Presbyterians, etc., the description of St. Vincent of Lerin, made in the Fifth Century, applies equally to the many denominations of today.

According to the early writers of Christianity, then, Tradition must be as equally respected and venerated as the written Word of God. For the Fathers place on an equal base and veneration these two great columns of truth, viz., Scripture and Tradition. On these two columns the arc of eternal truth is put up for our guidance and direction. There is no other way for mankind to find Jesus and His Church, but through that way. Through that entrance we shall enter into life. If we try another way, we shall wander "in darkness and in the shadow of death." Therefore, the Protestant contention that the first Christians

---

79. Lerin's *Commonit.*, C. II.

appealed to Tradition *because* and *in so far as* it conformed to Scripture is misleading, unhistorical and untrue.

6

Existence of Tradition

1

There is No Reason Why Revelation, from Its Nature, Should *Necessarily* Be Restricted to Scripture.

THE Word of God commands our respect and veneration; it is infinite truth. God spoke to man "at sundry times and in divers manners," (*Heb.* 1:1), and His word is good because He cannot deceive nor be deceived.

Being infinite in His attributes, all perfections which we perceive in His creatures are to be found in an infinite degree in the Creator. Hence, if it is man's privilege to communicate his thoughts by word or in writing or in other ways, how can we expect Almighty God to confine His Revelation only to writing? This is so evident that our separated brethren do not deny it. They fully admit that Revelation, as found in Scripture, may have been first made by God Himself to the Patriarchs, the Prophets and the Apostles, without any writing, and this is usually called "immediate Revelation." They deny, however, that Revelation, at least in the present order of things, long after its first promulgation, can be found except in Scripture. This is called "mediate or indirect Revelation"; that is, unless God reveals Himself to us, Revelation having come to an end long ago, we cannot find it except in Scripture.

This denial is entirely arbitrary: If God could render

His legates—whom He charged to promulgate for the first time a part of Revelation—worthy to be believed through *motives of credibility,* namely, through *evidence or certainty,* He could also constitute His legates for *all time* to keep and preach that same Revelation, *partly* by repeating or continuing those motives of credibility, *partly* and especially by connecting His first legates with all those who are placed by the Holy Ghost to rule His Church infallibly, thus rendering them worthy of faith and of being infallible witnesses.

In this case, man owes the same obligation to believe these infallible witnesses who exhibit, keep and witness Revelation—written or unwritten—as he does the first legates to whom God made His Revelation. So long as there are *motives of credibility* which make the legates of God and His infallible witnesses worthy of faith, so long also must man believe the legates of God and His infallible witnesses, whenever and wherever they are. It depends on God alone to choose the way and the manner of promulgating Revelation, and after its promulgation to keep it for future generations.

For this reason, when it is only a question of the nature of things, it depends on God alone, not only to choose the manner of promulgating Catholic Revelation to His first messengers, but also after its promulgation, to constitute the means and the manner of keeping it. If God chooses the Scriptures as the only instrument of promulgating and keeping Revelation, there must be sufficient *motives of credibility* by which we may be certain that the Scriptures alone *really contain* the unadulterated word of God. If He chooses the authority of witnesses to keep both the Scriptures and the already promulgated Revelation, it is then also necessary that for all time there must be sufficient *motives of credibility* to enable man to know that what is proposed to be believed is the sincere and uncorrupted word of God. In either case, man is obliged to believe Revelation—written or unwritten—as the infallible word of God. In the first case, it would be through the Scriptures; in the second, it is through the infallible testimony of those "Whom the Holy Ghost placed . . . to rule the Church of God." (*Acts* 20:28).

Therefore, besides the Scriptures, there may be other means by which God reveals Himself to us. It is not necessary that from the nature of things He should have chosen Scripture alone. God is eminently free.

2

After the Creation and Fall of Man, Down to the Coming of Christ, Tradition Always Existed.

It may be said in a certain sense that the Church—the Catholic Church—always existed. She began with the creation of man. All those who, even in the beginning of the world, worshiped God and obeyed His commands, formed the first nucleus of the Church. For the same reason it may also be truly said that the period which extended from Adam to Christ was the "Conception of the Church," just as the Day of Pentecost was her "Birthday."

From the beginning, man believed and professed certain truths. He believed in God, Creator of Heaven and Earth, a God who rewards the good and punishes evil. He expressed such belief in external worship and in the observance of the laws of God; he knew of the existence of good and of bad Angels; but most of all, he believed in a future Redeemer, who would not only cancel the sin of the first parents, but would pay the debt which, on account of their sin, he owed to God.

These truths were believed and professed at least by

those who in the general depravity of mankind were ruled by the spirit of truth. They were known as the "Sons of God," (*Gen.* 6:2), just as the people of Israel were afterwards distinguished from all the other nations as "God's Chosen People." All these truths were revelations of God. They were kept partly through the *ordinary ministry* of the successive Patriarchs, partly through the *extraordinary ministry* of the Prophets, who kept, enriched and explained the treasure of the Primitive Revelation.

We know very little of the Patriarchs who flourished before the Deluge. From the contents of the Scriptures, however, which began to be written by Moses, they appear as the "preachers of justice" and the "protectors of Religion." They did not write anything because they were not even proficient in the art of writing, as far as we know. The same may be said of the Prophets whom God sent before Moses.

Whatever may be said of this period of the human race, it is certain that Primitive Revelation, most of which was afterwards written by Moses, was kept and propagated exclusively by Tradition. This condition of things obtained for more than two thousand years.

Nevertheless, on account of the long age of the Patriarchs before the Deluge, the keeping of Primitive Revelation could never be in danger of corruption. For Abraham, being born in the year of Adam 2008, might have conversed with Sem, who died in the year of Adam 2158; while Sem's father, Noah, who was born in the year of Adam 1056 might have discussed with Enos, who died in the year of Adam 1140. The same Enos, on the other hand, was born in the year of Adam 235 and lived with his grandfather Adam for seven centuries.

With good reason, therefore, could Moses remind his people of the most ancient times of their origin: "Remember the days of old, think upon every generation: ask thy father, and he will declare to thee: thy elders and they will tell thee. When the Most High divided the nations, when he separated the sons of Adam, he appointed the bounds of people according to the number of the children of Israel." (*Deut.* 32:7-8).

If Revelation was kept *only by Tradition* after the creation and fall of man, through the advanced age of the Patriarchs down to the time of Moses, Tradition remained also *after* Moses to be a vital part in the religious life of the people of God, namely, in the Old Testament. For, after the Fall of man, God promised to all mankind a Redeemer and the eventual reward of eternal life. He never revoked this promise, nor did He restrict it to any one nation. This promise continued to be, in a *general way,* the hope and belief of all the peoples of the earth, even after God entered into a special pact with His Chosen People.

Suarez (1548-1617) understood this. He writes: "The Law, properly understood, did not promise an eternal reward—and still it is true that under the Law, man had the promise of eternal life and of all spiritual good—nor is there here any contradiction, because the Jews had this promise, not from the Law, but *'from the Fathers,'* so to speak, through *their* Tradition; for from the beginning of the Church, it was promised to all the Faithful, and its faith remained in them through Tradition, though it was renewed in Abraham and made more expressive. It reached, therefore, in this way the people of Israel and was afterwards written by the prophets, not as new, but as an *ancient doctrine.* This is abundantly proved by the testimony of the Apostle (*Heb.* 11) who, beginning with Abel and continuing through the Patriarchs to the Prophets, declares that all had this promise. The Law, therefore, did not add to this spiritual promise."[1] This is clearer still from the fact that after the first Divine Books had been written, God instituted a Ministry—an *ordinary* Ministry—that is, an explanatory Tradition and an authentic interpretation in the priesthood, as we read in *Deuteronomy* (*Deut.* 18:5) and in *Malachias*, "The lips of the priest shall keep knowledge and they shall seek the law at his mouth: because he is the angel of the Lord of hosts." (*Mal.* 2:7).

This *ordinary* Ministry was distinguished from the *extraordinary* Ministry of the Prophets, whom God at divers times sent to promulgate new revelations, as well as to explain and keep those which had been already accepted in the Old Law. There should be no doubt whatever that in this complex Ministry—*ordinary and extraordinary*—there were divine truths which were never written, or if they were written, they were vaguely indicated in the Scriptures. These were especially the traditions which belonged to the whole human race and were revealed by God before there *was* any Scripture. Our Lord Jesus Christ Himself intimates such doctrine: "The scribes and the Pharisees have sat on the chair of Moses," (*Matt.* 23:2), obviously not for new revelations, but to interpret the Law authoritatively.

Whatever we may think of this matter, it is certain that the canonical books of the Scriptures, their authority and divine inspiration, could not have been transmitted other than by Tradition. This is not only evident in itself, but it also appears from Josephus, who, having related how the books of the Scriptures written up to the time of Artaxerxes I (465-425 B.C.) were accepted by all, he refers then to other books of the same Scriptures, which afterwards followed, saying: "These were not equally accepted

---

1. Suarez, *De Legibus,* L. IX, C. VI, N. 21.

as the first, because of the inaccuracy of the succession of the Prophets."[2] The same Josephus then testifies how afterwards the Jews accepted and kept these latter books of the Scriptures and believed them as the Word of God.

Therefore, it is evident that dogmatic truths were carried on by Tradition from the creation and fall of man down to the Old Testament (the time of Moses), even *after* the appearance of the written Word of God.

This means that since the creation of man down to the coming of Christ, God did not restrict Revelation to the Scriptures.

3

The Church Always Believed Theoretically In Tradition.

Nowadays, most of the Protestant divines, pressed by the arguments of Catholic Theologians, begin to admit that before the Scriptures were all written, the Church, in its origin and infancy—from the beginning of the world and throughout the centuries down to the preaching of the Apostles—believed many dogmatic truths which, until then, never formed part of the Scriptures. They contend, however, that after the death of the Apostles, the Scriptures having all been written, the Church—the Church of the Apostles, the various Apostolic Churches—did not believe anything which was not contained in the Scriptures. This means that Revelation must now be restricted to the Scriptures.

That this contention is without foundation is proved by the perfection of the New Law compared to the Old Dispensation.

---

2. *Contra Appion,* L. I, N. 8.

Truly, the promises of the New Law given by God to the teaching ministry of the Church are much greater than those given to the Patriarchs and the priests of the Old Law. The distinguishing mark of the New Dispensation is that the belief of the Church is written by the Holy Ghost in *her heart*—in her Catholic Intellect—rather than on *paper and tables of stone.* The Apostle says: "You are our epistle, written in our hearts, which is known and read by all men: being manifested, that you are the epistle of Christ, ministered by us, and written, not with ink, but with the Spirit of the living God; not in tables of stone, but in the fleshy tables of the heart. . . . God also hath made us fit ministers of the New Testament, not in the letter, but in the spirit. For the letter killeth, but the spirit quickeneth." (*2 Cor.* 3:2-6).

This spirit has at all times been manifested by the Church in *theory,* or as others say, *speculatively speaking,* even after the completion of the Scriptures. This is the great principle which the Church always held and holds. Not only is it not necessary that what the Christian is to believe must *necessarily* be contained in the Scriptures, but also that *in fact* there are many truths—dogmatic truths—which exist and must be believed, and yet at the same time, they never formed part of the Scriptures.

That the Church *believed in theory* such a fundamental principle all the Fathers and Doctors of the Church testify in unmistakable words. Principal among them are Ignatius in Asia;[3] Clement in Alexandria;[4] Tertullian in Pontus;[5] Eusebius in Palestine;[6] Basilius in

3. In *Eusebius* III, 36.
4. In *Eusebius* VI, 33.
5. Tertullian, *De Corona,* CC. III, IV.
6. *Euseb. Demonst. Evang.,* L. I, C. VIII.

Pontus;[7] Epiphanius of Cyprus;[8] Chrysostom in Antioch and Constantinople;[9] Jerome, who practically belonged both to the Eastern and Western Churches;[10] and Augustine in the name of the whole Church.[11]

All these Fathers and Doctors of the Church, who in life and after their demise were and are forever the great luminaries of the Church, like one man, proclaim that they believe in Tradition and that they wrote for no other reason than safely to preserve Tradition. They even assert that what is believed and practiced in and by the Church, but not mentioned in the Scriptures nor declared by the Councils, is derived from the Apostles. Hence they warn us: "Nothing else must be further inquired; it is Tradition."

This has always been the belief of the Church expressed in her Councils. Thus, the Seventh General Council, Art. VII, affirms: "East and West, North and South, we all agree in the same Faith through the inspiration of the Holy Ghost—accepting all whatever the Holy Catholic Church received of old, whether it was written or unwritten," declaring moreover, "If any one denies Ecclesiastical Tradition, whether it is written or not, let him be anathema."[12]

Listen to Epiphanius, who wrote in the Fourth Century. Speaking on marriage, and having quoted the Scriptures, he says: "But we need also Tradition. For we cannot prove everything from the Scriptures, because the most holy Apostles left us some in writing and some by Tradition. This is what Paul affirms (*1 Cor.* 11:2): 'As I have deliv-

7. *De Spir.*, S., C. XXVII.
8. *Heres.* 61, N. 6.
9. In II Thess., Hom. 4, N. 2.
10. *Diag. c. Lucif.*, N. 4.
11. *De Bapt.*, L. II, N. 12.
12. In *Harduin* T. IV, pp. 471-479.

ered them to you'; likewise in another place (*1 Cor.* 14:33): 'as also I teach in all the churches of the saints'; and again (*1 Cor.* 15:2): 'if you hold fast after what manner I preached unto you, unless you have believed in vain.' The Holy Church of God has received it from the Apostles, that is to say, after one has emitted the vow of virginity, it seems a crime to contract marriage."[13]

All this evidently shows that after the death of the Apostles, the Church always believed *theoretically* in Tradition.

4

What the Church Believed Theoretically She also *Professed* Always in her Practice, that is, Truths and Rites Which are not Contained in the Scriptures.

The Universal Church always professed in her acts and practices certain truths and discipline which never were written in Scripture. As the dogmas contained in Scripture were always, on the one hand, declared and explained to the Faithful and, on the other, defended against heretics, so also the Fathers of the Church, individually or assembled in General Councils, solemnly confessed and testified that certain dogmas and usages universally believed or practiced, but not set forth in the Scriptures, must not be discarded, as if not belonging to the Faith.

This regards the solemn *formulae* or certain expressions drawn up to declare and explain certain dogmatic truths. Such are, for instance, *"one nature and three persons," "consubstantial persons,"* the efficacy of the Sacraments *ex opere operato* (i.e., by their very nature—literally, "from the work worked."), *"transubstantiation"* and so

13. Epiph. Heres. 61, N. 6.

forth. These formulae imply not only the existence of Traditions, but also the formal principle of Tradition, that is, *a living and teaching body, constituted by Christ, to guard and explain to the Faithful the Deposit of Faith.*

We are more particularly concerned with the solemn testimonies of antiquity about the unwritten dogmas and practices which are recognized and proclaimed only from Tradition.

The Fathers explicitly and candidly admit that certain truths and practices of the Church are not to be found in the Scriptures; consequently, they cannot be defended except by Tradition. Thus Origen, in his epistle to the Romans, writes: "The Church received from the Apostles the tradition of baptizing children in their infancy."[14] St. Augustine with regard to this *practice,* confessing that it cannot be proved from the Scriptures, says that there is in it only a "conjecture or supposition" drawn from circumcision. The convincing argument—*"if any one wants to know the divine authority"* for this *practice*—the holy Doctor derives from this principle: "What the Universal Church holds and was not instituted by the Councils, but was always retained, is rightly believed to be delivered by Apostolic authority."[15]

It will not be out of place to remark here that when the Anabaptists—"Rebaptizers"—a violent and radical body of reformers of the 16th Century, demanded from their Protestant brethren the testimony drawn from the Scriptures to prove the validity of infant Baptism, Luther, *not being able to prove it,* claimed that *through a miracle* infants emit an act of faith in order to receive Baptism validly. Asked however to demonstrate such a miracle

14. Origen, L. V, N. 9.
15. August., *De Bapt.,* L. IV, C. XXIV.

from the Scriptures, neither Luther nor his followers ever attempted to prove it.[16]

It is from Tradition that St. Augustine argues with regard to Baptism conferred by heretics. He writes, "What Cyprian and other African Bishops argued against 'the validity of such Baptism' must not be preferred to the confession of the whole Catholic Church, whose worthy members they were; nor by thinking otherwise did they cut themselves off from her communion, because it was only after many years that the truth was made more clear through a General Council, *not instituting anything new, but simply strengthening antiquity*. . . . The Apostles had not made any disposition about this matter (in Scripture); but the custom, which was opposed to Cyprian, was believed to have originated from their (the Apostles') Tradition, *just as there are many things which the Church holds and believes that were ordered by the Apostles, although we do not find them in the Scriptures.*"[17]

About this controversy, the response of Pope Stephen I (254-257) to Cyprian is famous: "Let nothing be introduced but what has been delivered."

Cyprian died a martyr of the Church, thus gloriously washing with his blood whatever guilt may have been imputed to him with regard to this question.

On the practice of praying for the dead, Epiphanius I (254-257), laying aside the question of the inspiration of the Books of the Machabees, says: "I declare that it is necessary for the Church to do it (to pray for the dead) because she received such a rite delivered to her by the ancients."[18]

Illustrious indeed on this matter is the statement of Tertullian, which he wrote more than 1,800 years ago: "We

16. Jörg., *Hist. of Prot.,* V. II.
17. August., *De Bapt.,* L. V, C. I.
18. Epiph. Heres. 65, N. 8.

offer oblations for the dead on their anniversaries; we do not fast or kneel on the Lord's Day. We enjoy the same immunity from Easter to Pentecost. We are anxious that not a particle or a drop (of the Holy Eucharist) fall to the ground. Before we start anything, when we come in or go out, at our rising and washing, at meal times, at our wakes, when we sit down or we go to bed, in our conversations, we make the Sign of the Cross. If you will ask for any law for this and other such discipline, you will find none in the Scriptures: Tradition is its author, custom confirms it, Faith helps to observe it."[19]

Finally, the Seventh General Council declares that from Tradition it approves the use and veneration of images. St. John Damascene, the champion and the greatest defender of this doctrine, acknowledges Tradition as its author.[20]

The Church, therefore, even after the completion of the Scriptures, publicly professed and believed dogmatic truths and practiced certain rites and disciplines which are not found in the Scriptures. She simply received them from Tradition.

---

19. Tertull., *De Corona,* C. III.
20. John Damascene, *De Fide Orthod.,* IV, 16, Art. 7.

7

Aberrations of Protestantism

1

Protestantism Is Inconsistent.

WE do not intend to discuss the living and burning questions which for the moment are agitating the internal structure of many a Protestant denomination. Those questions are being debated, not so much between the different Protestant Churches, as they are between the members of the same denomination. The issue is so formidable that it has caused serious dissensions in the Presbyterian, Baptist, Methodist and Episcopal Churches. In the opinion of some, the chasm between the conservatives or fundamentalists, on one side, and the liberals or modernists, on the other, is widening and forming a permanent division.

It is not out of place to give a passing glance at the present situation of these most important branches of Protestantism in order to show its greatest weakness.

The most ominous tendency at present is the effort of conservative leaders to insist upon *Creed-bound* dogmas—such as the verbal inspiration of the Bible, the virgin birth of Jesus, the vicarious substitutionary theory of the Blood of the Atonement, the physical Resurrection of Our Lord and His immediate, visible second advent—as essential to a saving faith and to Christian standing. All this the modernists, led by hundreds of clergymen and backed by a few bishops—often the most scholarly among them—deny or seriously doubt.

To be more specific, and singling out one denomination: the conservative element of the Episcopal Church has attempted without success to bring the clergy of that communion into doctrinal conformity with its Creed, threatening the recalcitrants with trial for heresy. But the Modern Churchmen's Union, which is said to be composed of 500 Episcopal clergymen, have accepted the challenge and assumed the defense of one of their clergymen—"an obscure clergyman from the southwest"—accused of questioning the Virgin Birth. He is said to have declared: "Consecrated Christian men differ much in their interpretation of the ancient creeds . . . for instance, there are those who cling with unquestioning minds to the doctrine of the Virgin Birth as a statement of physical fact, while others have been moved to analyze it and have discovered new spiritual truths that transcend what the form of words thus imperfectly express. There are those among us who believe that Jesus was in all things and in every way both God and man: the incarnation of God and the son of Joseph."

A more spectacular feature to this revolt is presented in the deliberate and dramatic utterance of a prominent minister who, appearing in the gown of a "Doctor of Theology" in his pulpit and publicly divesting himself of his clerical vestments, denied the Virgin Birth, suggesting that his bishop bring him, rather than the above "obscure clergyman"—a young man from the southwest—to trial for heresy. Now, in justice to the bishops of the Episcopal Church, it must be said that, with very few exceptions, they have reaffirmed in a recent declaration their faith in the Virgin Birth and the Apostle's Creed, and require conformity to these doctrines on the part of all their clergy. But without our entering into the intrinsic merits of the question at issue, we may simply ask: by what logic may the Episcopal bishops, or any other elders in any Protestant denomination, require conformity, or submission of the intellect on the part of their clergy or laity on any Christian doctrine which—no matter how orthodox or sound it may be—is based on the principle of "private judgment"? Was it not this very principle of private judgment that gave birth and life to Protestantism, by which all men and women have the right of making their own interpretation? Was not the principle of private interpretation of the Bible the cause of separation from the Old Catholic Church?

We assume that the rejoinder to all these questions is that every denomination has the right to form its own creed and live up to it. But here we must ask again: "By what right has any man, or any group of men, or any people who claim to be Christian, to form a new creed or start a new religion? If a new religion has been established on the right of private interpretation, why a creed that binds the thoughts of others into a bundle of words? The formation of a creed is the institution of an authority and the quintessence of that Tradition which all Protestantism has long ago rejected. It is true that Protestant creeds are changed from time to time, but they are always binding on the members of their respective denominations. Any minister who does not conform himself to the creed of his church is brought before the tribunals of his church and judged according to its creed. But is not a creed the product of a collection of private interpretation? Who gave the makers of a creed authority to bind or to judge others? Christ said to His Apostles: "As My Father sent Me, so also I send you." Who sent these modern "apostles" to start new religions or to make new creeds?

God has not sent them; Christ has not sent them; nor did the Catholic Church. Only to Peter, the head of the Church—and in the person of Peter to all his successors in office—Christ said: "Feed My Lambs . . . feed My Sheep." (*John* 21:15, 16, 17), The [Protestant] people may have sent them. But the people are not Christ, nor His ever-living and teaching Church. Consequently, if the judges appointed according to any Protestant creed render any judgment, their sentence is equivalent to a post-mortem examination. Their sentence will bring a new life neither to the living nor to the dead. It is only a phrase and is against the first principle which brought them into existence as a separate church.

Yet how mercilessly has this authority been exercised is a matter of history, and this history is still going on. Hence, the present existence of separations, divisions, unbridled Rationalism, Modernism and Freethought now rampant in cultured society, universities and in the press. Such is the result of inconsistent Protestantism.

Such inconsistency was recognized even by, among others, the Protestant J. H. Blunt, who writes: "The mere existence of such confessions of faith as binding on all or any of the members of the Christian community is inconsistent with the great principles on which the Protestant bodies justified their separation from the Church, *the right of private judgment.* Has not any member as just a right to criticize and to reject them as his forefathers had a right to reject the Catholic Creed or the canons of General Councils? They appear to violate another prominent doctrine of the Reformers, the sufficiency of Holy Scripture to salvation. If the Bible alone is enough, what need is there for adding articles? If it is rejoined that they are not additions to, but merely explanations of the Word of God, the further question arises—amid the many explanations, more or less at variance with each other, given by the different sects of Protestantism—who is to decide which is the true one? Their professed object being to secure uniformity, the experience of nearly 500 years has proved to us what may not have been foreseen by their originators, that they have had a diametrically opposite result and have been productive, not of union, but of variance."[1]

Therefore, Liberalism or Modernism in any non-Catholic denomination, while it is wrong, nevertheless, is more consistent with its principle of private judgment, carrying everything to its logical conclusion. The Conservatives or Fundamentalists, while they are right in upholding the truth of some fundamental doctrines of the Christian Religion, nevertheless, are wrong because they go only half-way and contradict themselves. While they glory in the proclamation of private judgment, which caused them to reject the authority of the Catholic Church, they deny to the individual the right of private judgment and assume to themselves an authority which no man can give them. They are inconsistent and contradict themselves.

2

The Principle of Protestantism—Considered as the Main Foundation and Reason for its Separation From the Catholic Church—Is an Open Contradiction.

Protestantism, no matter how vague and indefinite may be its various creeds, is based on three principles: The *first* consists in the *"sources of faith,"* according to which

1. J. H. Blunt, *Dict. of Sects, Heresies, etc.*

the Scriptures, and nothing but the Scriptures, must be accepted; the *second* lies in the *"means of justification,"* by which man is justified by faith alone; the *third* is the *"constitution of the church,"* according to which all believers constitute a universal priesthood, all having the right and the duty, not only to read and interpret the Bible, but also to take part in the government and public affairs of the church.

We are concerned here only with the *first principle,* that is, the *"sources of faith."*

As expressed in the Symbolic Books of all Protestant denominations, the principle of the "sources of faith" is proclaimed in the following words: "We believe, we confess and we teach that the only rule and guide, according to which all dogmas and all doctors must be considered and judged, are nothing else but the prophetical and apostolical writings of the Old and the New Testament."[2] This same principle was set forth by Chillingworth in this formula: "The Bible, the whole Bible, and nothing but the Bible, is the Religion of Protestants." This means the supremacy of the Bible and its exclusive *fountainhead* of knowledge and information concerning the Christian Religion by means of private interpretation. In another part, we have seen how this principle is fatal to Faith and destructive of Christian unity.

Moreover, it is *illogical* and *contradictory.* It is illogical: Faith consists in the *submission* of the intellect to a higher authority for what man must believe, whether he understands it or not. It implies dependence and reliance on something higher than man's intellect. It is evident that in this case reason is guided by Faith. On the contrary, when private interpretation constitutes reason as the

---

2. *Epitom. Form., Concord.*

sole judge, then the last word rests only with the intellect, that is, the reader or hearer. If only with the intellect, then there is no submission of the intellect to Faith; hence, there is no faith, because there is no teacher to direct the intellect. If no faith or no teacher, why and what is the intellect—the reader or hearer—trying to learn? How can it be guided? By excluding authority, the intellect excludes faith in God, or in His Church, and proclaims itself a little god. Reason is deified. St. Augustine is once more to the point: "He who believes whatever he likes, believes himself and not the Gospel."

Nor can it be said that, in the matter of private interpretation, reason constitutes as its teacher or higher authority the Bible itself. The Protestant reader or hearer, according to his own statement, constitutes his private intellect as the sole judge. Who tells him that he must learn religion from the Bible and only from the Bible to conform his life accordingly? If he persists in affirming that that is the creed of his church, he must confess that there is some authority higher than his intellect, namely, the creed of his church. But how can he logically admit the authority of the creed of his church over his intellect, when by his own confession he asserts that his intellect is the only judge? In such a case, he is the judge of his church and creed. Hence, St. Augustine again: "I would not believe the Gospel were I not moved to do so by the authority of the Catholic Church."[3]

But it is not only illogical, it is also contradictory when our non-Catholic brethren speak of faith in the Scriptures, for they must certainly mean a profession of *divine faith.* They declare that only the books of the Old and the New Testaments are the sole rule and guide by which all dog-

3. August, *Epist. Fund.,* C. V.

mas and all doctors must be weighed and judged.

This statement contains three points. The *first point* declares that, not only are all those books *sacred and divine,* but also that they are the *only* books, truly sacred and divine, which constitute the only "rule of faith." The *second point* proclaims that "there is no other word of God but those divine and sacred books which must be believed, nor any other doctrine of faith which is not contained in and which cannot be proved by those divine and sacred books." The *third point* asserts that every one of the Faithful is a sufficient interpreter of the true sense of Sacred Scripture and that all dogmas and all doctors must be considered and judged according to those divine and sacred books which form the only "rule of faith." Hence, they deny that the Church is the authentic interpreter of the true sense of Scripture; on the contrary, they claim that such right of interpretation belongs to every man and woman. This is what they call the right of *private judgment.*

Unfortunately, however, for our separated brethren, none of these three points—which, according to them, are the fundamental doctrines of their belief—is contained in Scripture. If they "search the Scriptures" from cover to cover, *they will not find any one of them.* The consequence is, therefore, that while they believe, declare and proclaim that nothing is to be believed which is not written in the Scriptures, at the same time they believe, declare and proclaim before the whole world, as a fundamental principle of their religion, *what was never written in the Scriptures.* This is something *affirmative and negative of the same principle.* It is a contradiction.

3

In the Belief and Practice of Religion, Our Separated Brethren Profess and Perform Many Things Which are not Written in the Scriptures. They Know Them Only from Tradition.

Sometimes man acts without much reflection. Not infrequently, he operates even "unconsciously" against the leading principles of his life or religion. By unconsciousness, we do not mean here the total inadvertence of a condition—like the act of the somnambulist, much less that of a state like the ox of his yoke—but rather, that certain inapprehension which is not realized nor brought home to one's intelligence. This lack of serious reflection or "unconsciousness" is derived from certain habits, from certain preconceived ideas, from certain surroundings, even after one has been able to judge and choose for himself. He who first asserted that peoples are said to be Mohammedans, Pagans, Protestants or Catholics "by birth" was not very much mistaken. Environment and prejudice work to a great extent on man's views and actions.

Now, if we consider the fundamental tenet of Protestantism—that is, private judgment—at first sight, we are inclined to conclude that such a deleterious principle must unavoidably lead to a dissolution of all creeds and to a complete destruction of all non-Catholic faiths. Our conclusion is right.

However, we are faced by the fact that, if private judgment broke the unity of faith, Protestantism has lived several centuries, and until lately, it has been active at home and abroad.* This seems an incongruity—which, how-

* The reader should continue to bear in mind that this book was published in 1928. Msgr. Agius is not the only author to have observed a decline in the vitality of Protestantism in that era. However, it

ever, is only apparent—for private judgment was never allowed full play in the life and course of any religion.

From the beginning of the Protestant Reformation down to our own times, the exercise of private judgment has been limited to those who, by dint of strong character, have been able to create new denominations and creeds. "Private Judgment"—that is, "the open Bible and nothing but the Bible, with a free interpretation for all"—is nothing but a *lure* to entice the masses. It only serves to flatter the pride and to deceive the ignorant people. In reality, it does not belong to the masses, but it is the privilege of the few. The masses are always moved and led to do the work of others. Their reflection and conscience are too often formed by *adventurers,* who have much to gain and not much to lose. As time lends stability and the color of truth to their achievement, particularly when they are born and brought up in such unhappy surroundings, the people take for granted that they are right and others are wrong.

This lack of serious reflection and of a sound consciousness is nowhere better revealed than in the belief and practices of our Separated Brethren. The principal denominations which are still proud of their Christian origin and name have retained, even in our days, many doctrines and practices which they have inherited from no other source than Tradition. Some of these doctrines and practices are not even mentioned in the Scriptures. If they *are* mentioned, the Scriptures rather disapprove of them. They are simply transmitted by Tradition. Yet the Protestant masses believe that they are acting, not according to Tradition, but according to Scripture.

---

displayed a resurgence of energy starting about the 1960's.—*Publisher,* 2005.

They believe that Baptism may be validly administered by heretics and infidels, or that infants should be baptized. They believe that the Lord's Day is Sunday and not Saturday, as it was under the Old Law. They believe that, under certain conditions and for a good motive, it is lawful for Christians to take an oath. They believe that the use of *strangled* food or of blood is permissible. Although these practices seem to be rather disapproved of by Scripture, most Protestants act and interpret them according to the Tradition and authority of the Catholic Church. Hence, no wonder that a certain denomination observes not Sunday, but Saturday, as the Lord's day. (*Ex.* 20:10-11; *Matt.* 5:33-34; *Acts* 15: 28-29).

All the above mentioned practices, as well as many other practices, our dissenting brethren believe and comply with, without their being written in the Scriptures. Why? Because they always did so, and their fathers and forefathers did so before them—back to *before* the Reformation.

There are still many other things which our Separated Brethren believe, contrary to the teaching of the Catholic Church, which are not written in the Scriptures. Such, for instance, is man's justification by *faith alone,* that is: faith is the only requisite and means of obtaining salvation.

According to this theory, neither repentance, nor love of God, nor good works, nor any other virtue is required. When Martin Luther, in his German translation of the Bible, falsified *Romans* 3:28 by interpolating or adding the word *alone*—"For we account a man to be justified by faith [*alone*], without the works of the law"—he thus answered to his critics: "I want it this way. Papist and ass are the same thing: so I will, so I command; my will is a reason for it."[4]

---

4. Cath. Encycl. V, VIII, p. 575.

Finally, our Separated Brethren have somehow evolved a system of distinguishing what articles of faith are *fundamental* and *not fundamental* to be necessarily believed. Such a system is nowhere to be found in the Scriptures. Still they approve of it, and they wonder why the Catholic Church does not even take much notice of it. Their reasoning is strange indeed! When we consider that there are many things known only from Tradition which are not approved by them, because not found in Scripture, while on the other hand they act and live according to certain Traditions which are not found in Scripture, we understand the lamentable spiritual condition of all non-Catholic denominations, and we dread with horror the labyrinth in which all Protestantism is miserably lost. There is only one way out of it: a speedy return to Old Mother Church.

8

Incorruption of Tradition

Introduction

THE Constitution which Christ Himself instituted and which the Apostles, faithful to the command of the Master, established in every part of the then known world continued to exist in the first centuries of the Church. When the Apostles died, their commands were carried out by their successors.

In the first centuries it was impossible that the principles and fundamentals of Christianity could have become so corrupted as to make place for a different order of things in the government of the Church. For not all the Apostles died the same year, nor could the generation which they gained for Christ have been possibly substituted at once by another generation. Some of the Apostles and some of their immediate successors lived to an old age. One generation lived and intermingled with another, only to be all brought up and instructed as were the first generation of Christians.

For this reason, whatever has been affirmed about the impossibility of change in the government of the Church, may also be applied to the impossibility of corruption of the Apostolic doctrine in the early centuries—and thus also in the course of time, down to our own days. We must take the writings of the Fathers for what they are worth, that is to say, as historical documents, not as revealed truths. No man can reject historical documents. It would destroy all historical certitude. We take the Fathers' writings just as we accept, for instance, the writings of Josephus Flavius (c.37-c.100), of Caesar (100-44 B.C.) or of Livy (59 B.C.-17 A.D.). Josephus Flavius describes the political and religious conditions of his contemporary brethren, just as Caesar and Livy give us a good account of the civil war, which divided the Romans before the fall of the Republic. There is no reason why we should believe those authors more than we do the early writers of the Church.

What a presumption it was on the part of the Reformers of the 16th Century to claim that they knew better than the Fathers what the government and doctrine of the Church had been during the first three centuries! Generally speaking, the Fathers were men of great learning and piety. They enlightened the Church and glorified the Faith with their great works. They were the great men of their times, writing first-hand about their contemporaries. And they testify that, besides the Scriptures, which they saved from oblivion and total loss, there is also in the Church another "Rule of Faith," and that is the Church herself, to which Christ and the Apostles delivered the Deposit of Faith.

1

The Traditions of the Church are not Subject To Corruption.

At the beginning, Protestants rejected Tradition. Lately, however, there are so many of them that admit some of the traditions—such as Lutherans, Episcopalians and Evangelicals—that their separation from Rome seems to have been more political than religious. They are governed by a certain supreme authority, not very unlike the Roman

Jurisdiction. The King of England is the head of the Anglican Church; the King of Prussia was at the head of the Reformed Lutherans; and there is scarcely a non-Catholic denomination in which a so-called *board of directors* is not vested with a supreme authority in its administration. Many denominations believe in the Apostles' Creed, recognize the decrees of the early General Councils, and revere the writings of the Fathers. But they explain them according to their sectarian standpoint. Others reject *all the Traditions,* on the grounds that they are subject to corruption. When any doctrine, they claim, is carried on for generations—from father to son—necessarily so many legends and myths arise that little truth is left.

This is an affirmation on their part that the Church is not infallible. Had they believed that the Church is infallible, they would not have forgotten so soon the assistance promised to the Church by Christ.

They forgot that, strictly speaking, all Revelation, whether contained in the Scriptures or in other documents, on monuments, in usages, and so forth, were all written down and transmitted to posterity. The Apostles wrote that part of Revelation which is contained in the Scriptures, while their disciples wrote what the Apostles preached, taught or instituted in the Church, but which had not been written by the Apostles.

It is a mistake to dream only of an oral tradition carried on from generation to generation through the help of word of mouth. *For Tradition, in the first place, is not "oral" in the sense that it is maintained and propagated "only" through man's lips.* It is oral in the sense that in the beginning it was received by the Faithful from the Apostles themselves, *not in writing,* but through their preaching, teaching or institutions, established in the Church by the same Apostles. What the Apostles did not write, but preached, taught or instituted, was *afterwards written* by their immediate disciples, and sometimes by the disciples of these immediate Apostolic disciples.

Tradition, in the second place, is "oral," not in the sense that it was never written, but in the sense that "what in the beginning was not written" by the inspired authors was written "afterwards" by their disciples. What the disciples heard or were taught by the Apostles and not committed to the Scriptures, they afterwards laid down in writing.

In the third place, Tradition is "oral," as distinguished from that part of Revelation which was written by the Apostles—namely, Scripture. For what the Apostolic disciples afterwards wrote, as heard, learned or as instituted by the Apostles, is what we call, properly speaking, Tradition. We must remember that not all the truths which the Apostles preached and taught were written or discussed in their Epistles, because most of those truths were plain enough and accepted by all. They simply wrote, as the occasion demanded their further attention, to confirm the brethren in their absence.

Moreover, as the Apostles were not only Apostles but also the "ancients" and the legislators of the Church, they instituted certain days of the week or certain seasons of the year as the time of penance, of joy or of rest, to be observed by all. Abstinence from meat on Friday, fasting in Lent, the Sunday observance instead of Saturday, Easter Joys, the ceremonies of Holy Mass, were instituted by the Apostles as a help to the Christian to save his soul and as an ornament to divine worship. All these things were a part—so to speak—of the routine of the Church. All accepted them as a matter of course and as a part of the daily life of the Church. Hence, there was no necessity on their part to write them down; they preached and taught the Faithful what they must do as members of the Church of Jesus Christ. Hence, it was natural that what the Apostles did not write, their disciples, in order to refresh their memories, as well as to transmit it to other generations, did write, according to the warning of the Apostle, "to teach others also." (*2 Tim.* 2:2). "Hold the traditions, which you have learned, whether by word, or by our epistle." (*2 Thess.* 2:14).

Traditions, therefore, according to the Apostle, are of two kinds, *written* and *unwritten.* The *written* are the Scriptures, because *tradition* means anything that is delivered or transmitted to others. In this case, the Scriptures *are* traditions, although improperly so called. The *unwritten* are all those other Traditions which are not contained in the Scriptures, but which, as the Apostle says, his disciples received through his preaching. These are properly called "Traditions."

As both kinds of Traditions—received, as the Apostle says, "through my preaching" (properly called Traditions) "and through my Epistle" (the Scriptures—improperly called Traditions)—come to us from the Apostles, both are to be accepted, both are to be believed, both must be lived up to because, according to the command of the Apostle, we must hold both.

The written Traditions, or the Scriptures, contain the greater part of Revelation. *But it is not less true that what the Apostles preached, taught or instituted in the Church, but did not write, are a very important part of the Deposit of Faith. They were written by their disciples.*

Therefore, the objection collapses, that Traditions, being oral, become corrupted in the course of time. Tradition, strictly speaking, is not oral. It was only such in its first proclamation. *All Traditions have been written, if not by the Apostles, certainly by the Church.* As pastors and doctors, or as writers of the Church, the first Christians wrote what they heard or learned from the Apostles, or what was practiced in the Church. They wrote not as inspired writers, but simply as common teachers or believers who had nothing else in view but to defend and protect the Deposit of Faith. God, in His Providence, induced those men to write, to be witnesses of that Faith which is always old and always new, feeble and still strong. Although written in the documents of old, Tradition is still better written in the hearts of the Faithful and deeply engraved in the religious practices and belief of the Church.

2

Tradition, Approved by the Church, Is a Supernatural and Absolute Certitude in Every Century of the Church.

God, in His infinite wisdom and Providence, gave the Church in all times so many learned and holy men that their knowledge seems to have been more supernatural than human. Those personalities were illustrious, not only for their wisdom and prudence, but also for their learning in the divine and human sciences. They were the men of their day. They were the guardians of that Faith which the Apostles planted in the principal parts of the Roman Empire. Of one thing they were solicitous more than of anything else: to keep inviolate the Deposit of Faith. They so loved antiquity and detested innovation that so many of them—such as Ignatius of Antioch, Polycarp, Lactantius, Cyprian and a great host of bishops, priests, and confessors—even gave up their lives in defense of the Faith.

Others, like Jerome, left the world and repaired to the desert, there to write and explain in sublime contemplation the principal articles of the Christian Religion.

They were one in their consent and union of the Faith. For this they employed all their talents and made use of the best ways and means in their possession.

It was for this reason that the Fathers of the Lateran Council (First Lateran Council–1123), having first recited the unanimous sentences of the doctors and pastors who preceded them, exclaimed: "These holy Fathers, accepting with the greatest love the word of Our Lord God and Saviour Jesus Christ, have not hidden under the bushel of unfaithful obscurity the light of grace which He gave them, but placed it upon the candelabrum of the doctrine of salvation, in order that it may shine before all those who are in the house, that is to say, before all the people of the Catholic Church."[1] Augustine, speaking of the bishops who ruled the Church of God and lived before him, says: "They are bishops, learned, grave, holy, fearless defenders of the truth against loquacious vanities, in whose reason, erudition and liberty—the three most important qualities in a judge—you can find nothing to reproach. If a synod of all the bishops of the world could be assembled, it would be a wonder if all could easily gather together. For they lived not in the same time, but as faithful and most excellent ones, they were sent by God in different ages to different places, as the same God pleases and sees fit to send them. They are to you the more terrible because you attack the Catholic Faith, which they sucked with their milk, which they partook in their food, and which milk and food they administered to the little ones and to the great."[2]

With such holy, prudent and learned men at the helm

---

1. *Lat. Council under Pope Martin I.*
2. August, *C. Jul.,* L. II, N. 37.

of Peter's bark; with the most perfect consent and union among those whom "the Holy Ghost placed to rule the Church of God"; with such watchful eyes on the part of the pastors to lead their flocks to wholesome pastures and to keep them away from the poisonous weeds of heresy; with such contempt for innovation and such love and reverence for antiquity that "Nothing be introduced but what has been delivered" [Pope St. Stephen I—254-257]; with the most severe and protective means, to hold "what they received from the fathers in order to deliver it to their children"; it was impossible that any novelty could either at once or by degrees ever infect the illustrious antiquity of doctrine.

And if ever novelty did succeed, it was a local occurrence, never a general event. History does not register even one single innovation *in the whole Church,* because the whole Church cannot be subverted. There *have been* extensive defections—as in the Orient after the Eighth Century—and in the North of Europe in the 16th Century. But these were partial. Large, though dead branches seem to be part of a tree, but the sooner they are cut down, the better it is for the tree. It becomes more vigorous in size, in foliage, in life. So it is with the Church, the great "Tree of Life." It is planted in the garden of God and watered by the graces of the Holy Ghost. It will live unto the End of Time.

The peoples of the earth need the Church, but the Church does not need anybody. Woe to those nations which separate themselves from the Church. As dead branches, they will wither away and will only be good to burn. History cannot designate one single instance of general innovation in the Church. That would be the end. The gates of Hell would prevail. But it is impossible. "Let nothing be introduced but what has been delivered."

The solicitude of the pastors of the Church, their detestation of novelty, their sanctity, science and love of antiquity, and still more the supernatural protection which Christ promised to His Church, all force us to the conclusion that whatever is found in or approved by the Catholic Church is true and according to the truth. Nothing can be more certain. It came down to us from the Apostles through the watchful learning of the bishops, whom "the Holy Ghost has placed to rule the Church of God." (*Acts* 20:28). Whatever is the bishops' doctrine, that is also our doctrine. It is based on the promise of Christ and the guidance of the Holy Ghost. And our certainty is a supernatural and absolute certainty. Such is the Tradition approved by the Church. It can never be corrupted. It will live until the End of Time.

3

The Canon or Rule of St. Vincent of Lerin is True In an *Affirmative,* Not in an *Exclusive* Sense. It is Simply the Way to Find Out the Apostolicity of a Certain Doctrine in Order to Repel Novelty.

Famous among the writings of the Fathers is the Canon of Vincentius, or as others call him, St. Vincent of Lerin (c.400-c.450). Contained in his *Commonitorium,* the Canon draws a line, intended to discern what is pure from what is corrupt, to distinguish the truth from what is simply an opinion, to determine what is orthodox from what is faulty. "We must hold what has been held *always, everywhere,* and *by all;* this is truly and properly Catholic . . . this can be obtained if we follow universality, antiquity, consent." (N. 3, Emphasis added). These are the three characteristic notes of the so-called Vincentian Canon or Rule.

There is nothing in this world however, which may not be abused. For this reason, in order to cut off as corruptions all usages, tenets and dogmas which are not sanctioned by primitive times, Protestants appeal to this rule, by which they strike at Rome, never thinking that it is an assault against Protestantism itself. Cardinal Newman, in the last book which he wrote before he became a convert to the Catholic Church, speaking of this rule and proving that "scanty as the Ante-Nicene notices may be of Papal Supremacy, they are both more numerous and more definite than the adducible testimonies in favor of the Real Presence," and adducing himself as a believer in the Real Presence, he exclaims: "I betake to one of our altars to receive the Blessed Eucharist; I have no doubt whatever on my mind about the Gift which that Sacrament contains . . . the Presence of Christ is here, for it follows upon Consecration; and Consecration is the prerogative of priests; and priests are made by Ordination; and Ordination comes in direct line from the Apostles . . . therefore, we are blessed with the great Gift. Here the question rises in me: who told you about that Gift? I answer: I have learned it from the Fathers: I believe the Real Presence because they bear witness to it . . . and then the thought comes upon me a second time: and do not the same ancient Fathers bear witness to another doctrine (Papal Supremacy), which you disown? Are you not as a hypocrite, listening to them when you will, and deaf when you will not? How are you casting your lot with the Saints when you go but halfway with them? For, of whether [i.e., which] of the two do they speak the more frequently, of the Real Presence or of the Pope's Supremacy? You accept the lesser evidence, you reject the

3. Newman, *Develop. of Christian Doctrine,* Introd. NN. 17, 18 seq.

greater."[3] Then he proceeds to show the contradiction of his Episcopalian brethren when they discard many truths and practices of the Catholic Church because they were not believed or practiced "always, everywhere, and by all," as if so many principles professed by the Anglican Church were likewise not believed "always, everywhere and by all." No wonder that even before the publication of this, Newman became a loyal child of the Catholic Church.

And what of the arch-principle of all Protestantism, the private judgment of the Bible? Was it *"always, everywhere* and *by all* believed" in the Church? The history of the Church, long before the "Reformation" of the 16th Century, asserts that very few were its followers, and the Fathers, whenever they mentioned it, severely condemned it. Therefore, why try to make the Rule of Vincentius a weapon against the Church of Rome? If it apparently strikes at some truths of the Catholic Church, it is certainly irresistible against all Protestantism. Well, then, what is the Vincentian Canon good for? Just for the very purpose it was composed by its author. To help our memory and guide us in our belief according to the *Traditions* of the Fathers; *to determine the value of a doctrine prior to the Judgment of the Church; to test a novelty arising in the bosom of the Church.*

To understand this Canon and apply it rightly, bear in mind: 1) *Universality,* for Vincentius means the "one, true Faith, which the Church believes in every part of the world." That is, the Church consent to a certain doctrine at the time of the appearance of a new doctrine, different from the old one. 2) *Antiquity* means *relative* antiquity: the consent of the Church, just before the novelty begins to gain a foothold in the Church. To arrive at an *absolute* antiquity, namely, to the true doctrine's *apostolicity,* opposed to the novelty, you appeal to the consent of the Fathers or to the decrees of the General Councils; 3) A canon or rule may be applied in either an *affirmative* or in an *exclusive* sense. It is applied in an affirmative sense when the rule is applied to what has been defined, not to what has not yet been defined, by the Church. It is applied in an exclusive or negative sense when nothing can belong to the Deposit of Faith which has not been explicitly believed "always, everywhere, and by all" the Faithful. 4) A truth may be *implicitly* contained in Revelation, hence not proclaimed by the Church; or *explicitly* contained in Revelation, when believed by all the Faithful or proclaimed universally by the Church. 5) The question is not about an implicit, but an explicit doctrine, because whatever is contained in the Deposit of objective Revelation has been believed "everywhere, always, and by all," at least implicitly, nor could one be a Catholic, who is not disposed to believe also explicitly whatever he believes implicitly, after what is implicitly believed is sufficiently proposed to him as divinely delivered.

We say that: 1) The Vincentian Rule is always true in an *affirmative* sense. That is, if a doctrine is already defined, it certainly belongs to the Deposit of Faith; consequently, it has the three characteristic notes of *universality, antiquity* and *consent,* because the universal consent on any doctrine of Faith "always, and everywhere" has always been held in the Church as a proof of the doctrine's being divinely delivered. 2) The Vincentian Rule *cannot be applied in an exclusive sense.* There may be doctrines implicitly contained in Revelation which were not always sufficiently known, hence *not always explicitly* declared and believed as such by the Church. Before the Church's declaration, those doctrines could be denied without shipwreck of the Faith. After the Church's declaration, however, they are to be held as revealed; consequently, they belong to the Deposit of Faith and must be explicitly believed. There may be, therefore, a time when some revealed truths were believed implicitly, but not always explicitly believed. Vincentius, to be consistent with all his writings, could not and did not apply his Rule *indiscriminately,* that is, to what was or was not defined by the Church. That shows that the Rule cannot be applied *exclusively,* that nothing can belong to the Deposit of Faith or that nothing can be defined which is not explicitly believed "always, everywhere and by all." 3. That Vincentius did not really propose his Rule in such an exclusive or negative sense is evident from the aim of the author: to guard himself against novelties, which are neither Catholic nor Apostolic. He is mindful of the words of the Apostle to Timothy: "And the things which thou hast heard of me by many witnesses, the same commend to faithful men, who shall be fit to teach others also." (*2 Tim.* 2:2). Vincentius wanted to keep immaculate the Deposit of Faith against those who in the future "will indeed turn away their hearing from the truth, but will be turned into fables." (*2 Tim.* 4:4). He knew there would be religious rebellions in the Church, as for instance, the Donatist heresy, as he affirms in his *Commonitorium.* He could not then have in mind what belonged to the Deposit of Faith only in an affirmative sense, that is, what was already defined and what belonged to the past, but also to what might take place in the future, according to the Apostle: "For there shall be a time when they will not endure sound doctrine, but according to their own desires, they will heap to themselves teachers, having itching ears." (*2 Tim.* 4:3). When such controversies arise, Vincentius warns us: Look at the consent of antiquity existing immediately before the controversy. You will thus arrive at older antiquity, an absolute antiquity. That is the apostolicity of the doctrine attacked by heretics. Vincentius did not and could not exclusively apply, nor did he intend to have us exclusively apply his Rule—"always, everywhere, and by all"—indiscriminately to whatever doctrines are found in the Church, in order to be truly and properly Catholic. What is already defined belongs already to the Deposit of Faith, was and is believed, at least implicitly, "always, everywhere and by all." On the other hand, what has not yet been defined may still be defined in the future or, what lies obscurely and implicitly in the explicit may in the course of time be brought out of the explicit and through the consent of the Faithful or the definition of the Church become an explicit part of the Deposit of Faith. Hence what is not yet defined may be defined afterwards. What is not yet explicitly believed may still become an explicit part of the Deposit of Faith.

All this notwithstanding, it seems that the application of the Vincentian Rule to historical facts, despite its lucidity, is sometimes difficult. Cardinal Newman thinks that it determines what Christianity is, rather than what it is not. Anyhow, it is not a mathematical measure. It must be applied by practical judgment and good sense.

9

Means and Ways by Which Tradition Is Safely Transmitted

Introduction

IT IS A matter of the greatest importance for a Catholic, not only to know the fundamental articles of the Catholic Religion, but also to render a good account of that knowledge. When Catholics live in a community which is composed of all creeds and of no creeds, it is expedient that they give a reason for their belief and practice. "But sanctify the Lord Christ in your hearts, being ready always to satisfy everyone that asketh you a reason of that hope which is in you." (*1 Peter* 3:15). Is it not perhaps the contention of Rationalists that Catholic Dogma sprang and grew up in a natural or fantastic way, like all human systems? Do not many non-Catholics claim that Catholic doctrine became corrupted in the course of time? It will be well then to retrace the course of centuries, to stop at the different stations of the life of the Church, and to reach the very source whence Christianity had its origin. There one may see how the first Christians lived, what they believed, to what extent they labored to keep immaculate the Faith they received from the Apostles. The soul of the Church is there in its fullness. The waters which flow from the fountain of Life are still pure and refreshing. Were we to admit that those waters were contaminated in the First, Second or Third Century, it would be just as well to assert that Christ founded His Church, not on the rock, but on the sand of human frailty.

Behold, then, the Bride of Jesus Christ, beautiful, pure, immortal; behold His only Bride, the Bride of "yesterday, and today, and the same forever," (*Heb.* 13:8), the only one who can legitimately claim that the Son of God is hers and hers alone. By documents she proves that claim beyond any doubt and to the exclusion of all others.

Without excluding the Scriptures, we maintain that the history of the Church, the General Councils, the writings of the Fathers, the Liturgies, the monuments of Christian art in painting, sculpture, crypts, coins, epigraphs, inscriptions, catacombs—all evince the Faith of the first Christians in such a manner that, failing other proofs, "the stones will cry out"—*"Lapides clamabunt."* (*Luke* 19:40).

These documents of Christian antiquity contain in one way or another the word of God. They manifest the daily life of the Church, her doctrine, her faith, her practices, and what is most important, the *identity of the faith and doctrine of the early Church with the Catholic Church of today.* In other words, the life of the true Church is one and always the same: her heart, as it were, beating in unison in all generations. No change of Faith, no substantial alterations in her practice, no vital change of doctrine.

Still, important as all these documents and monuments are—Holy Scripture not excluded—they are not the principal organ of Tradition; that is, they are not the principal means by which Religion is and must be known. The infallible and ever-living Apostolic Succession, that is, the Magisterium, or the living, teaching body of the Church is the one visible organ which, utilizing all this immense material, brings men to the true knowledge of Christ. It is the principal channel through which all Christian doctrine flows. Scripture and Tradition are certainly the word of God, and consequently the Rule of our Faith. But they are not so, considered in themselves, but as *approved* by the common consent of the Church. As the Vatican Council proclaims [Vatican I, 1869-1870]: "By divine and Catholic Faith, all those things must be believed which are contained in the written or delivered word of God and which are proposed by the Church through her *solemn judgment* or *ordinary* and *universal teaching* as divinely revealed."[1]

To her *solemn judgment*—besides the canon of the Scriptures—belong the dogmatic definitions of the General Councils and of the Roman Pontiffs, as well as the definitions of particular Councils solemnly approved by the Holy See; the professions of Faith emitted by the Church and imposed upon the Faithful; and the most ancient Symbols [Creeds].

To her *ordinary* or *universal teaching* belong the liturgies, Church history, the Acts of Martyrs, the monuments of Christian Art, the consent of the Faithful and of her Theological Schools, and the writings of the Fathers.

As it is not in our province, however, either to relate here the history of the Church, the Acts of the Martyrs, the different Liturgies, or to enumerate the dogmatic definitions of the Roman Pontiffs and of the General Councils, it will be enough to state that, even a superficial knowledge of all these matters is most useful to the student of religion who is in search of the truth. For instance, as Liturgy was and is today the outside and practical expression of the internal faith of the Christian, one may discern what the first Christians believed and practiced by comparing the practices and ceremonies of the Church today with the practices and ceremonies related and

---

1. Vat. Council I, Session III, C. III.

described in the ancient Liturgies of the Church. Hence the great dictum of the Fathers: "The manner of praying shows the way of our belief." *"Legem credendi, lex statuat supplicandi."* [Also, *Lex credendi, lex orandi.*]

We shall therefore limit ourselves to those documents, which are necessary for the keeping and the propagating of the True Religion—documents and monuments which are invaluable instruments in the hands of the Church, being intimately connected with the Apostolic Succession. It is our task to describe what are the solemn judgments and the ordinary teaching of the Church; what is the import of the writings of the Fathers; what Symbols [Creeds] are; of what value is the consent of Catholic Schools and of the Catholic Christian people; and what is to be learned from the Catacombs and from other Christian monuments. As the Fathers of the Church are the main source, we shall give them a Chapter for themselves.

1

The Solemn Judgment of the Church is an Infallible Proof of Divine Tradition.

The teaching of Christianity must be kept intact from all error. Faith must be safeguarded. This is implied in the commission which Christ gave to the Church: "Going therefore, teach all nations . . . and behold I am with you all days, even to the consummation of the world." (*Matt.* 28:19-20). On the other hand, the members of the Church are called on not only to believe the teaching they receive, but also to express that belief. "With the heart we believe unto justice; but with the mouth, confession is made unto salvation." (*Rom.* 10:10). This becomes a necessity in time of danger. For this reason the Church, according to circumstances and the nature of heresy, has from time to time warned her faithful, safeguarding their faith through her precautions, either by her infallible declarations, her public profession of the truth, or her solemn proclamations. All these may be called the solemn judgments of the Church. To these solemn judgments belong all Dogmatic Definitions, declared and proclaimed by the Roman Pontiff as Head of the Church, or by General Councils approved by the Holy See.

Dogmatic Definitions are oracles of the Church. That is, they are infallible pronouncements, based on the infallibility granted by Christ to the Roman Pontiffs and to the Church. Such is, for instance, the Dogmatic Definition of the Immaculate Conception. On December 8th, 1854, Pope Pius IX pronounced, decreed and defined that Mary, the Mother of God, "in the first instant of her conception, by a singular privilege and grace granted by God, in view of the merits of Jesus Christ the Saviour of the human race, was preserved exempt from all stain of Original Sin."[2]

Professions of Faith and Symbols [Creeds] are also within the realm of the special jurisdiction of the Church. Of the different Symbols, we shall speak later.

Professions of Faith manifest what the Church believes and practices at the time of their emission. They are a fuller exposition of some articles of the Faith. When some fundamental truths are attacked or denied, the Church enjoins upon those whose duty it is to defend and protect what has always been held by the Faithful a full and public profession of her doctrines. The most famous Professions of Faith are: the *Tridentine Profession,* so called because it is a summary of what the Council of Trent defined and declared as matters of Faith. It was prescribed

2. Constit., "*Ineffabilis Deus.*"

by the same Council under Pius IV in 1564. It ends with these words, "In the same manner, all the other things which have been delivered, defined and declared by the Sacred Canons and Ecumenical Councils, without doubt, I accept and profess." In 1877 the Congregation of the Council ordered the following words to be added: "and by the Ecumenical Vatican Council [Vatican I, 1869-1870] delivered, defined and declared, especially about the Primacy and Infallibility of the Roman Pontiff."

Following are three other famous Professions of Faith: one was prescribed for the Greeks by Pope Gregory XIII; another was imposed on the Orientals by Pope Urban VIII and by Benedict XIV; the last Profession of Faith was prescribed for the whole Catholic Clergy by Pope Pius X against the errors of the Modernists.

All these Professions, as well as all Dogmatic Definitions, are solemn judgments of the Church; consequently, they are an infallible proof of Divine Tradition, because they emanate from the Roman Pontiff as Head of the Church, who is infallible in matters of Faith and morals when he is explicitly teaching the entire Church, *ex cathedra*—"from the Chair" of Peter, i.e., as Head of the Church. Moreover, whenever a solemn document of the Church exhibits a doctrine in such a manner that the consent of the Apostolic Succession is thereby indicated, it also happens that those same members of the Apostolic Succession are not *private,* but *public witnesses,* belonging to different ages of the Church; hence, they are, as it were, *present witnesses,* giving not their own private opinion, but pointing to a unanimous testimony of Tradition.

Augustine to the point: "If an episcopal synod could be convened from every part of the world, it will be a wonder if all of them could take part in it. For nor did they exist in the same time, but God calls forth some of

His faithful ministers, more illustrious than others, according to different times and distances of place, as He pleases and as it is expedient in His judgment. These, however, you see from different times and countries, from the East and from the West, convened, not in places which cannot go to men, but in books, which can go to men. The more lenient judges they may be to you if you hold the Catholic Faith; the more they are terrible to you if you oppose the Catholic Faith; which they sucked like milk in their infancy, of which they partook as food, which milk and food they administered to children and adults; which they openly and firmly defended against enemies when you were not yet born, and now against you, for such you are revealing yourselves. After the Apostles, with such plant growers, irrigators, builders, shepherds, nurses has the Church grown up."[3]

Such always has been and is the authority of the bishops of the Catholic Church. Their unanimous testimony in consent and union with the Head of the Church is, as we shall see, a proof of Divine Tradition. Their solemn Judgment is a proof of Divine Tradition.

2

The Symbol [Creed] of the Apostles is truly "Apostolic," Not Only in Doctrine, But in Origin.

The word *Symbol,* generally speaking, has three significations: It may mean either a *collection* of many things; an *emblem,* by which the military are distinguished from the civilians; or a *mark,* by which contracts were considered as authentic or genuine. These three significations are admirably adapted to the Symbols [Creeds] of our

---

3. August., *C. Jul.,* L. II, C. X, N. 37.

Faith. Symbols are a collection or summary of what must be believed, an emblem by which Christians are distinguished from infidels, a mark of that pact which we entered into with God in Baptism. Symbols, therefore, are brief and simple collections of what must be believed fundamentally by all Christians. They are three in number, as approved by the Church. They are the Symbol of the Apostles, the Nicene or Constantinopolitan Symbol, and the Symbol of St. Athanasius. They are so universally known that even the Greek Church and many Protestant bodies acknowledge them.

How useful they are may be inferred from the fact that famous teachers had symbols which were useful both to teachers and disciples. Both the Apostles and the Ancient Church adopted this method for their disciples. It is simple enough for the ignorant to understand; short enough to be committed to memory; and deep enough for the learned to study, meditate upon and be edified with.

The "Symbol of the Apostles," or the "Apostles' Creed," as it is commonly called by the Faithful, is by far the best known and the most important of Christian Symbols. Notwithstanding the subtle disquisitions of our modern "high critics"—both Catholic and Protestant—it is truly "Apostolic." This is true, not only of the doctrine it contains, but of its origin. It may be true that each of the twelve articles, of which the Symbol is composed, may not be separately and exclusively assigned to any individual Apostle. It may be true that it did not come down to us entirely in its present form. But no critic, however great, will be able to disprove the golden rule of St. Augustine, that "Whatever comes down to us from the ancients, and does not emanate from the Councils or from the Church, is of Apostolic origin."

The last command which the Apostles received from

Christ before His Ascension was to teach and baptize: "Go ye into the whole world and preach the Gospel to every creature. He that believeth and is baptized shall be saved; but he that believeth not shall be condemned." (*Mark* 16:15-16).

Notice first of all the connection between the belief in the Gospel and the reception of Baptism. One had to believe before he could receive Baptism. The Apostles were sent into the world, not to convert children, but an adult generation. And what had one to believe? Just what the words of Baptism mean and imply: whatever concerns the Father and the Son and the Holy Ghost. One had therefore to believe the Mystery that contains all other mysteries, *i.e.,* the Mystery of the Most Blessed Trinity, with all its signification, its bearing and its import. This requisite before the reception of Baptism is as essential today, as it has been in every century, and as it was at the time of the Apostles. That the Apostles demanded some explicit belief in God before admitting anyone into the Church may be inferred from the profession of faith in Christ which the Apostle Philip exacted of the eunuch as a preliminary to Baptism. (*Act*s 8:37). That explicit belief was a summary of the existence and the attributes of the Three Divine Persons. The Faithful called it after the Apostles. They did so because the Apostles, as Founders of the Church and Supreme Legislators, imposed it upon all those who wished to become members of the Church. If anyone in those days of universal idolatry had to believe anything, it had to be something that dealt a blow at the very heart of idolatry: the belief in one God in Three Divine Persons. That was the least that could be expected of those who entered the Church in the name of the Three Divine Persons: the Father, as Creator; the Son, as Redeemer; the Holy Ghost, as Sanctifier.

The Symbol of the Apostles is therefore a fuller exposition of the Mystery of the Holy Trinity. In the course of centuries, the Church, as in the Council of Nicæa, made new additions to the Apostolic Creed to offset innovations contrary to the Faith. The provident Apostles, also to guard against heresy, set forth the Mystery of the Trinity in its most essential points. We cannot even for a moment entertain the idea that the Apostles were less provident than their ever-living Apostolic Succession.

A few additions have been in the course of time affixed to it. But they are not very important. They are details of the principal doctrines contained in the Creed.

These few minor additions, originating principally in Rome during the Sixth Century, were fully approved and adopted by the Universal Church.[4]

No one, however, should wonder that the Symbol, being the work of Apostles, could have undergone even these slight modifications. For the Apostles exacted belief in the Holy Trinity when they taught it by word of mouth. *Had it been given in writing, then it would have been a part of Scripture.* Thus, being in constant use in the Church, it became an *oral tradition,* and as such is subject to the Keys of Peter. Whatever gap may therefore exist between the old Roman form and the time of the Apostles should be filled by the golden rule of St. Augustine, as we have already stated above. ["Whatever comes down to us from the ancients and does not emanate from the Councils or from the Church, is of Apostolic origin." Cf. page 169].

The question is whether it really and originally comes down to us from the Apostles themselves. There should be very little doubt on this point. If some think that in the first years of Christianity no trace of the Symbol

---

4. See Burn. Introduction, p. 239.

appears in the Church, they should know that the Christian policy of those days, called the Discipline of the Secret—*Disciplina Arcani*—was then in full operation. The knowledge of the most intimate mysteries of Christianity was carefully kept from heathen and Jew, as well as from those who, for some time, underwent instruction in the Faith. The Discipline of the Secret necessarily prevented the preservation in writing of the Creed, which contained the principal mysteries of Religion. According to that ancient precaution, the Creed was to be learned by heart and never to be consigned to writing. The Discipline of the Secret is of Apostolic times. It is mentioned by Origen against Celsus[5] in the Third Century, and before him by Tertullian,[6] who belonged rather to the Second Century. Such reserve was applied to all the Sacraments, but most particularly to the Holy Eucharist and to the doctrine of the Most Holy Trinity. Not until the truth of the Unity of God had sunk deeply into the heart of a heathen, could he be safely instructed in the much deeper Mystery of the Trinity. For that reason, it was never taught to the Catechumens before they were ready to receive Baptism. We know this from St. Ambrose in the Epistle to his sister Marcellina. He says that on the Lord's Day, in dismissing the Catechumens, he taught the Creed only to those, who were sufficiently advanced.[7] St. Cyril also writes: "Not to every Gentile do we declare the secret mysteries, which concern the Father, the Son and the Holy Ghost."[8] This fact is most significant when we consider that St. Ambrose lived in the Fourth Century and St. Cyril in the Fifth—in times when there was not much danger

---

5. Origen, *Contra Celsum,* L. I, N. 7.
6. Tertull., "Prescript," C. XLI.
7. Ambrose Ep. 20.
8. Cyril. Cath. C. N. 29.

of persecution. Still, even then, it was deemed prudent not to divulge indiscriminately the teachings which concerned the Holy Trinity. It was preferred rather that all should commit the Creed to memory, in order to guard it against the mockery of an infidel mob and to have the Faithful discerned from heathen and Jew. This commitment to memory also explains why this doctrine of the Trinity, as contained in the Creed, has been preserved in a *continuous form.*

But it is not true that no evident trace of the Apostles' Creed is found in the first years of Christianity. Before the middle of the Second Century, we find in Rome a Creed which, in its completeness, is substantially identical with the Creed we recite every day.[9]

It is a striking fact that in the Fourth Century the Eastern Churches are found in possession of a Creed which strictly harmonizes with the old Roman Creed. These two facts show a common origin: they could only originate from the Apostles in their itinerary throughout the world.

Toward the end of the Second Century, we find in Northern Africa, as well as in Southern France, a Creed which closely resembles and agrees with the same Roman Creed. In his work, *De Præscript,* Tertullian reproduces the *"Regula Doctrinæ"*—the Rule of Doctrine—and after elaborately describing that by this *"Regula Doctrinæ"* he understands what is practically substantial with the Roman Creed, he insists most emphatically that this "rule" was instituted by Christ and delivered to us (*tradita*—"by transmission") by the Apostles.[10] In a similar way writes St. Irenæus, disciple of St. Polycarp, who in turn was a disciple of the Apostle St. John.

9. See Burn., *Journal of Theological Studies,* July, 1902.
10. See *Migne* P, L. II, 26, 27, 33, 50.

We may easily conclude that the Roman Creed was delivered to the Roman community by the Apostles Peter and Paul, that the Eastern and African Churches had received a similar Creed from the same Apostles or from some other one of the Apostles, and that in a short time it had spread throughout the world.

It is also to be noted that the monk Rufinus in the Fourth Century, having visited the Orient, wrote that the Symbol [Apostles' Creed] in the Eastern Churches was received from an early age—*tradunt majores nostri* ["our forebearers have handed (it) down"]. He may not be correct in stating that the Apostles composed it together on the Day of Pentecost. But he could have scarcely made such a declaration were it not that the Symbol was everywhere believed to have originated from the Apostles and that it fully corresponded with the Roman form.

Ancient and Modern Apostles' Creeds

This defense of the Creed's Apostolicity would not be complete without placing side by side the Old Roman Creed and the one which, since the Sixth Century, has been in use in the Church.

The Old Roman Form	*More Recent Roman Form*
1. I believe in God, the Father Almighty.	1. I believe in God the Father Almighty, Creator of Heaven and earth;
2. And in Jesus Christ, His only Son, Our Lord;	2. And in Jesus Christ, His only Son, Our Lord;
3. Who was born of (De) the Holy Ghost and of (ex) the Virgin Mary;	3. Who was conceived by the Holy Ghost, born of the Virgin Mary;
4. Crucified under Pontius Pilate and buried;	4. Suffered under Pontius Pilate, was crucified, died and was buried;
5. The third day He rose again from the dead;	5. He descended into Hell: the third day, He arose again from the dead;
6. He ascended into Heaven;	6. He ascended into Heaven, sitteth at the right hand of God, the Father Almighty;
7. Sitteth at the right hand of the Father;	7. From thence He shall come to judge the living and the dead.
8. Whence He shall come to judge the living and the dead.	8. I believe in the Holy Ghost,
9. And in the Holy Ghost,	9. The Holy Catholic Church, the communion of saints,
10. The Holy Church	10. The forgiveness of sins,
11. The forgiveness of sins,	11. The resurrection of the body, and
12. The resurrection of the body.	12. Life everlasting.

The Symbol of the Apostles is therefore truly Apostolic, not only in doctrine, but also in origin.

3

The Nicene, Constantinopolitan and Athanasian Symbols are a Vindication of the Mystery of the Most Blessed Trinity.

The great persecutions of the first three centuries against the Church had one good effect: They confirmed the divinity of the Church. Hell and heresy had gone their limit to uproot from the earth the tree which Christ and the Apostles had planted and sprinkled with their blood. The combination of evil forces was so formidable that the Church would have succumbed were it not that it is the work of God. The victory of the Church, however, was so complete that peace was at last granted to her throughout the whole Roman Empire. The Cross surmounted the temples of the false gods.

I. The early part of the Fourth Century affords a spectacle which, in its brilliance and future consequences, is unrivaled in the history of civilization. The Church dealt Paganism a blow from which it never recovered. Civilization, from being pagan, became Christian.

But peace was not to last long. With Julian the Apostate, Paganism again appeared [for a very short time, only one and a half years—361-363], while the Serpent of heresy also threatened the very life of the Church. With the help of God, she came out triumphantly in both conflicts. She had on one side the Dragon of Paganism breathing his last and on the other the bleeding heads of the multifold Serpent of heresy.

The heresy was Arianism. A new enemy! It was not a speculative doctrine that it denied. It was not some Church attribute which it contradicted. It was the diabolical attempt to rob the Son of God of His divinity.

Arianism refused to acknowledge that Jesus Christ is

God, God of God, true God of true God. Bishops of great name followed Arius, its founder. Constantine, who granted peace to the Church, protected him. Some of his [Constantine's] own successors avowed his cause. The new doctrine, like a prairie-fire, soon spread out to the four corners of the Empire. It conquered many nations before it could be successfully coped with. It was so universally spread that St. Jerome, a Father and Doctor of the Church, seeing such devastation in the Church, exclaimed, although with some exaggeration: "The whole world groaned and marveled to find itself Arian."

But God helped His Church. If Arius was a genius and a winning personality, there was Athanasius, the young deacon, and the future great Patriarch of Alexandria! God called him to sustain His Church in the long period of her greatest trial. Athanasius personifies a crisis in the history of the Church. His active life may be said to have begun and ended for the cause of Christ's divinity. His conspicuous ability, the courage he displayed in the defense of the Catholic dogma, the stormy career of his long life, rendered him one of the greatest champions of militant Catholicism the Church has ever known. He consecrated his whole being to what he believed to be the first and most essential truth of the Catholic Creed. Five times he was ejected from his See at Alexandria by his enemies and sent into exile, and five times he was enthusiastically received back by his people. Finally, the dogma of Christ's divinity triumphed. The great Primate of Alexandria, after more than 40 years of a stormy episcopal career, died peaceably on his own bed, surrounded by his clergy and mourned by his people.

In the meantime, however, Christianity seemed to be helplessly divided and torn into factions. Emperor Constantine, having conquered Licinius, became the only ruler of the whole Roman Empire. Having re-established civil order everywhere, he was anxious to restore also religious peace. To that end, and most probably in concert with Pope St. Sylvester I (314-336), he called a General Council of the Bishops of the Church. The great assembly met in Nicaea in the year 325, known as the First Ecumenical Council of the Church. Three hundred eighteen Bishops, most of them belonging to the Eastern Church, and many more hundreds of theologians, were in attendance. Among these was the young deacon Athanasius, who accompanied St. Alexander, the Primate of Alexandria, to the Council as his secretary and theological adviser. Arius was also there. He was summoned frequently before the assembly, but after many sessions and discussions, all the Bishops save two declared and defined that Jesus Christ, the Son of God, is "consubstantial" or co-essential with the Father. That is, He is of one substance or essence with the Father, although the "Father" and the "Word" are two different Persons. Arius refused to submit. He was exiled to Illyria and his writings were burned.

The peace which the Nicene Council gave to the Church did not last long. In the year 330, a campaign of intrigue, carried on chiefly through the imperial household, induced Emperor Constantine to recall Arius and the Arian bishops from their exile, insisting on their readmission to communion. But St. Athanasius, who by this time had become the Primate of Alexandria, refused to comply with the imperial request.

It is enough here to observe that when the Church, on account of certain circumstances, is obliged to rely on earthly princes, events have shown that their intervention has, as a general rule, done more harm than good to the Church. The interference of Constantine and of many of his successors many times forced Athanasius and many other orthodox bishops to leave their sees and go into exile, to the detriment of Christianity. The Popes of the time, Sylvester, Julius, and Liberius, did all they could do to help the defenders of Orthodoxy; but being far away from the seat of the controversy, and the selection of bishops being in those days left to secular princes and to the people, they could scarcely call to task the great catechumen, Constantine, or his powerful successors. It was only after the death of Athanasius, that Emperor Theodosius convoked another Council of the bishops to confirm and enforce the Nicene Creed and bring to an end the Macedonian heresy, which denied the Procession of the Holy Ghost. It was held in Constantinople in the year 381.

This First Council of Constantinople was originally a Council of the Orient. It was attended by 150 Catholic and 36 heretical bishops, and was presided over first by Meletius of Antioch and after his death, by his successive Patriarchs, St. Gregory of Nazianzus and Nectarius. But the ecumenical character of this Council dates from the Council of Chalcedon, held in the year 451. Pope St. Gregory the Great (590-604), as well as Popes Vigilius and Pelagius II, recognized it as a General Council, but only in its dogmatic decrees.

This Council, according to the oldest Latin versions, had four canons, the first being of the greatest importance and dealing with our case. It condemned all shades of Arianism.

To this Council is usually ascribed the formula of the so-called Nicene-Constantinopolitan Symbol. The Council of Chalcedon designated the Symbol as the "Creed of the Council of Constantinople of 381." However, according to the most common opinion,[11] the Constantinopoli-

11. See *Vossius and Hort.*

tan formula includes the most important Nicene statements concerning the Holy Ghost. Its author seems to have been St. Cyril of Jerusalem (315-386).

However that may be, it is certain that both the Jerusalem and the Constantinopolitan formulas are simply an enlargement of the Nicene Creed. If the formula now in use did not really originate with the Constantinopolitan Council, it is certain that the Council of Chalcedon (451) attributed it to the First Constantinopolitan Council. Whether this Council actually composed it, or simply adapted and authorized it, the fact remains that that formula is a true expression of the Faith of the Fathers assembled in that Council.

But, as the Church does not generally render any solemn definition without necessity, so it is that the Council of Constantinople did not mention the double Procession of the Holy Ghost from the Father *and* the Son: it only declared and defined this Procession from the Father. In the course of time, we find in the Spanish Church, after the conversion of the Goths, which took place in the Third Synod of Toledo, the addition of the *Filioque*—"and the Son" (Procession also from the Son) sung in the Creed. This practice spread slowly to every part of the Western Church, and by the Eleventh Century it gained such a firm foothold, even in Rome, that Pope Benedict VIII, at the instance of Emperor Henry reluctantly, but freely and solemnly, allowed the Symbol with the addition of the *"Filioque,"* to be sung in his presence in the year 1014.

This Catholic doctrine was accepted by the Greek bishops at the Second Council of Lyons in 1274, and at the Council of Florence in 1439. On their return to their sees, however, the Greek bishops failed to carry their people with them, and the schism which Photius, the Patriarch of Constantinople, started in the year 870, on account of the addition of the word *"Filioque,"* became a heresy and continues to this present day. The Patriarchs of Constantinople and the other Greek bishops found in the doctrine of the *Filioque* ["and the Son"] too good an excuse for throwing off all dependence on Rome, Head of the Universal Church, which they jealously viewed as their rival. They preferred to be ruled by the turban of the Turk than by the tiara of the Successors of St. Peter. Their desire became an accomplished fact, and this fact holds to this day. [Constantinople was conquered by the Turks in 1453, and remains under their control, being renamed Istanbul.]

The following is a translation in the singular personal number of the Greek text of the Constantinopolitan form. The words in parentheses are an addition to the Western Liturgical form as it is in present use. "I believe in one God, the Father Almighty, maker of heaven and earth, and of all things, visible and invisible. And in one Lord Jesus Christ, the only begotten Son of God, and born of the Father before all ages, (God of God), light of light, true God of true God. Begotten, not made, consubstantial with the Father, by Whom all things were made, Who for us men and for our salvation came down from Heaven. And was incarnate of the Holy Ghost and of the Virgin Mary and was made man; was crucified also for us under Pontius Pilate, suffered and was buried; and the third day He rose again according to the Scriptures. And ascended into Heaven, sitteth at the right hand of the Father, and shall come again with glory to judge the living and the dead, of whose Kingdom there shall be no end. And in the Holy Ghost, the Lord and giver of life, who proceedeth from the Father (and the Son), who together with the Father and the Son is to be adored and glorified, who spoke by the prophets. And one, holy, Catholic and Apostolic Church. I confess one Baptism for the remission of sins. And I look for the Resurrection of the Dead and the life of the world to come. Amen."

II. A few, but important statements must be made with regard to what is commonly called the "Creed of St. Athanasius." This Creed is a clear exposition of the doctrine of the Trinity and of the Incarnation. It was framed in its present shape to manifest unmistakingly the Trinity of Persons in God and the two-fold nature in the one Divine Person of Jesus Christ. Up to the 17th Century it was attributed by all to St. Athanasius, the Patriarch of Alexandria. Now, many critics think that it was composed only under Athanasian influences.

Gerard Voss says that "no early writer of authority speaks of it as the work of this great Doctor of the Church; hence, it should not be attributed to St. Athanasius." Now, if we examine well the internal literary evidence of this Symbol and the time it first made its appearance in the Church, there is no reason why it should not be attributed to the Primate of Alexandria. For in the first place, the literature of the Symbol exhibits expressions and doctrinal coloring akin to the literature of the latter half of the Fourth Century, in which St. Athanasius lived, and with the writings of the Saint. Moreover, recent inquiry resulted in the firm opinion that the Symbol must have been composed in the latter part of the Fourth Century, during the life of this Great Eastern Patriarch. It is an historical fact that at Antioch the Primate of Alexandria had an interview with the Emperor Jovian, who asked him to prepare an exposition of the Orthodox Faith. This happened in the month of September 363. Although the Emperor died the next year, there should be no reason why Athanasius did not comply at once with the request of the Emperor, with whom he was on friendly terms. Who could ever make such a statement better than Athanasius? Are not the "damnatory" or "minatory" clauses with which the Symbol opens and concludes most proper for the Saint, who fought so much for the Faith?

As all objections against the authorship of Athanasius are not plausible, and as no convincing reason was ever given against the fact that the Faithful and the Church herself, down to the 17th Century, attributed this Creed to St. Athanasius, we should not doubt that the author of the Athanasian Creed is St. Athanasius, Primate of Alexandria. We must not, however, forget that the authorship of the Creed is of secondary importance. What counts is the fundamental truth which it contains and its approval by the Church.

4

The Common Belief of the Faithful Is a Safe Rule of Divine Tradition.

Above the great chaos of opinions and problems and theories which now agitate the Christian world, there is something abiding and singular in the Catholic Church, and in that Church alone! It is the faith of the Catholic people.

We will not speak here of the Faith, which comes from above and is preached by God's ministers, but of the faith, existing in the common people: that faith, which is *one* in all the length and breadth of the earth; which is such a conviction that, while the rest of the Christian world is in doubt, the Catholics are firm in their belief. Whatever the Catholic Church teaches, they accept. The Church is the mouthpiece of God, who cannot deceive nor be deceived. Such belief may not always be very prominent, nor does it always appear on the surface. It lies deeper. It is in the mind and heart of the people. It forms, in a sense, the columns on which the Apostles have erected the edifice of the Church.

The Catholic Church is not concerned with the religious problems of the other so-called churches. She cannot, however, but take notice of the dangerous ground on which they tread. She knows well that she is the only one that can and ultimately will save society. Neither socially nor politically does the Church, as a Church, interfere with the temporal affairs of any nation. She helps, but she does not impose herself on society in its material affairs. However, when her doctrine is attacked violently from outside, or a new doctrine is advanced within her own fold contrary to what has always been believed or practiced, then the whole Church is in commotion. The people themselves are stirred. They are resolved and determined to keep whatever was handed down to them by the ancients and to reject the innovation, at whatever cost.

This is the point. When the Catholic people believe that a doctrine or an institution is true—and practice it—then we proclaim that this belief is a sign or a mark that this doctrine or institution is a part of divine Revelation, whether contained in the Scriptures or not. We refer to the consent of the Faithful generally. We do not speak of a consent of a *part* of the Faithful. Individual churches—or *even* nations, as the English and Scandinavian peoples—may fall away. Nor do we speak of a consent which has not always been certain and clear. It must be as universal as the Church herself and also believed without ambiguity.

All this does not mean that the Catholic people have the right to reject or retain by their own authority any doctrine or any part of Revelation, nor that the gift of infallibility lies with the Catholic people.

It means that the view, understanding and belief of the universal Church on any doctrine, is a *proof* or *criterion* that such doctrine is a part of divine Tradition.

Christ constituted the Apostles and their successors in office at the head of His Church. He commanded them to preach, teach and baptize. He promised to be with them until the End of the World. He sent the Holy Ghost to abide with them forever. All this means that Christ made the Apostles and their successors *infallible teachers.*[12] Christ, however, rendered them infallible, not only for their own sake, but especially for the benefit of all the Faithful. The purpose of this divine institution is the conservation and integrity of the Faith, not only in those who are commanded to teach, but more so in those who are enjoined to hear. These gifts were given by Christ for the utility and necessity of all the body of His Church. Hence, if those teachers on the one hand are ordered by Christ to rule and to teach, their subjects on the other hand *are bound to obey* them in whatever belongs to the Deposit of the Faith. If the teachers are immune from teaching false doctrine, their disciples cannot be taught false doctrine. If the teachers teach infallibly, their disciples, who *listen to* and *obey* what they are taught, are infallible in their belief.

Teachers and disciples are the members of one Body—joined by one Faith—the Head of which is Christ Himself. The actions of these members are in perfect harmony with one another under the supreme direction of their Head, Jesus Christ. There can be no divergence, no disagreement, no contradiction in the actions and sentiments of this Mystical Body. The members are joined by Faith with the Head, so long as they remain in unity and consent with their pastors. These in turn are in harmony with the Head of the Church upon earth, Peter, and his successors in office. Hence the members are immune from error in matters of faith and morals.

---

12. See Chapter 4, 7-8).

This perfect unanimity among the members of this Mystical Body is beautifully expressed by St. Ignatius in the First Century: "First I admonished you to be of one mind in the sentence of God. For Jesus Christ, our inseparable Life, is the sentence of the Father, just as the bishops in every part of the world, are in the sentence of Jesus Christ. You must be, therefore, of one mind in the sentence of the bishop."[13] By *sentence* the Saint means *doctrine* or *creed.*

Hence, whatever the Catholic people believe is like the responding echo of the sentence [belief] of that infallible teaching body which Christ established upon a rock for the benefit of the Faithful. Nor can it be otherwise. As Tertullian says, Christ promised the Spirit of Truth to the Churches, that they may not "differently understand, differently believe, than what He preached to the Apostles."[14]

All this is confirmed by that necessary bond, which exists between teachers and disciples. The Apostle writes: "The word is nigh thee even in thy mouth, and in thy heart . . . for whosoever shall call upon the name of the Lord, shall be saved. How then shall they call on him, in whom they have not believed? Or, how shall they believe him, of whom they have not heard? And how shall they hear, without a preacher? And how shall they preach, unless they be sent? . . . Faith then cometh by hearing; and hearing by the word of Christ." (*Rom.* 10:8-17). The Faithful are therewith taught to keep whatever Christ commanded, but they are to be taught by those who are *"sent."* "As the Father hath sent me, I also send you," (*John* 20:21), and He will be with them even "to the consummation of the world." (*Matt.* 28:20).

Therefore, whatever the Faithful have learned from those

---

13. *Ignatius to Ephes.* N. 3.
14. Tertull., Preser., C. XXVIII.

who are sent cannot be error. The Faithful, scattered all over the world, would be poor disciples indeed if, having been taught by infallible teachers, they would hold, not what is true, but what is contrary to the truth. That would mean that "the gates of Hell" prevailed "against the Church." The promise of Christ would be void. The common belief of the Faithful must be a safe Rule of Divine Tradition.

5

The Writings of the Fathers and the Analogy to Reason Prove That the Consent of the Faithful is a Rule of Divine Tradition.

The Holy Fathers of the Church were so convinced that the "sense and consent" of all the Faithful in communion with their legitimate pastors is a proof of Divine Tradition that, in their controversies with the heretics of their times, they made of this a strong argument for the defense of Catholic Dogma.

I. St. Augustine in his refutation of Pelagianism, writes: "It is not the complaint alone of the people that we oppose against you, although the people themselves complain against you for the reason that it is not a question that can escape popular opinion. Rich and poor, high and low, learned and ignorant, men and women knew what, and at what age, is remitted in Baptism. For this reason, every day, in every part of the world, mothers hasten with their children [for the Sacrament of Baptism], not only to the Christ that is the Anointed One, but to the Christ Jesus that is the Saviour. As if it were of little importance that in a most solid and most ancient fundamental, the Faithful, scattered in every part of the world, do not disagree."[15]

15. August., *C. Jul.,* L. I, N. 31-36. Ep. Fundam. N. 4.

In the same vein St. Gregory of Nazianzus wrote his Second Epistle to Cledon in the Fourth Century. So also Tertullian,[16] and St. Vincent of Lerin.[17]

Likewise, the Fathers of the Church prove the absurdity of the hypothesis that all the Faithful could ever err in what belongs to the Deposit of the Faith. St. Vincent of Lerin argues: "If all the Faithful could be induced to accept the innovations of heretics, or what is conflicting with the doctrine of antiquity, then it must be declared that all the Faithful of all ages, all the Saints, all the chaste, the continent, the Virgins, all the Clergy, Levites and Priests, so many thousands of Confessors, the great army of Martyrs, the celebrity and multitude of so many cities and peoples, so many islands, provinces, kings, countries, kingdoms, nations and—finally—almost the whole world, intimately united with Christ through the Catholic Faith, all these had for so many centuries ignored, erred, blasphemed and never recognized what they believed."[18]

This "sense and consent" of all the Faithful is for some Theologians such a "Rule of Divine Tradition," that they do not hesitate to assert that Infallibility has an *active* and a *passive* element. By the former they mean that the Church can never err in teaching the Faithful; by the latter, they mean that the Faithful, as a body, can never err in believing.

For this reason Pope Pius IX (1846-1878), before solemnly proclaiming the Dogma of the Immaculate Conception of the Blessed Virgin Mary (1854), among other preparatory requisites, asked all the Bishops of the Catholic Church to inform him "what piety and devotion their

16. Tertull., "Prescript," C. XXIX.
17. Vincent of Lerin, *Commonit.,* C. XXIV.
18. Vincent of Lerin's, *Commonit.,* C. XXXIII.

Faithful have toward the Immaculate Conception of the Mother of God." All the Bishops having given a favorable account in this matter, the Sovereign Pontiff, among other rules of Divine Tradition, enumerated and declared "the singular agreement of Bishops and Faithful."[19]

II. Secondly, the common "sense and consent" of all the Faithful in matters of Faith may be compared, according to Hurter,[20] with the common "sense and consent" of mankind in the natural order. As "common consent" is taken by all as a rule for the well-being of all, the admirable assent of all the Faithful in communion with their legitimate pastors, in matters of Faith, originates from and is based on the Holy Spirit of God, who cannot deceive, nor allow His Church to be deceived.

We shall conclude this subject with the wise remark of Melchior Canus: "There are two classes of truths that are believed in the Church: One belongs equally to all. Here it is not difficult to know the common faith and the sense. . . . The other is that which does not interest the average man, but the scholar and the student. If you ask the opinion of the ordinary man on these matters, you may as well ask a blind man to distinguish colors. They must profess what they believe and think in these things, just as the Church believes and thinks . . . Now in a common controversy, a certain argument can be obtained from this sense of all the Faithful, but it is not necessary to examine the sense of each and every one of the Faithful. In the Faith, however, of those things which properly belong to the doctors and the learned, only the opinion of such men, and not that of the people, should be taken into consideration. But in decrees and laws dealing with these

---

19. Pius IX, *Bulla Ineffabilis Deus,* 1854.
20. Hurter, *Theol. Dogm.*, Vol. I, N. 201.

matters, neither the lay nor [the] learned have much to say. Only those, who are the pastors of the Church."[21]

6

The Constant and Unanimous Consent of Catholic Schools on Matters of Faith is a Certain Proof of Divine Tradition.

The Catholic Church has always been the teacher of mankind. After the invasion of the Roman Empire, civilization was all but destroyed. The only refuge of literature, science, and art was the cloister of the monk. Those monasteries were few and far between, but they saved from complete destruction the Scriptures and the great literary works of civilization. The common and plain doctrine of the Church softened the rude manners of the victorious barbarian and made possible a new progress in the history of the world. Hundreds of years rolled on, but under the direction of religious men, schools of all kinds were everywhere reopened. Progress was slow. But it was sure. And so the tender plants of knowledge which those good men laid down in the shade of their cloister, increased in the meantime a hundredfold. In the 12th Century the first universities were established at Paris and Bologna. Paris became famous for its Theological School; Bologna for its School of Civil and Canon Law. Other universities in the course of time were founded and chartered by Popes and Catholic kings. A revival of studies took a firm hold on the Continent of Europe.[22]

---

21. Melchior Canus. De L. Th., L. IV, C. VI.
22. *Note.* It will not be out of place here to note that the first universities on the Continent of America were established under Catholic auspices. The University of Lima, Peru, was founded by Decree of Charles V in 1551 in the Monastery of the Holy Rosary. The University of Santo Domingo in the West Indies was established by a

The Council of Trent was held in the 16th Century, inspiring and encouraging the erection of Catholic seminaries. Not only the elementary schools, but the general studies of higher education, especially Theology, Civil and Canon Law, from the 12th to the 16th, nay to the 18th Centuries, were under the sole direction and vigilance of the Catholic Church. In Northern Europe, however, the Reformation handed over to Protestant princes the direction of already flourishing universities, which consequently became Protestant. In Catholic countries in the 18th Century, the civil authorities usurped to themselves supreme control of education. For this reason, we speak here only of those great institutions which were not only founded under Catholic auspices and chartered by the Apostolic See, but were always, until recently, under the supreme direction of the Church. These centers derived from the Church the authority to teach Theology and always maintained toward the Church that filial devotion which a child owes to its mother.

Founded and authorized by the Church to teach her best children, selected as it were from her flock, these Schools became the lights of the centuries and, to a certain degree, the successors of the Fathers [of the Church]. For, if according to Vincent of Lerin,[23] the Fathers kept, explained and defended what they received from the ancients, the Theological Schools also had to keep, explain and defend the doctrine which *they* had received. If any of the teachers advanced a theory dangerous or contrary to the Catholic intellect, he was at once warned and—if

---

papal Bull seven years after. The next in importance was that of San Antonio Abad founded in 1598 at Cuzco, Peru. Between 1586 and 1620 two great universities were established at Quito, Ecuador: the former by the Augustinians and the latter by the Jesuits.

23. *Commonit.*, C. XXII.

persisting in his error—expelled by the local Bishop or by the authority of the Supreme Pontiff.

This connection between Church and institutions of learning becomes more evident when we consider that from those Theological Departments came most of the bishops and the best element of the clergy. It was there that they learned how to teach and direct the flock committed to their care.

These Schools, however, do not exhibit an authentic testimony of the truth: that is, they are not the immediate and official witnesses of the Church. That belongs to the Apostolic Succession, in union and consent with the Head of the Church. But we are able to arrive at the same knowledge of [i.e., possessed by] the Apostolic Succession through the sufficient testimony of these Schools. For if the Head of the Church and the Apostolic Succession constitute the divine-human testimony of the truth, the Catholic or Theological Schools are the historical and human authority under the control of the ecclesiastical authority.

This assertion does not in the least minimize the statement that Catholic or Theological Schools are a sure proof of Divine Tradition. Nor does it matter that the teachers and doctors of these Schools were not Bishops. We must not think that truth can be found only in the Apostolic Succession, nor that every Bishop, considered individually and apart from the Head of the Church, is infallible. It was for these reasons that St. Augustine, distinguishing the testimony of St. Jerome, who was simply a theologian, from the testimony of a number of bishops, who had declared their sentence, writes: "Never think that St. Jerome may be discarded, because he was simply a priest. . . . He read all or nearly all those who in every part of the world wrote on ecclesiastical doctrine, nor did he differ from their (the bishops') sentence."[24]

Moreover, Ecclesiastical history teaches us that Roman Pontiffs and Bishops, before and after they convened in General Councils, consulted the doctors and teachers of these Theological institutions as a certain preparation for authentic definitions. They consulted them, not about mere philosophical matters, but about doctrines, which strictly belong to faith and morals; they conferred with them, not about the manner of defending, but about the very truths of Christian doctrines; they sought information about their *constant and unanimous consent* on doctrines which, in relation to the Scriptures and the Fathers, were accepted by all the Schools: consent which must not be limited to some, but is seen to include practically all of them; and not of one or more generations, but of all the ages of such noble institutions.

Such being the case, no one can fail to perceive the intimate connection of Theological Schools with the Supreme Pastors of the Church and the other Successors of the Apostles. It indicates the high place which Theological Schools held in the Church and the great import of their teaching.

Hence, if we consider their principal aim, namely, of keeping and defending Catholic truth; if we remember, generally speaking, what an illustrious and learned body that the teachers and doctors of Theology must be; if we reflect upon the special care which Supreme Pontiffs and Bishops exercised upon those Schools; if we keep in view that the constant and unanimous consent of Theologians in matters of faith and morals has always been sought by Popes, as well as by National and Ecumenical Councils; then we cannot but see that the constant and unanimous

---

24. August., *C. Jul, L. 2, N. 36.*

consent of such eminent Catholic Theological Schools in matters of faith and morals reflects and corresponds to the very consent of the whole Apostolic Succession, and consequently of the Church in all ages. For if the consent of the Faithful in matters of faith and morals is a mark of Divine Tradition, how much more so should be the consent of the learned in union with their bishops?

The constant and unanimous consent of Theologians on matters of Faith and Morals is not, therefore, subject to error—not that theologians or Theological Schools are under the special assistance of the Holy Ghost and consequently infallible. Rather, *under the special care and direction of the Apostolic Succession, they manifest the infallible consent and the Catholic Intellect of the same Apostolic Succession and of all the Church.* The gift of Infallibility was promised to none but to the Head of the Church, and to the Apostles' Successors *in union and consent with the same Head.* Therefore, the *unanimous and constant testimony* of Theological Schools on *matters which belong* to the Faith bears, *not directly,* but *indirectly,* a legitimate testimony of Divine Tradition. We say *indirectly* purposely because the direct and authentic witnesses of the Faith are the Pope and the bishops of the Church in union and in consent with the same Head of the Church. It was also for this reason that Pope Pius IX declared: "Even if we had in mind the submission which in our acts we owe to the Divine Faith, it is not, however, to be limited to the particular decrees which have been defined by Ecumenical Councils or by Roman Pontiffs, or by this Apostolic See; but it must also be extended to those doctrines which are taught by the common teaching of the Church throughout the whole world, as revealed by God, *and consequently by unanimous and constant consent proclaimed by Catholic Theologians* to belong to the Faith. (Emphasis added)."[25]

On all other matters which do not strictly belong to the Faith, the authority of the Schools is very grave. It is not permissible to depart from their sentence when their consent is equally constant and unanimous. These Schools were the noblest part of the Learning Church under the direct supervision of the Teaching Church.

We may summarize the teaching of Theological Schools in four classes: 1. When unanimously they propose anything *de Fide,* or "of Faith," they are *indirectly* infallible, because we may then consider them as the voice of the Apostolic Succession, under whose auspices they lived and taught. 2. When they teach something as *Fidei Proximum* or "Nearly of Faith," we cannot depart from their doctrine, because such is the Intellect of the Church Universal, whose belief cannot be erroneous. In this case, the doctrine they teach is by common consent contained in Divine Revelation, but only lacking the solemn decision of the Church. 3. When they declare some doctrine as true, but not *de Fide* or "of Faith," it is dangerous to deny it. For when Theologians, through inquiry and human science, come down to deductions even of their own from revealed truths and propose their sentence as true by unanimous consent, their authority is certainly grave. No one may reject it without at least a note of *temerity.* But we cannot say that their inquiry and human study are under the immediate assistance of the Holy Ghost. Hence, we may call that sentence which they declare as *true, certain,* but not *de Fide* ("of Faith") or *Fide Credenda.* ("must be believed in Faith"). To reject their teaching is rash. But it is not heresy. 4. When they do not agree, anyone may follow his own opinion

25. *Pius IX. ad Episc. Monach., A. 1863.*

until the Church gives her decision.

Finally, it must be observed that the relations between the Church and Theological Schools were more firmly held together from the 12th to the 16th or even to the 17th Centuries, than they have been recently. Through royal patronage and interference, many Theological Schools, especially in certain universities, emancipated themselves from the influence and control of the bishops. The consent, therefore, of the older Theological Schools is a safer rule of Divine Tradition, although the consent of the more modern is not to be despised.

In making this statement, we do not in the least mean to impair the authority of truly Catholic Universities, nor of those Theological *Cathedras* ["Chairs"], which at present flourish in so many well-conducted seminaries, under the direction of the bishops and for which we have the greatest respect and admiration.

7

The Ancient Ecclesiastical Monuments Are an Ever-Living Expression and a Visible Confirmation of Catholic Christianity.

Divine Providence did not leave the Church without irrefragable documents to show to the world that she is the greatest work in creation. This we have already seen in another part of this work. It is still more evident through the ancient monuments of Christian art.

These are of all kinds: paintings, statues, crypts, tombs, sarcophagi, coins, inscriptions, epitaphs. They may not all describe in words the faith and practice of the first worshippers of Christ; they may not exhibit a distinct notion of the Christian truths; they may not speak to us as the written books. But more than the written books, they speak to us in a silent language that fills the soul with light and unction and places before our eyes the religious life of the first Christians.

These glorious testimonies are nowhere more precious, more abundant or more significant than in the Roman Catacombs. The Catacombs are a veritable underground kingdom of the dead. It is asserted that, if placed in a straight line, they would extend the whole length of Italy. Having been completely forgotten by the 12th Century, Anthony Bosio, a native of the Island of Malta and justly called the Christopher Columbus of the Catacombs, labored for nearly forty years (1593-1629) in the exploration of the Roman Catacombs. Later on, other men appeared on the scene, and in our own times, Armellini, Stevenson, Marucchi, Wilpert and above all, De Rossi, the prince of Christian archeologists. Their labors led to a wider diffusion of Christian Archeology and an increased interest in and veneration for the Catacombs. Besides the Roman Catacombs, there are also several smaller Catacombs—in Naples, Sicily, Malta and one in North Africa. It was in such places that the first Christians prayed, sacrificed and were buried. To this very day, the odor of sanctity, the spirit of sacrifice, the perfume of the blood of Martyrs seem to emanate from these cities of the dead. It was in these quiet enclosures that the first Christians sang together the sublime Psalmody, celebrated the august Sacrifice of the Mass and, having received the Bread of the Strong, hastened to the battlefield of Martyrdom.

It is not our province to deal minutely with the treasures of Christian art. A few words will suffice. The Roman gravestones alone of the first three centuries furnish so many proofs for the fundamental dogmas and practices of the Catholic Church that they could illustrate every page of a modern Christian catechism. It is true that very few inscriptions and epitaphs speak clearly enough of their age. But there are other means of ascertaining this. The place of discovery, the names, the form of the letters, the style, the emblems, permit us to trace them to times of persecutions, or simply to the Third, Second or First Centuries. Most notable are the recent excavations in the Catacomb of St. Callistus and the finding of the inscriptions which describe the work of St. Peter in Rome and the low place of the baptistry in which the first Pope used to baptize the first Christians.

The same principle applies more or less to all other monuments of Christian art.

Here we are concerned not so much about the different monuments as about their meaning. After the Scriptures, Symbols [Creeds], and Liturgies, they furnish the Church with so many evident and visible proofs, that they may be placed on a par with the writings of the Fathers for the conservation and preservation of Divine Tradition. They are the Grand Seal of Catholic Christianity. They are a visible part of that assistance with which the Holy Ghost helps the Church to keep intact the Deposit of Faith and not to fall into error. It is not that they are necessary for the Church. The Church existed without them. But they came to us from times of persecution, or trying days. They are an expression of the belief and sentiments of our ancestors in the Faith. They help future generations to make the truth more resplendent. They cannot be but in harmony with God's designs.

The Teaching Church—that is, the Apostles and their successors in office—consigned a part of her preaching to writing. The Learning Church, wished to express her faith in sentimental and tangible works of art. We shall consider a few examples.

I. The most celebrated is the *Fractio Panis* —"The

Breaking of the Bread"—a title given to a fresco in the so-called "Greek Chapel," discovered in the Catacomb of St. Priscilla, situated near Rome. It dates from the first half of the Second Century. It is of the highest liturgical and theological importance. It was discovered by Wilpert in 1893 upon the face of the arch immediately over the Altar tomb of the Chapel. It represents a picture of seven personages at table: six men and one woman. The seventh personage sits in a dignified manner with his head thrown back, his arms stretched out in front of him, and his hands holding a small loaf in the act of breaking it. Before him there is a two-handled cup; farther along the table there are two large plates, one with two fishes and the other with five loaves. At one side of the picture, there are four baskets and at the other side three baskets, all filled with loaves.

Without any doubt this picture represents the Eucharistic Sacrifice. The priest, in the name and person of Christ, takes bread in his hands, lifts up his eyes to Heaven, gives thanks, blesses it and pronounces the words of Consecration on the bread, which is distributed to the Faithful after it becomes the Body of Our Lord. This act of the Catholic priest was called by the first Christians *Fractio Panis*—"The breaking of the bread." It is mentioned by the four Gospels and by other Apostolic and post-Apostolic writers. St. Paul writes: "And the bread which we break, is it not the partaking of the body of the Lord?" (*1 Cor.* 10:16). And in the *Acts of the Apostles:* "And they were persevering in the doctrine of the apostles, and in the communication of the breaking of bread, and in prayers." (*Acts* 2:42). This is the Catholic Holy Communion.

This "Breaking of the Bread" represented in this picture, not only describes the Eucharistic Sacrifice, which is the center of all Christian worship, but it also proves that the first Christians observed Sunday instead of Saturday as the Lord's Day, according to the Scriptures: "On the first day of the week, when we were assembled to break bread . . ." (*Acts* 20:7). This "breaking of the bread" demonstrates also that they went to Confession before receiving Holy Communion, because the author of the *Didache*—that is, of the "Teaching of the Apostles"—like so many other post-Apostolic writers, inviting the Faithful to assemble together to break bread on Sunday, warns the Faithful: "And on the Lord's Day, come together and break bread and give thanks, having first confessed your transgressions that your Sacrifice may be pure."[26] How many fundamental truths of our Religion are included in these few lines: The Holy Eucharist as a Sacrament and a Sacrifice of thanksgiving, the duty of observing the Lord's Day, the Sacrament of Penance! Everything on the table in this picture is symbolic of and belongs to the Sacrifice of the Mass.

There is in the same room, on one side of the picture, the representation of the Sacrifice of Abraham, and on the other side, the portrait of the prophet Daniel, who was fed miraculously by the prophet Habacuc in the lions' den. For the loaves in the baskets are the material for the Sacrifice or, as in the opinion of others, the "Bread" already consecrated; the cup suggests the chalice of wine for the Blood of the Lord; the fish is an allusion to Christ as the food of the soul. The Early Church, since the Second Century, regarded the five letters of the Greek word for fish—that is, *iχθvs*—as the first letters of the words making up the phrase in the Greek language, "Jesus Christ, the Son of God, the Saviour," because Christ fed the multitude with the loaves and fishes. We may truly affirm that the *Fractio Panis*—"Breaking of the Bread"—found in the Greek Chapel corresponds to and represents the

"Elevation of the Host" during Mass, as well as Holy Communion. When De Rossi, the master of Wilpert, heard and observed in his old age this new find, he exclaimed: "It is truly the pearl of all Catacomb discoveries."

II. The primacy of the Pope, who is the successor of St. Peter, not only in honor, but also in jurisdiction, is delineated, where Peter, as another Moses, strikes the rock with a rod. As Moses was the legislator, the leader and the head of the Chosen People of God, so also is Peter in the Church of Christ upon earth. The word *Petrus* is therewith plainly visible. Besides this, the rod is a sign of jurisdiction.

III. That there should be no distinction between the Deuterocanonical* and the Protocanonical Books of the Scriptures is indicated by the paintings, relating to *Tobias* and *Daniel.* They show that the Early Church accepted them all as inspired. Hence, as the Protestants rejected the Deuterocanonical Books, such as of *Tobias* and *Daniel,* the Protestant Bible is evidently incomplete.

IV. The raising of Lazarus from the dead is used as the "type" of our Resurrection from the Dead. Death is also represented as having entered this world through the sin of Adam and Eve. Escape from death is indicated by the rescue of Noe from the Deluge, of the three Hebrew children from the fiery furnace, and by Susanna's deliverance from false accusation. All of these show the belief of the early Christians in a future life.

V. The devotion we owe the Mother of God is vividly and repeatedly depicted in the art of the Catacombs. A fresco found in the Cemetery of Priscilla represents the

---

* These are *Tobias, Judith, Wisdom, Ecclesiasticus, Baruch, 1* and *2 Machabees,* part of *Esther* and part of *Daniel* in the Old Testament. "Protocanonical" books are all the rest of the Old Testament books. —*Publisher,* 2005.

Virgin with her Divine Child, while the Prophet Isaias stands before her and points to the star above her head. Another painting of the Third Century, found also in the same cemetery, represents the Annunciation. One or more pictures of the Virgin Mary are attributed to St. Luke by the best scholars and artists. One of the most famous pieces of ancient Christian art is a glass fragment kept in the Borgian Museum in the Palace of the Propagation of the Faith in Rome. Mozzoni ascribes it to the Second Century. It delineates the Blessed Virgin praying for us. On one side is St. Peter and on the other St. Paul. The figures of the two Apostles are smaller than the Virgin's, who is thus given greater prominence in Heaven than the two principal Apostles. They are also designated by their own names. This shows the veneration, esteem and reverence which the Apostles had towards the Mother of God.

Truly, therefore, the ancient ecclesiastical monuments are an evidence and a confirmation of Catholic Christianity.

10

The Fathers and Doctors of the Church

1

The "Fathers" and "Doctors" Were in Every Century the "Luminaries" of the Church.

APART from the Scriptures, the principal sources through which the Church has received her material Traditions are chiefly the writings of the "Fathers." By "*material* Traditions" we mean the *objective* "Deposit of the Faith," for the Church herself is governed by the voice of a Living Magisterium, namely, by an ever-living Apostolic Succession.

Divine Providence called forth in every age men who by their erudition, piety and high position, strengthened the Church of Jesus Christ. As in the Old Testament, God from time to time sent the Prophets to keep His people faithful to the belief in the one, true God, so also in the New Testament, the same God, after the establishment of the Church, selected in every century eminent men who, under the direction of the Holy Spirit, expounded and kept intact the Deposit of Faith.

The Fathers of the Church deserve our unlimited respect, gratitude and veneration. While most of them are illustrious for their sanctity and high position in the Church, they are all renowned for their erudition and antiquity. Their writings enable us to render a better account of our Faith because they were closer to the fountain of truth.

In the first centuries, bishops and doctors applied the title of "Fathers" to all their predecessors who, by their doctrine, sanctity and defense of the Christian Religion, became well-known to the Universal Church. That custom prevailed to a great extent up to the 12th Century, for St. Bernard, who by common opinion is the last of the Fathers, died in the year 1153. All that time is called the "Age of the Fathers."

Most of the "Fathers" are honored by the Church as Saints, such as Clement of Rome, Ignatius of Antioch, Polycarp, Justin, Ambrose, Augustine, Jerome, Cyprian. Others were loyal children of the Church, such as Papias, Lactantius, Clement of Alexandria. Others became infected with heresy, like Eusebius of Cæsarea, who fell into Arianism, and Tertullian who, after he had so valiantly defended the Church against heretics, embraced the Montanist sect in his old age. Origen is only *suspected* of heresy.

They are all, however, called "Fathers of the Church" because all of them gave testimony in their writings of what the Church believed and practiced in their time.

All those, therefore, who in the first twelve centuries gave testimony of Apostolic and Church doctrine by writing on important ecclesiastical matters, even those who lack the note of sanctity or who had lapsed into heresy, so long as they were in harmony with the rest of Christian writers, are commonly called "Fathers of the Church." Properly speaking, however, only those whom the Church acknowledges as competent writers and sincere witnesses of Apostolic and ecclesiastical doctrine are in the true sense of the word "Fathers of the Church." For, as the Church has the right to declare which are in reality the inspired writers of the Scriptures, so also she has the right to point out which are the competent teachers and qualified witnesses of the doctrine that comes down to us from Christ and the Apostles. It is only the Church that always knew and knows all about it; it is only the Church that is able to judge whether or not any doctrine is truthfully contained in ecclesiastical writings because—like any other Society that is conscious of its rights and duties—she is the only one that can competently declare in matters that regard her well-being which are her teachers, her judges and her witnesses.

Sublimity of doctrine is necessary. No matter how brief is the doctrine contained in his writings, the ecclesiastical author commands our respect when he transmits truths of great import. Those truths may not be related in a brilliant style. They are important on account of the antiquity of the author. Such are the writings of the Apostolic Fathers and of the first Apologists of the Church.

Sanctity is required, because it is the sister of Sacred Science. Although common or profane science may be found in any man, a pure life renders one able to see better what belongs to the Kingdom of Heaven, according to Christ's words: "Blessed are the clean of heart, for they shall see God." For this reason, if any writer whom we call "Father of the Church" lacks the note of sanctity, he is improperly so-called.

Antiquity is required. The nearer that ecclesiastical writers are to Christ and the Apostolic times, the more revered is their testimony. What they heard from the Apostles or from the Apostles' disciples of what the Rule of Faith was in their times could be nothing but the truth. The most ancient ecclesiastical authors were always cited by Ecumenical Councils and by Roman Pontiffs to illustrate, to defend and to prove the integrity of the Faith.

Approval of the Church is practically included in the above three requisites, nor is it necessary to have a solemn decree to that effect. The tacit consent of the Church is sufficient.

There is some difference between *"Fathers"* and *"Doctors"* of the Church. The prerogative of *Doctor of the Church* does not necessarily include *antiquity,* but rather a *brilliant exposition* of the Christian doctrine and a crushing refutation of the enemies of the Church. The title of "Father and Doctor" is something more than is implied in the title of *"Father of the Church."* For the most notable ecclesiastical writers may be considered as *witnesses or as teachers.* As *witnesses,* they proclaim what the Church of their times believed and practiced. What they assert is not their own opinion or doctrine, but specifically or equivalently they declare that what they say, they heard or learned from the ancients, presenting the articles of Faith to be believed, and the opposite doctrine to be rejected; these are the "Fathers of the Church." As *Teachers* or *Doctors of the Church,* they defend and illustrate with arguments what belongs to the Faith, although they may also bear testimony to the belief and practices prevalent in their days.

This difference indicates, on the one hand, how it is that certain eminent writers whom we call "Doctors" are never enumerated among the "Fathers," and on the other hand, how other great writers, who without doubt are always counted among the "Fathers," are also declared "Doctors of the Church." That means that they are both *witnesses* and *teachers.*

In comparatively recent times, the following learned and holy writers were declared "Doctors of the Church": St. Thomas Aquinas (1225-1274) by St. Pius V; St. Bonaventure (1221-1274) by Sixtus V; St. Peter Damian

(1007-1072) by Leo XII; St. Bernard (1090-1153) by Pius VIII; St. Hilary of Poitiers (c.315-c.368), St. Alphonsus Liguori (1696-1787) and St. Francis de Sales (1567-1622) by Pius IX. Other Doctors of the Church are St. Cyril of Jerusalem (c.315-386); St. Cyril of Alexandria (c.376-444); St. Leo the Great (c.400-c.461); St. Peter Chrysologus (c.406-c.450); St. Isidore of Seville (c.560-c.636), St. Anselm (1033-1109), St. Bede the Venerable (c.673-735), St. Peter Canisius (1521-1597), and St. John of the Cross (1542-1591) by Pius XI.

The greatest Doctors of the Church, however, all lived in the "Age of the Fathers" and are consequently both "Fathers and Doctors." They are distinguished according to the number of the Evangelists. Four belong to the Latin Church: St. Ambrose (c.340-397), St. Augustine (354-430), St. Jerome (c.342-c.420), and St. Gregory the Great (540-604); the other four belong to the Greek Church: St. Athanasius (c.297-373), St. Basil the Great (c.329-379), St. John Chrysostom (c.347-407), and St. Gregory of Nazianzus (c.329-c.389).*

All the "Doctors" are honored as Saints of God. The explicit or equivalent declaration of the Church is necessary to call anyone "Doctor of the Church." Hence it is that every Doctor of the Church is a Saint of God; but not every Father of the Church must necessarily be a Saint.

The Fathers and Doctors of the Church were "not the Light, but to give testimony of the Light." (*John* 1:8). They are to keep it ever burning for all, especially for those who sit in darkness and in the shadow of death.

Infallible they were not. Infallibility was only granted to the Apostles, to the Head of the Church, and the Apostles' successors under Peter.

---

* A complete list of the 33 Doctors of the Church appears on page 325.

2

The Fathers Distinguish the Scriptures from Tradition as Two Different Parts of Revelation.

Most of the Traditions have come to us through the writings of the Fathers. The Fathers were in every century the foremost exponents of Christian doctrine. They were the lights of Christianity in the Catacombs; in the great convulsions that submerged and changed the old civilization of Europe, Asia and Africa; in the social and national birth of so many nations after the break-up of the Roman Empire. They were, above all, the bulwark of Christian truth in all the religious upheavals that rent—alas, how many times and in how many places!—the beautiful mantle of the Spouse of Jesus Christ.

They had to contend with all kinds of difficulties. All the powers of Hell were arraigned against the Church. All kinds of enemies arose in the bosom of Christianity itself. But God in His wisdom was with His Church in her days of trial. Errors arose and may yet arise, but thanks be to God, we can say with certainty that all errors—past, present and to come—have already been valiantly combated and refuted by the Fathers of the Church. They had many times to accept battle on the enemy's ground and use his own weapons to defend the truth.

Since their writings furnish the most eloquent testimonies on Tradition, it will not be out of place to set forth their teaching. They distinguish Tradition from the Scriptures, as two distinct objects, one completed by the other. Scripture and Tradition appear in their writings like two different hands, both holding fast the deposit of Revelation. They are two streams with a common origin. They flow over separate ground. But both lead to and form the same Revelation.

What they *received from the elders* but did not find in the Scriptures, the Fathers call "Tradition"—either *Dominical,* or *Apostolic.* Thus, St. Basil in his work *"On the Holy Ghost,"* writes: "Of the dogmas and preachings which are kept in the Church, some came to us in writing (the Scriptures); others we received in mysteries from the *Tradition* of the Apostles."[1] So also Tertullian in *The Crown;*[2] and Augustine in *The Baptism.*[3]

In the second place, the Fathers speak of Tradition as a *separate means* of information, propagation and conservation of the truth, regardless of the Scriptures. "What then," writes Irenæus, "if the Apostles did not even leave us the Scriptures? Would it not have been necessary to follow the order of Tradition which they left to those to whom they entrusted the Churches? Many illiterate peoples adapt themselves to such an order of things, [people] who without paper or ink believe in Christ, but have written in their hearts, through the Holy Ghost, what belongs to salvation, and diligently *'keep the old traditions,'* believing in one God, Creator of Heaven and earth"; and after reciting the Apostles' Creed, he continues "these peoples, who believed without any writings, as far as our language is concerned, are foreign to our tongue; while in what regards the Faith, in its construction and custom and conversation, they are very learned indeed, and they please God, serving Him in all justice and chastity and wisdom. If any one relates to them, even in their own tongue, what heretics have devised, they will at once shut their ears and flee from him, not to hear such blasphemous talking. Thus, through that *'ancient tradition of the Apostles,'* they do not even want for one moment to entertain in their mind

1. *Basil,* C. XXVII.
2. Tertull., C. IV.
3. August., C. VII.

what such persons have to say."[4] Note that Irenæus, writing in the Second Century, is speaking of peoples who could not even read or write. They had nothing to direct them on the road to salvation except the ancient traditions: the preaching and practices of the Church. Preaching is not reading. Preaching came to them not through the Scriptures, but by hearing the word of God preached to them by the priests of the Church, as the Apostle says: *Fides ex auditu*—"Faith cometh by hearing." (*Rom.* 10:17).

The Fathers, comparing Scripture with Tradition, declare that they are both *equal in authority.* St. Basil, after having testified that some dogmas came to us through the Scriptures and others from the Tradition of the Apostles, declares: "Both of them (Scripture and Tradition) have the same strength toward piety; no man can contradict them. Certainly no one, even with [no] little experience, should [be able to] know which are the institutions of the Church [and which came down to us from Our Lord].* For if we begin to reject the custom which has not come to us in writing, as if not important, we will hurt the Gospel in its most principal parts. Rather, we reduce the preaching to a mere name. For example, to mention what is first and most common, the Signing of the Cross by those who hope in Christ—who taught us that in writing? The words of invocation during the Consecration of the Eucharistic bread and the cup of benediction, what Saint has left them to us in writing? We are not satisfied with what the Apostles or the Gospel commemorates. We also say other things before and after, as having relation of great importance to bear towards

4. Iren., L. 3, C. IV, N. 1.

* This sentence, without the words in brackets, is exactly how it appears in the original edition of this book. The bracketed words give the sentence a correct meaning in the context of this paragraph.
—Publisher, 2005.

the Mystery, and still we received them from the unwritten Tradition." "We bless the water of Baptism and the oil of Unction," the Father continues, "nay even him who receives Baptism. By what writings? Is it not by a silent and secret Tradition? And the very same Extreme Unction . . . the unction itself, or the words used in anointing the sick . . . what written word has taught it to us? . . . is it not from that unpublished and secret doctrine which our Fathers kept in a quiet and non-inquisitive silence? They learned very well that reverence to mysteries is kept by silence. On account of that, which one of them could agree to divulge in writing what was forbidden to the initiated even to look upon? . . . This is the reason why certain things have not been delivered in writing, that without neglecting the knowledge of dogma, that same dogma (had it been written) would be depreciated by the people with its constant use. Dogma is one thing, preaching is another. For dogmas are kept silent, and preaching is public. A certain kind of silence is obscurity, of which the Scripture avails itself, rendering the interpretation of dogmas hard to understand. The day is not long enough to enumerate the unwritten mysteries of the Church."[5] Thus St. Basil in the Fourth Century.

It is evident, then, that the Fathers of the Church suppose and declare that besides the Scriptures, the written Word of God, there is also the unwritten word of God, as another source of information, totally distinct from the Scriptures. *This is Tradition,* a source of information or revelation, distinct from the Scriptures.

---

5. *Basil on Baptism,* C. XXVII.

3

The Unanimous Consent of the Fathers of the Church in Matters of Faith and Morals is a Rule of Divine Tradition.

In the supernatural order, no matter how wise and learned he may be, a person is subject to error. Certainty is reached only by Revelation or Infallibility. When the Apostles died, Divine Revelation came to an end. The gift of Infallibility, according to the solemn promise of Christ, was given only to those who are charged with the government of the Church: the successors of St. Peter, the origin and center of all jurisdiction in the Church of God, and the whole Episcopate, as far as they act and agree with the Head of the Church. No single bishop, however, as a private person, is infallible. Only the Bishop of Rome, acting as head of the Church [and teaching on Faith or morals], is infallible. In a similar manner, the Fathers and Doctors of the Church may be considered with regard to Infallibility.

For the Fathers of the Church may be regarded either as a body of good and learned men, writing in defense of the Church, or as particular persons explaining Christian truths. As "Fathers of the Church," they are her *witnesses,* showing the same consent. Hence, they are infallible, because their testimony exhibits a consent *which is the same consent of the Church.* As particular *persons or doctors,* they act on their own authority. What they affirm or deny individually may not always go unchallenged. These statements need some explanation:

I. When the Fathers of the Church consent on certain doctrines which evidently belong to the common Faith of the Church—and all the Faithful believe them—then, that consent of the Fathers shows the Divine Tradition of those doctrines. It is the same consent of the Universal Church.

Consequently, the common consent of the Fathers is infallible, because the Church itself is infallible.

For this reason, when the Fathers propose certain doctrines in such a way that they evidently assert them as belonging to the Faith, their common consent evinces the Divine Tradition of those doctrines. No Christian can reject them without falling into heresy.

II. Likewise, if the Fathers of the Church, explain a certain doctrine, as theological and true, but do not propose it as explicitly belonging to the Faith, it is a dangerous sign and a note of temerity to depart from their doctrine and belief.

III. When the Fathers are really divided on some particular doctrine and grave reasons are given for both sides of the question, we are free to form a different opinion. There is no *common consent.* It is plain that in such a case the truth has not come to light thus far. In the course of time, the unanimous consent of the Church, or its solemn decision, may render it evident.

Hence, the Church always looked, in *theory and in practice,* at the Fathers as her defenders and leaders: *in theory,* threatening to expel from her communion whoever despised their authority or the solemn profession of the General Councils; *in practice,* proving through the Councils, the Dogmas, by the unanimous consent of the Fathers, or condemning the opinions of those who were or are contrary to the common teaching.

The Council of Chalcedon (451) affirms: "In any ambiguous question, we permit ourselves to render what we believe conformable to the interpretations of the Fathers and not to teach anything contrary to what they taught, but rather, we make use of these witnesses to confirm our faith." The Lateran Council under Martin I (649-655) declares: "If anyone does not properly and truthfully admit whatever has been delivered and proclaimed to the holy Catholic and Apostolic Church of God according to the Fathers, and hence, does not recognize by word and mind whatever the Fathers and the Five venerable General Councils declared, *let him be anathema" [i.e., "excommunicated"].*

The VIII General Council states: "In order to keep on the right and royal way of divine justice, without falling into error, we must follow the writings of the Fathers as unquenched and ever-resplendent flames. For this reason, we profess that the sanctions of the Catholic and Apostolic Church must be observed and kept as received through the Traditions, not only of the Apostles, but also of the orthodox and Ecumenical Councils, or by any divine Father and Doctor of the Church. For Traditions—whether by word or by writing of our ancestors, who distinguished themselves by the sanctity of their life—the great Apostle Paul (*2 Thess.* 2:14) explicitly declares must be upheld."[6]

Therefore, whatever the Fathers of the Church state and declare by common consent, can be nothing else but the truth. That is Divine Tradition.

4

The Consent of Some of the Fathers, When the Others Are Silent, Or Not Contradicting, Is a Sure Argument of Divine Tradition.

To reach moral certainty in a Christian truth, it is not necessary to have the consent of *all* the Fathers. Quite often what the Apostolic or ancient Church thought of a doctrine may be safely inferred from the consent of a few.

It happened that certain Christian truths—some of them not unimportant—were defended not by all, but by a few of the Fathers against heretics of their times. When cer-

6. *Act.* 10, can. I.

tain dogmas were attacked, the whole Church was thereby affected, but she left the whole matter to a few, knowing well into what hands she committed the defense of her truths. She approved their conduct, commended their action and rejoiced at the defeat of their enemies.

This happened, for instance, in the doctrine of the Most Blessed Trinity. The name of Athanasius was sufficient in the defense of Christ's Divinity. Basil, Gregory of Nazianzus, Hilary, Augustine, are more than sufficient for the defense of the Catholic truth against the Arians, Semi-Arians, and Pelagians. Cyril of Alexandria, Leo the Great, Agatho and Sophronius defend the mystery of the Incarnation against both Nestorians and the Monophysites. Each name of such eminent Fathers has more weight than a legion of modern writers. Thus Augustine, speaking of Gregory of Nazianzus, declares: "He is such a great man that neither would he say this but from a Christian faith well-known to all, nor would they (the contemporary bishops of his province) have him for so illustrious and venerable a personage unless they knew that he said these things through the celebrated rule of truth."[7]

During the discussion of such vital questions, the whole Church was breathlessly watching and praying without ceasing for the triumph of the truth as expounded by her leaders. They attacked heresy in its multiform error, defended the Faith so valiantly and explained Catholic Dogma so completely, that there was no need of too many leaders.

This explains why some Fathers offered little defense or none at all on some doctrines. Their silence was a tacit consent, a mighty approval of the action of the more eminent Fathers, an expression of the general feeling of the Universal Church.

---

7. August., L. I., *C. Jul.*, N. 16.

The silence, therefore, of the rest of the Fathers and the acquiescence of the Faithful were a silent but eloquent sanction of the other Fathers' teaching and defense. From experience and past history, we know that none of the Fathers remained silent when an innovation had crept into the Universal Church; they gave at once the alarm and never ceased to oppose it until it was entirely crushed.

Hence it is, that some of the Ecumenical Councils, as well also as some of the Fathers, in order to prove certain dogmatic truths, did nothing but present the sentences of ten or twelve Fathers of the Church. They gave no other proof but their simple, plain, authoritative statements. The Councils of Ephesus (431), of Chalcedon (451), and of the Third and Fourth of Constantinople (680-681 and 869) are cases in point. St. Augustine himself in the controversy against Julian, Cyril of Alexandria in "The Right Faith," Gelasius I in his third treatise on the "Two natures in Christ," Cassianus in his book against Nestorius—all used the same method.

No one will affirm that Ecumenical Councils and men like Augustine did not know how to defend the Christian Faith. Hence, Vincent of Lerin, speaking, of the Ephesine Council (431), says: "A much greater number (of Fathers) could have been presented, but it was not necessary. It was not expedient to crowd the session with a multitude of witnesses. No one thought for a moment that those ten differed from the rest of their colleagues."[8]

It is therefore certain that Christian antiquity believed that the consent of several of the Fathers of the Church, when the others remained silent or did not contradict, was a sure proof of Divine Tradition. This is also the belief of the Church today.

---

8. Vincent of Lerin, *Commonit.*

5

The Consent of Either All the Western, Or of All the Eastern Fathers, Or Even of Very Few of the Fathers, When the Rest Do Not Contradict, Is a Sure Argument Of Divine Tradition.

After the Scriptures and the solemn decisions of the Church, there is nothing more authoritative, nothing more beautiful in the Church of God than the doctrine of the Fathers. When we consider the esteem and reverence in which they were held in the Universal Church, in life and after death, the sublime doctrine which they so clearly explained to the people and so ably defended against heretics, and which was so universally accepted by the Councils and the Faithful as part of the Deposit of Faith delivered by the ancients, we may safely say they labored and wrote under the assistance of the Holy Spirit. Their testimony cannot be but true and their doctrine nothing else but the orthodox teaching of the Church.

Now Truth and Faith are not confined to one place nor to any group of persons. Neither can the teaching of the Fathers be considered as better in any group of the Fathers, whether from the East or from the West. This is so true that even a small number of the Fathers, affirming or testifying to the same doctrine, must have our whole confidence and assent when the rest of the Fathers do not contradict them. It may happen, and it has happened, that some dogmas of the Christian Religion were attacked in some districts only. And only the Fathers of those places refuted such local heretics; or a few testified to certain Christian doctrines, while the others by silence gave their full approval. Had it been otherwise, they would have at once protested, and their protest would have come down to us.

The Oriental Church professed the same Faith as the Western Church. So long as that unity of Faith remained, it was impossible that with such watchful vigilance of pastors and Faithful, the Greek Fathers could sustain a doctrine which the Fathers of the Latin Church rejected. And it was equally impossible that the Latin Fathers could ever teach a doctrine which the Greek Fathers repudiated. "One Faith, one Lord, one Baptism" (*Ephesians* 4:5) was up to the Eighth Century, the bond of union between East and West.

Augustine, defending the Catholic dogma of Original Sin against Julian, says: "Do you perhaps despise them because they are all Western Fathers or bishops, and not one Oriental bishop has been mentioned? . . . It is useless for you to look for Oriental bishops, for they also are Christians, and Faith *is one* in both parts of the world, because Faith is also Christian, while you were born in a Western land, and the Western Church had regenerated you."[9]

Revelation comes to us through the Tradition of the ancients, who received it and guarded it most carefully.

The Fathers—East and West—were the most eminent writers and the great Saints of their times. They were, moreover, when bishops, successors of the Apostles. They transmitted Revelation to the Faithful as they themselves received it from the ancients. They kept it unadulterated, explained it to their flocks and defended it from the attacks of the enemy. Supernatural grace, high position in the Church, natural proximity to the main source of truth, natural talents, all conspired to render the Fathers well acquainted with the truth. What else could be expected to keep immaculate the Deposit of the Faith?

Moreover, we must not forget that the Deposit of Faith was not all attacked at one single time or place. In every generation it has been the target of heretics. And in every

9. August., *C. Jul.,* L. I, C. IV, N. 13.

generation, God came to its rescue with eminent and holy men. Hence, while truth shone more brightly and became better known, its defenders became more renowned. They were few. But the importance of the matters involved, the confidence placed in them, the brilliance of their arguments, made them stars in the firmament of the Church. Had a great part of the Church become Arian? Behold Athanasius replacing on Christ the aureola of Divinity of which Arius divested Him! Had Nestorius denied the Queen of Heaven her most exalted title? Behold Cyril of Alexandria in the Ecumenical Council [of Ephesus in 431], in the name of the Roman Pontiff, proclaiming Mary "the Mother of God." Had Pelagius and his immense multitude of followers so deified man as not to need God's help? Behold Augustine, like a new Solomon, magnificently illustrating on the one hand man's frailty, and on the other insisting on the necessity of God's grace. Thus, even one Father of the Church may be sufficient authority on some article of the Faith. A very ancient practice or belief may be known through the writings of a solitary witness. Cyril of Alexandria could say of St. Athanasius: "Indeed, he is such an able man and so worthy that we place in him our full confidence, that he never proposed anything at variance with the divine letters."[10]

Similar testimonies could be repeated for many other single Fathers, eminent in science and sanctity, or illustrious in the defense of the Church's doctrine. It is evident, then, that even from the testimony of a few, we may know what were the Faith and practices of the Church in their own times—that is, the Tradition of the whole Church. And the Tradition of the whole Church is a sure argument of Truth.

---

10. *Cyril of Alexandria, Ep. I.*

6

Although the Fathers of the Church Are Not Infallible, Their Authority Is so Great That, Whenever Any One of the Fathers Does Not Appear To Be of One Mind with the Others, We Must Be Very Cautious Before Declaring That He is in Error, Or Not in Accord With the Rest of Them.

In immunity from error, the Fathers and Doctors of Christianity—considered as individuals—may be rightly compared to the individual bishops of the Church. The bishops, considered as one body, acting under and with the Head of the Church, are infallible, because it is through Peter and Peter's Successors that the bishops cannot fall into error in faith or morals. It is the Head of the Church that communicates infallibility to the other principal members of the Body—the bishops of the Church.

The Father or Doctor of the Church, *in a similar way,* is immune from error—so long as his consent agrees with the *consent of the others.* For when all the Fathers and Doctors of the Church agree on a certain doctrine, their consent is not a private one: it exhibits the consent of the Church, which is infallible.

In the case where a particular Father of the Church does not agree on some proposition with the rest of the Fathers, we must conclude that he departed from the truth. But we must be very slow before we come to that conclusion. They are all Fathers; hence, we must first see whether or not the Father's opinion could be made to harmonize with the others. The following rules are to be observed:

I. The authority of one, or even of several Fathers of the Church, is not infallible because—with the exception of the Successor of St. Peter on matters of dogma and morals—no man is infallible. Nor must we ever consider the writings of the Fathers as canonical Scriptures. Although the testimony of only one inspired writer is sufficient, the same, however, cannot be said of any of the Fathers—for the reason that no one of them wrote under the inspiration of the Holy Ghost. St. Augustine writes: "Rendering, therefore, due reverence, and paying all the honor I possibly can to the peaceful bishop and glorious Martyr Cyprian, I hold [that] in the rebaptizing of schismatics and heretics, he thought differently from what the truth proved afterwards to be—not through my own opinion, but from the doctrine of the Universal Church, which doctrine was afterwards strengthened and confirmed by the authority of a Plenary Council."[11]

II. Truth—more than authority—is always and in everything the principal motive. St. Augustine and others affirm that they are moved, not so much by the authority of the Fathers, as by the reasons and proofs which they present for their statements. In this vein Augustine writes in his Epistle to St. Jerome.[12] Thus also, the same Father of the Church warns his readers not to consider his writings as canonical Scripture nor to correct them according to their own opinion, but according to *"divine writings* and incontestable reason."[13] Hence, Cardinal Franzelin says, "Where there is consent, the authority of every single Father cannot be compared with the sufficient authority of every single inspired writer; but the *reason* and *proof* of the Tradition—whether historical, philosophical or theological—is contained in that same consent."[14]

III. Quite often the dissent of one or more from the general consent of the rest of the Fathers is *apparent or*

11. August., *De Bapt.,* L. 6, C. II.
12. August., Ep. 82, N. 3.
13. August., *De Trinit.,* L. 3.
14. Franzelin, *Scr. et. Trad.,* Th. XV, N. I.

exaggerated by the ill-disposed enemies of Tradition. St. Athanasius writes: "They are all Fathers. It would not be holy to declare that these have spoken well and the others wrong, because they all died in Christ; we cannot accuse them, because they all took care of what belongs to Christ; all used their best efforts against heretics."[15]

For this reason, when some of the Fathers apparently seem to contradict what has always been believed by the Faithful, while on the other hand the same Fathers proved to be the leaders in the defense of the doctrine—which sometimes they assert in an obscure way or in an ambiguous form—their sentence should be reconciled with the doctrine of the Church and made clear through other statements which are plainer and more intelligible. Obscure sentences of any writer are made clear through the general context of his work. St. Ambrose says: "Do his words seem strange to you? Well, ask for his profession; a clear mind shields and defends from fault even a doubtful discourse."[16]

On this theory, some of the Fathers have explained and defended what other Fathers had less accurately expounded. Thus, Augustine elucidates Chrysostom;[17] Athanasius interprets Dionysius.[18]

IV. As none of the Fathers is to be blindly followed, so none of them is to be on any question regarded of little importance or discarded without sufficient reason. On the authority of a Father of the Church, considered individually, follows the rule of St. Augustine: "What you see as true, hold and attribute it to the Catholic Church; what is false, reject and do not mind me who am only a man; what is doubtful, believe until reason will persuade or

---

15. Athanas., *De Synod,* N. 43.
16. Ambrose, Ep. 48, N. 4.
17. August., L. I, *C. Jul.,* N. 22.
18. Athanas., L. Sent. Dion.

authority will demand that it must be either rejected or declared true or always to be believed."[19]

V. It is certain that the consent of all the Fathers in any period of the history of the Church never was or is in opposition to the consent of all the Fathers of another age or epoch. Truth is always one and eternal. According to the promise of Christ, no false doctrine could ever be believed by all the Faithful in any time of the Church. There may be, in a preceding period, an apparent, not a real opposition; a weak, not a firm common consent; but never a different profession of Faith.

VI. We must admit that some of the sentences of some of the Fathers on some doctrines can never be harmonized with the general consent of the rest of the Fathers. In such cases, their sentences are to be rejected: they have simply erred. We must not wonder, however, at some errors of some of the Fathers. This teaches us that no individual Father is a canonical or Scriptural writer. Each one wrote as a human being, not as the Truth itself, nor as an infallible instrument in the hands of God. Some wrote when a question was obscure and before the Church issued a solemn declaration, putting an end to that question. Others wrote under the impression that some books (like the *Shepherd of Hermas* or the *Epistle of Barnabas*) were a part of Scripture. Those books proved afterwards to be Apocraphal and not the Word of God. No wonder that some of the Fathers, drawing their knowledge from such books, could have written certain things which were afterwards found to be at variance with the infallible and common consent of the Fathers and of the whole Church.

VII. No matter how erroneously the Fathers may have written, it is a fact that they never erred on revealed doc-

---

19. August., *De Vera Relig.*

trines, which are the fundamental and vital doctrines of the Church. These were always believed and are always to be believed, because contained in the symbols [creeds], or in the public professions of Faith.

VIII. Finally, it is also certain that whenever the Fathers erred, their error was not about Tradition—but namely, about truths which they received from the ancients. The errors of some of the Fathers concern, in most cases, their own *private opinions* on some *doctrinal* matters. They cannot in such cases be considered as *witnesses* of the Truth, transmitted from the ancients, but simply as common writers and just as fallible.

7

The Fathers Did Not Advocate the Sufficiency of the Scriptures to the Exclusion of Tradition.

The defense of a bad case only makes it worse. When Protestants endeavor to prove the sufficiency of Scripture to the exclusion of Tradition, they show up the weakness of the whole Protestant system. This we have already seen. But when they bring forward the Fathers as witnesses to their doctrine, the weakness becomes an open contradiction. If common witnesses must tell the truth, the Fathers cannot fail. And if they have already declared themselves, what a crime it is to compel them to contradict themselves! This is what Protestantism would do. Protestant writers leave no stone unturned practically to force the Fathers to testify against the Church, which they have defended in a thousand ways against thousands of enemies.

When a witness has given his testimony, the whole testimony—and not merely a part of it—must be considered. The context of the whole deposition, the spirit and the letter of the attestation, go together. One sentence, illustration or affirmation taken out of its proper setting may express a different or an opposite view. As the Fathers have written so many works, opposed so many enemies, in so many different circumstances, it is little wonder that isolated statements taken out of context might seem to admit the sufficiency of Scripture. But on every page they insist on Tradition and the authority of the Church. If the Fathers seem to advocate the sufficiency of Scripture in some of their statements, that sufficiency is not *absolute,* but *relative.* Thus:

I. When they affirm the sufficiency of Scripture, they do not exclude, but *suppose* Tradition. After Athanasius says that "the Sacred Scriptures are sufficient to indicate the Faith in Christ," he adds, "There are *many books of our teachers* which, if any one will read, he will in some manner understand the interpretation of the Scriptures and might know what he desires."[20] When Vincent of Lerin states that "the canon of the Scripture is perfect and is abundantly sufficient to itself and to anything else,"[21] he does not include all Revelation. He only speaks of doctrines which were then attacked and which he mentions by name. Even then, he adds that Faith must be safeguarded, "first, by the law of Divine Authority (*viz.* the Scriptures), and then by the Tradition of the Catholic Church." He declares the reason for this double security in his famous sentence, "because not all men accept in the same sense the Sacred Scriptures, on account of their loftiness . . . hence, it is most necessary, on account of so many different errors, that the line of prophetic and apostolic interpretation be drawn according to the rule of the ecclesiastical and Catholic sense."[22]

20. Athanas., *Orat. C. Gent.,* N. 1.
21. *Commonit.,* CC. I-II.
22. *Commonit.,* C. II.

II. If a truth is clear in the Scriptures, the Fathers did not deem it always expedient to prove it from other sources. Defending the Divinity of Christ against the Arians, the Fathers cite only the Scriptures, because that dogma is splendidly illustrated in Holy Writ, which is a common ground to Catholics and heretics. Augustine, in his controversy with the Donatists about the catholicity of the Church, quotes only from the Scriptures, because this "mark" of the Church is evident in those sacred pages.

III. When the Fathers extol the sufficiency of the Scriptures, describing them as nothing more divine, nothing more true, nothing more sublime, so as that nothing must be believed than "what has been delivered," they are making no reference to Tradition, but to spurious sources from which heretics tried to prove their assertions. They referred them to the Scriptures—as to common ground—proving that only the Scriptures, not the apocryphal books, are the written Word of God. What Origen says of the Two Testaments as sufficient, "from which we can derive all science, and no other third Scripture must be accepted as authority to science,"[23] must be understood of the sufficiency of the Divine Scriptures *to the exclusion of apocryphal books,* to which heretics appealed. Such was also the case of Augustine against the Manichæans and the Montanists.

IV. At least in the first centuries, whenever heretics endeavored to prove anything beyond the Scriptures, or also against the Scriptures, through human inventions and sophistic argumentations, the Fathers taught that we must stand only by the Scriptures. Thus, when the Fathers say that "we must not speak through our own argumentations, but according to the Scriptures," or "the conviction of the hearer goes lame if anything is said without the Scrip-

23. Origen. In *Lev. Hom., 5,* N. 9.

tures and only from our own reasoning," it is evident that the Fathers oppose the authority of the Scriptures to human inventions and silly arguments. When Montanus and the other so-called prophets of the Montanist sect claimed to be possessed by God and spoke in His person, the Fathers proved to them that Revelation is only in the Scriptures and in Tradition.

V. It is true that the Fathers affirmed that the Scriptures contain whatever must be *explicitly* believed. For that reason they called the Apostolic Creed a "Symbol, or abridgment of the Scriptures," and advised the catechumens to have it "first written in their hearts" and later on, "as the opportunity presented itself, to derive from the Scriptures also what each article affirms."[24] Thus also Augustine.[25] This does not mean that the Fathers wanted the Faithful instructed in the Faith independently of the Teaching Church, nor that everyone should derive his doctrine only from the Scriptures, to the exclusion of Tradition. They spoke of the Scriptures, which *must be explained,* not as *already explained—"explicandæ,* not *explicatæ,"* as the Theologians say. That is, the Fathers wanted the Scriptures explained through the Church. Who does not know that as soon as a controversy arose about the true sense of the Scriptures, even about the articles of Faith which must be explicitly believed, the Fathers wanted all the Faithful to follow the teaching of the Church? This we have abundantly seen in another part of this work.

VI. When on some occasions the Fathers seem to proclaim the absolute sufficiency of the Scriptures, they simply wanted the Faithful to have recourse to the Scriptures, because they know that the Scriptures refer the Faithful

24. Cyril of Jerus., *Catech.* V, N. 12
25. August., *De Symb. ad Catech.,* C. I.

to the Church, to learn from her, namely, what they must believe and practice. Augustine is once more to the point: "Although the Scriptures do not speak with certainty on this matter (of the validity of the Baptism conferred by heretics), we hold, however, the truth of the same Scriptures in this matter when we act according to the direction of the Church, *whom the authority of the same Scriptures commends.* For this reason, since the Scriptures cannot deceive, if any one is afraid to err on account of the obscurity of the question, let him consult the Church, which the Scriptures show without any ambiguity."[26]

The statements of the Fathers are therefore different from the Protestant contention, which declares that "the Scripture contains all that is necessary to salvation, so that if anything is not read in it, or cannot be proved through it, it must not be exacted from anyone to be believed as an article of faith, nor to be regarded as necessary to salvation."[27] The Fathers have always in mind the Apostolic Succession, whose teaching and understanding is to be the course and rule in the interpretation of the Scriptures. They do not separate the Scriptures from Tradition.

Therefore, according to the Fathers of the Church, not all the truths are clear in Scripture. What is clear is not clear enough to all the Faithful, that they may understand it without the help of Tradition. If any controversy arises, it cannot be settled without the authentic judgment of the Church, which is the rule and the final tribunal to define and declare the true sense.

Scripture and Tradition go together. Hence, the illogical accusation of Protestants that Catholic theologians defend the necessity of Tradition theoretically, but have recourse,

---

26. August., *C. Crescon,* L. I, N. 39.
27. VI "Anglican Article."

first of all, to the Scriptures to prove the doctrines of Catholicism. Protestants fail to understand that the defense of the truth from the Scriptures, with *the Catholic Intellect* as a guide and rule for its understanding, is very different from the constitution of private judgment as the only rule and the sole judge of the true sense of the Scriptures, *with the rejection of Church authority.*

It will be well for the student of Religion to read Cardinal Bellarmine, who gathered together all the texts taken from the Fathers by Protestant divines in favor of the sufficiency of Scripture.[28] See also Franzelin.[29] All such Protestant objections may be solved either by keeping in mind the whole context of the Fathers' statements, or by the *supposition* of the authority of the Church, which the Fathers proclaim in all their writings, or by the Scriptures themselves, which demonstrate the authority of the Church as the universal guide and rule for the knowledge and the acceptation of the Faith.

Therefore, what the Fathers say about the sufficiency of the Scriptures does not exclude Tradition.

8

The Opinion or Doctrine Approved by Some of the Fathers that Christ Will Reign Upon Earth With the Just for a Thousand Years Does Not Impair the Statement that the Consent of the Fathers, or of the Faithful, Is a Sure Proof of Divine Tradition.

"Things are not always what they seem." Such are certain texts of Scripture, taken in their literal sense. Many Christians in the Second and Third Centuries wrongly

28. Bellarmin, *De Verbo Dei,* L. IV, C. II
29. Franzelin, *Scrip. et Trad.,* Th. XIX.

interpreted certain texts of the Scriptures, falling an easy prey to heresy. They thought that by relinquishing something material in this life they would receive it a hundredfold in the next. Influenced by Judaism, from which they adopted many rites and doctrines—especially the expectation of a glorious Messias—they believed that before the General Resurrection of the human race on the Last Day, the just will rise and reign with Christ upon this earth for a thousand years, having restored and rebuilt the great City of Jerusalem. Prominent among them were the Cerinthians, the Nazarenes and the Ebionites in Asia Minor. They called it the first resurrection, to distinguish it from the Last Resurrection on the Last Day.

Papias, a saintly bishop, divested the doctrine of all sensuous pleasures, approved of it and taught it to the Faithful.

Many Catholics followed his opinion as a doctrine revealed by God, delivered to the Church by the Apostles and contained in Scripture, especially in the *Apocalypse*. "And I saw an angel coming down from heaven . . . and he laid hold on the dragon, the old serpent, which is the devil and Satan, and bound him for a thousand years . . . that he should no more seduce the nations, till the thousand years be finished. . . . And I saw seats . . . and the souls of them that were beheaded for the testimony of Jesus . . . and they lived and reigned with Christ a thousand years. The rest of the dead lived not, till the thousand years were finished. This is the first resurrection." (*Apoc.* 20:1-5).

We must admit that such a glorious Kingdom of Christ upon earth with the just for a thousand years or more seems to be in harmony with many parts of the *Psalms,* plus the prophetic and the Apostolic letters concerning a Kingdom of Christ. If such a Kingdom is not acknowledged, their interpretation is more difficult. That part of the Symbol of the Apostles [Apostle's Creed], "He shall judge the living and the dead," seems to suggest a seemingly fair interpretation through the acceptance of Christ's earthly Kingdom.

Therefore, we should not wonder that even great writers of the Church in the Second and Third Centuries, such as Justin and Irenæus, accepted Papias' doctrine. Augustine believed it for some time, but afterwards discarded it. It was also believed by many Christians who during the time of persecution had trusted in it and had expressed their hopes in Christ's earthly Kingdom. It was believed by so many that St. Jerome complains in his works, that "many of the ancients," "many of the Clergy," "many of our own people" believed it in the past, and many in his own times still believed it, following on this point only the heretic Apollonius, who revived it in the Fourth Century.

Among the recent heretics who adopt Papias' doctrine are the Mormons, the Irwingians and the Adventists.

The followers of this doctrine were called Chiliasts by the Greeks (believers in one thousand years), and *milliars* by Augustine[30] and the other Latin writers. We call them the *Millenarians.*

We would take no notice of this doctrine were it not that its adoption by Fathers of the Second and Third Centuries and by many Catholic people seems to impair the statement that the common consent of the Fathers in every century and the general belief of the Faithful is a rule of divine tradition. For it is well established that after the Third Century practically all the Fathers and the Faithful rejected it. Therefore, did the Fathers and the Faithful after the Third Century disagree with the Fathers and the Faithful of the Third and Second Centuries, were it even in the case of one single dogma?

30. *De Civit. Dei,* XX, 7.

Such was not the case. The belief in a Kingdom upon earth for a thousand years was not only rejected by the Fathers and the Faithful after the Third Century, but even in the Third and in the Second Centuries, *it was not* universal. But it was never condemned by the Church. St. Jerome writes: "Although we do not follow it, we cannot, however, condemn it, because many churchmen and martyrs believed it."[31] Cornelius a Lapide, Ribera, and others state that they do not dare to call it heresy.

That such a doctrine was not universal in the Second and Third Centuries is evident from the statements of the Fathers and other writers of the same period.

I. Justin himself, believing in and writing on that doctrine, says: "I have already informed you that such is my opinion and the opinion of many others . . . ; however, I have also told you that many other Christians . . . do not admit it."[32]

II. Irenæus, who took it from Papias, asserts that *those who do not believe* in the future Kingdom of Christ upon earth furnish heretics with the means of denying the Resurrection of the Dead. This is an admission on his part that in his time there were also many Christians who denied his opinion.

III. Origen, who lived in the Second and Third Centuries, openly condemned and combated Millenarianism.[33] It was mostly due to him that it disappeared gradually from the minds of Oriental Christians.

IV. When Nepos, Bishop of Arsenoe, introduced it into Egypt, many Christians who believed it and who afterwards became schismatics were not readmitted into the Church by St. Dionysius, the Bishop of Alexandria, unless

31. Jerome L. IV in Jer. 19, 10.
32. Justin, *Dial. cum Tryph.*, N. 80.
33. Origen, *De Princ.*, L. II, C. II, N. 2.

they first rejected that doctrine. This happened about the middle of the Third Century.

V. There is no record that the doctrine of the Millenarians was ever introduced in Rome. Rather, it was opposed. The Roman priest Caius, writing in the beginning of the Third Century against Cerinthus, not only condemns it, but ironically also says: "Cerinthus induces great wonders when he affirms the future Kingdom of Christ upon earth after the Resurrection, and the flesh again to serve concupiscence in Jerusalem!"[34]

VI. If we consider the origin of Millenarianism, we may observe that nearly all of its Catholic authors lived in or were in some way connected with Asia Minor. Papias, the first prominent Catholic to adopt it, was Bishop of Hierapolis, a city of the province of Phrygia, in Asia Minor; Justin held a dialogue about it with Tryphon in Ephesus, formerly a great city of Asia Minor; Irenæus was born and brought up in Asia Minor; Methodius was formerly bishop of Olympus in Lycia, another province of Asia Minor. These were the most prominent exponents of Millenarianism among Catholics in the first centuries of the Church. Tertullian defended that doctrine only after his defection from the Church. The works of Lactantius on this matter are considered *apochraphal,* that is, they are not related among the writings of the Fathers.

Papias is said to have received his doctrine from disciples of St. John the Evangelist, whom he had seen, heard and conversed with. Eusebius narrates how Papias misinterpreted the Apostolic accounts, which are not to be taken literally, but symbolically.[35]

Most of the Fathers and the Theologians of the Church

---

34. Caius, *In Euseb. H. E.* III, 28.
35. *Eusebius,* C. XXXIX.

since the Fourth Century interpret the text of the *Apocalypse,* on which the Millenarians based their belief, according to St. Augustine. In his *De Civitate Dei*—"*City of God*"—the holy Doctor takes the chapter as allegorical.

1. The number of one thousand years is intended to express the *plenitude of time* by a *perfect number,* that is, the time between the first advent of Christ and the seduction by Antichrist. 2. The binding of the devil means that the former dominion of Satan is broken—not absolutely, but so diminished that God may not permit him to tempt man above his forces because of Christ's grace. "But if I by the finger of God cast out devils, doubtless the kingdom of God is come upon you." (*Luke* 11:20). "Now is the judgment of the world; now shall the prince of this world be cast out." (*John* 12:31). 3. "*The souls of them that were beheaded . . . and lived and reigned with Christ a thousand years*" (*Apoc.* 20:4) are the souls of the Saints who, after Christ's death, reign with Him in Heaven until the advent of Antichrist; for this is the first resurrection, namely, the translation from the present to the heavenly life. Nor can it be properly said that *resurrection* belongs only to the souls that were beheaded, when it belongs rather to the body: "I believe in the resurrection of the body." 4. "*The rest of the dead lived not, till the thousand years were finished.*" (*Apoc.* 20:5). Sinners after their death are not allowed to enter Heaven until Christ's second advent, when "He shall come to judge the living and the dead," that is, until the second Resurrection—that of the just on the Last Day. Nor shall they enter Heaven *after* the coming of Christ, because on that day Christ will judge the living and the dead: "And they that have done good things, shall come forth unto the resurrection of life; but they that have done evil, unto the resurrection of judgment." (*John* 5:29).

There are, therefore, two resurrections: the first is the *resurrection of the souls,* that is, the translation of the souls of the blessed from this world into Heaven, mentioned in the *Apocalypse;* the second is the *Resurrection of the Body* on the Last Day. St. Augustine is to the point: "As there are two regenerations, one according to faith, which takes place now through Baptism; the other according to the flesh, which is effected in its incorruption and immortality on the Great and Last Day: so also there are two resurrections, the first, which exists now and belongs to the soul and does not permit [a person] to come to a second death; the other, which does not exist now, but which shall exist in the future and belongs not to the soul but to the body, and which through the Last Judgment will send some to a second death and some into that life which has no death."[36]

In any case, the Kingdom of Christ of which the *Apocalypse* speaks can only be applied to the Church.

Millenarianism was then practically confined to Asia Minor. Comparatively few Catholics followed it. If some of the Fathers believed it, others rejected it. There was never a common consent of the Fathers or of the Faithful. It was an opinion. The Church neither condemned it, nor approved of it. And it was never regarded as an article of faith based on Apostolic traditions.

Since the Fourth Century, all the Fathers of the Church and the vast majority of the Catholic Faithful discarded Papias' doctrine. Nowadays, it is restricted only to Adventists and Mormons.

---

36. August., *De Civ. Dei,* C. VI, N. 2.

11

The Intellect of the Church

1

The Catholic Church is the Subject of Divine Tradition; the Deposit of Faith is the Object.

TO GET an intimate notion of Tradition, we shall consider the terms by which the Fathers—writing not under the inspiration, but under the assistance of the Holy Ghost—called the Universal Doctrine of the Faith: They speak of the "Rule of Faith," the "Ecclesiastical Preaching," the "Catholic Intellect," the "Ecclesiastical Sense." These are only some of the beautiful and expressive names.

St. Ignatius, disciple of St. John the Evangelist, warns his people to be all "of one mind in the *Sentence* of God"—that is, in the doctrine of God—"for Jesus Christ, our inseparable Life, is the Sentence (the Doctrine, the Word) of the Father, as are also the bishops throughout the whole world constituted in the Sentence of Jesus Christ."[1] The word *Sentence* means unanimity and union of the Faithful with their bishops, as these are united in doctrine with Jesus Christ.

Irenæus, speaking of the Universal Doctrine which came to us through the Apostolic Succession and which was transmitted to the first Christians in the Apostolic Sym-

---

1. *Ignat. ad Ephes.,* N. 3.

bol [Apostle's Creed], calls it the *"immovable rule of truth,"*[2] by which heresies and false interpretations of the Scriptures are always discerned. He also calls it the "Church Preaching, everywhere constant and equally persevering";[3] the "true and firm Church preaching";[4] the *"Præconium* ["Proclamation"] of the Church, which the Prophets foretold, Christ perfected, and the Apostles delivered, from whom the Church received it. She alone kept it well through the whole world, transmitting it to her children."[5]

Tertullian calls Tradition "the only Rule of Faith"[6]—"the Rule which the Church received from the Apostles, the Apostles from Christ, Christ from God."[7]

Clement of Alexandria names it "the Ecclesiastical Rule" according to which the Scriptures must be understood. He also terms it "the non-written of the written Tradition."[8]

Origen, in the Preface of his book *De Principiis* [*Concerning First Things*], declares the *"Ecclesiastical Preaching* delivered by the Apostles through the order of succession and lasting to the present time"[9] as the only course according to which all doctrine must be conformed. In his Commentary on the 36th *Psalm,* he also christens it "the Apostolic Rule of Truth."[10]

The author of the ancient book bearing the name of *Little Labyrinth* names Tradition the "Ecclesiastical Sense and the Rule of the Primitive Faith."[11]

---

2. Iren. L. I, C. IX, N. 4.
3. Iren. L. III, C. XXIV, N. 1.
4. Iren. L. V, C. XX, N. 1.
5. Iren. L. V, Praef.
6. Tertull., *De Vel. Virg.,* C. I.
7. Tertull., "Prescript," C. XXXVII.
8. See Strom. VI, pp. 645-679.
9. Origen, *De Princip.,* praef.
10. Origen, *Commentar.,* Ps. 36. Hom. 4, N. 1.
11. In Euseb., H. E. L., IV, C. XXVIII.

Likewise, the universal doctrine by which the Church and the Bishops are animated, molded and apprised is called by Athanasius the "Intellect by which we think";[12] by Hilary the "Conscience of Faith," which he opposes to the *"wicked intelligence"* of heretics;[13] by Augustine, the "Rule of Faith,"[14] the "Rule of Piety,"[15] the "Canonical Sense" and "the Catholic Intellect."[16]

All these titles are easily divided into two classes, as is evident from their meaning: When they convey the idea of *intelligence* or *conscience* in the Teaching Church under the charism of the Holy Ghost, they mean that "Divine Tradition" which animates, apprises and acquaints the Church with the necessary knowledge to understand, keep and explain the Deposit of Faith. *In this sense, the subject* which is imbued, apprised and molded by Tradition is the Teaching Church—called with the names of "Catholic Intellect," "Conscience of Faith," "Ecclesiastical Sense," "Ecclesiastical Intelligence." All other titles, designating the *Deposit of Faith*—which is kept, explained and delivered *by the same Teaching Church*—signify that "Divine Tradition" which is the object of our Faith and which must be kept and explained by the Teaching Church. Hence it is termed the "Ecclesiastical Preaching," the "Rule of Piety," "the Rule of Apostolic Truth," the "Rule of Faith," etc.

All the above phrases, however, do not constitute two different things. They refer to the same thing: *"Tradition,"* considered either as the *object* delivered, or *the manner of delivery.* St. Vincent of Lerin, after he asserts that Faith

---

12. Athanas., *Orat,* 2, C. Arian., N. 34.
13. Hilar., *De Trinit.,* L. VIII, C. I.
14. August., *In Johan.,* Tract. 18, N. 1.
15. August., *Genes,* C. XXI, N. 41.
16. August., *Serm. 294,* C. XX.

must be safeguarded, "first by the authority of the Divine Law (the Scriptures), and then by the *Tradition of the Catholic Church,"* immediately adds, "Here perhaps some one will ask: if the Canon of the Scriptures is perfect and is always sufficient to itself for everything, of what use is it to join authority to *ecclesiastical intelligence?"* He answers that, on account of difficulties and the many interpretations by which the Scriptures are explained, it is necessary that "the method of prophetical and Apostolic interpretation be directed according to the *Rule of the Ecclesiastical* and Catholic Sense."[17]

Not without reason have we enumerated these different titles. The Church, animated by Divine Tradition, is the *subject.* This Church is informed and assisted by the Holy Ghost to interpret and teach the Deposit of Faith. This Deposit is the *object* of our belief. There is therefore a *subject* and an *object* in Tradition. The subject is the Church. The object is the Deposit of Faith. The "Catholic Intellect," the "Ecclesiastical Intelligence or Sense," the "Conscience of Faith" refer to the subject. The "Church Preaching," the "Rule of Faith," the "Rule of Truth" show the object of our belief. The "subject" and the "object" of Tradition of necessity go together. They are like *matter and form.*

Hence the error of Protestants: By rejecting the authority of the Church, they have rejected the subject of Divine Tradition, which is the Teaching Church, and kept only the *object,* or rather, a part of the object of Revelation.

Even if the Scriptures were the only object of Faith, rejecting the authority of the Church is an error. It would always be true that there is no "subject" to understand, interpret, keep and teach them truly. In the rejection of

17. Vincent of Lerin, *Commonit.,* CC. I-II.

authority, they have eliminated the "Catholic Intellect," the "Ecclesiastical Intelligence," the "Conscience of Faith"—in effect, the "subject" of Divine Tradition. They have taken the heart out of the Scriptures and rendered them a dead body—without intelligence, certitude or life. To substitute "Private Judgment" for the Church as the "subject" of Divine Revelation is to destroy the subject. But they no longer take it [the subject of Divine Tradition, i.e., the Church] seriously. Actually, they form creeds, symbols and synods to supersede "Private Judgment." Those creeds, symbols or synods are *their* "ecclesiastical sense," *their* "conscience of faith." Whoever does not conform to one of those forms is brought to trial, and if he persists in his "private judgment" of the Scriptures, he may be summarily expelled. In other words, *"their creed,"* not "Private Judgment," is their subject of *Revelation—their* "ecclesiastical intelligence," *their* "catholic intellect," *their* "conscience of faith." But was it not on account of the "Ecclesiastical Intelligence," the "Conscience of Faith," the "Catholic Intellect"—that is, on account of the Authority of the Catholic Church—that their forefathers *left* the Church? Why return to the first principle? Or if they do return, why not do so completely and come back to the Catholic Church?

2

The "Catholic Intellect," Instructing and Moving the Church in her Solemn Definitions, or Manifesting Itself in the Consent of the Apostolic Succession Under the Assistance of the Holy Ghost, is the Infallible Interpreter of Scripture.

It is the "Catholic Intellect" that, under the assistance of the Holy Ghost, directs the Church in an infallible manner. When we affirm with Irenæus that the Church is in possession of what may be called a "Depository of Truth," when we assert that the Church is the infallible custodian of the Deposit of Faith, we certainly do not limit her possession and guardianship to its material part. It must be extended to what is therein contained for the preservation and transmission of the "discipline by which we are made Christians."[18]

This is the reason why the Fathers speak so brilliantly of the "Catholic Intellect," "Conscience of Faith" and "Catholic Sense." The real and principal Tradition is the conservation and propagation of that genuine intelligence of the revealed truths, through the common consent of the Apostolic Succession, under the special assistance of the Holy Ghost. This is Divine Tradition.

Since the Church is in possession of the Deposit of Faith, of which the Scriptures are the most important part, it follows that it is the Holy Ghost who keeps forever in the Church, not only the material part of the Scriptures, but also the "Catholic Understanding." For in order that the Church may render an authentic and infallible judgment on these Scriptures, her guardianship must not be limited to mere words and forms. It must include whatever sense those words and forms have, their true sense and their genuine intellect. Instructed by that "Intellect," the Church is the infallible interpreter of the Scriptures, although the cause of her infallibility is ultimately attributed to the assistance of the Holy Ghost.

This is evident from the conservation of the universal doctrine of the Faith through the consent and unity of the Apostolic Succession, under the assistance of the Holy Ghost. Such consent or unity in doctrine excludes dis-

18. Tertullian.

agreement. This can only exist among private persons. Hence, it is only the ministry instituted by Christ to be under the guidance and assistance of the Holy Ghost which has the right and power to interpret the Scriptures infallibly. Whatever is its interpretation, that interpretation is true. It is derived from the Spirit of Truth, who does not let that ministry fall into error. "No prophecy of scripture is made by private interpretation," says the Prince of the Apostles, "for prophecy came not by the will of man at any time; but the holy men of God spoke, inspired by the Holy Ghost." (*2 Ptr.* 1:20-21).

Therefore, God, not man, has the right and the power to interpret His words. This He does through the "Catholic Intellect" of that ministry which Christ instituted in the Church. For "Catholic Intellect"—it must not be forgotten—is the antithesis of "Private Interpretation," for the reason that Private Interpretation, as the very name implies, is opposed to "Catholic Interpretation," which emanates from the "Catholic Intellect," or more plainly, from that "Universal Intellect" under the assistance of the Holy Ghost. It is therefore the "Catholic Intellect" and the "Catholic Intellect" alone which, under the assistance of the Holy Spirit, enables the Church to declare infallibly which is the true sense of the Scriptures.

By rejecting the infallible authority of the Church, Protestantism has had recourse to "Private Interpretation" and has established human means that have only the semblance of churches.

Tertullian is to the point: "Now, who knows better the flower of the Scriptures than the very same School of Christ? Those disciples whom He adopted to Himself to know all and, as our Masters, to teach us all?"[19]

---

19. Tertull., *Ad Scop.*, C. XII.

The words of St. Jerome, written in the Fourth Century, seem to be addressed to all the Protestant churches of today. After having related that the eunuch did not understand the Scripture, although he had carefully read it, but that he understood it after God sent Philip to interpret it for him, the holy Doctor says: "I have briefly written this that you may understand that without anyone showing you the way, you cannot understand the Holy Scriptures. . . . I make no mention of the grammarians, rhetoricians, philosophers and Doctors. . . . I only mention some artists, who work with their own hands. . . . Peasants, cement mixers, blacksmiths, metal and wood cutters . . . all those who are engaged in trivial and low work cannot accomplish without a master what they wish to make. 'Doctors promise, blacksmiths handle their tools,' as Horace says. (L. 1. ep. 1.). The Scriptures are the only one art which everyone claims to himself. 'Whether we are learned or unlearned, we all write poetry,' as the same Horace says. (L. 1. ep. 1). The loquacious blubberer, the delirious old man, the verbose sophist, all presume, rage, teach before they learn."[20]

Private interpretation of the Scriptures should therefore be condemned. St. Peter himself gives the reason for this condemnation, that is, because they are *divinely* inspired.

When we declare, however, that private interpretation of the Scriptures should be rejected, we do not mean that the Church is the supreme judge of the Scriptures and of Tradition in the sense that she possesses in herself a higher authority than either the Scriptures or the monuments of Tradition. This is a calumny of her enemies. The word of God, which is contained in the Scriptures or in Tradition, is above all. It is in itself a supreme authority. It is the

---

20. Jerome Epist. 53, N. 6, 7.

word of the Infinite Truth. Hence it is the supreme Rule of Faith in the Church. The Church simply discerns which is and which is not the word of God. She gives the right interpretation to what she decides is truly the word of God and what God thereby commands. Was it not the Church of the first centuries that discerned *"what and what not"* must be the Scriptures? This is a result of the "Catholic Intellect" under the assistance of the Holy Ghost. The Church does not judge the word of God. She discerns the true interpretation from the false. She kept and she keeps what is true. The word of God directs the Church. For, the word of God will always be true. Christ says: "Heaven and earth shall pass away, but my words shall not pass away." (*Luke* 21:33).

The Church, therefore, does not claim to be superior to or the judge of the word of God. She is rather directed by the word of God and is subject to it. Having the word of God as her richest inheritance, she explains it to the Faithful and demands from them absolute consent to her infallible interpretation. The Church is not above the Scriptures. But she is above the private and fallible intelligence of the individual.

3

The Authentic Interpretation of the Church on Any Scriptural Texts is the Supreme "Rule of Intelligence," Which Must Simply be Followed.

When the supreme authority of the Church issues a decree declaring its purpose to determine the sense of a Scriptural text, this definition is without doubt the true sense which the Holy Ghost intended to convey in that part of Scripture. It is then the Pope who speaks *ex cathedra.*

There are many texts whose genuine sense the Church

has declared and defined by its authentic interpretation. Such are the following: "I and the Father are one," (*John* 10:30); "Going therefore, teach ye all nations, baptizing them in the name of the Father and of the Son and of the Holy Ghost," (*Matt.* 28:19); "Is any man sick among you? Let him bring in the priests of the church, and let them pray over him, anointing him with oil in the name of the Lord. And the prayer of faith shall save the sick man; and the Lord shall raise him up; and if he be in sins, they shall be forgiven him," (*James* 5:14-15); "Amen, amen I say to thee, unless a man be born again of water and the Holy Ghost, he cannot enter into the Kingdom of God," (*John* 3:5); "Whose sins you shall forgive, they are forgiven them; and whose sins you shall retain, they are retained." (*John* 20:23). These and many others passages have been interpreted, declared and explained by Roman Pontiffs and by the Councils of the Church. Their judgment is the fruit and the result of that "Catholic Intellect," under the assistance of the Holy Ghost, which animates, informs and moves the Church to act. This judgment or definition, being infallible, must therefore be simply accepted as the only "Rule of Intelligence" by which we can understand and know the sense of a certain text. Hence, all other auxiliary means assumed from philology, archeology, grammar, context, aim of the author and all other instruments of interpretation must be subordinated and conformed to it. If they are so directed, they will show that the sense declared by the Church is also scientifically true. Consequently, if through any human or scientific means we reach a different sense than the one of which we are made certain of through the authority of the Church, we should admit the fallacy of our own interpretation, either because of the improper use or of the insufficiency of the means at our disposal. Something is wanting or not properly applied.

Since the "Catholic Intellect" may become known to us, not only through the supreme authority of the Church, but also through the unanimous consent of the Fathers and Doctors, such consent—in a dogmatic interpretation of a Scriptural text or law pertaining to morals—leads us unmistakably to the truth. But the definition rendered already by the Church may be easier to our understanding or more openly indicated.

This has been declared by the Council of Trent: "With regard to matters of faith and morals belonging to the upbuilding of Christian doctrine, no one, confiding in his own prudence, should dare to bend to his own sense the Sacred Scriptures against that sense which our Holy Mother the Church always held and holds, to whom belongs the right to judge the true sense and the interpretation of the Holy Scriptures, or also against the unanimous consent of the Fathers."[21] The Council only confirmed what had always been held and understood as a matter of course throughout the centuries. The historian of the Council, Pallavicini, speaking about the above decree, affirms: "The Council did not state anything new, nor did it intend to impose any new obligation. It simply wanted to teach and confirm the obligation already existing which our faith effects of its own nature."[22]

However, although the mind of the Church is very clear on this point, some recent interpreters of Scripture did not fail to bend to their own erroneous sense what the Church always held and holds. They said that the decree of the Council of Trent was only disciplinary and that it was issued simply on account of the circumstances which

21. Session IV.
22. Pallavicini H. C. Trid. L. VII, C. XVIII, N. 3-6.

prevailed in those times of revolt against the Church; hence, it was only a precautionary measure; that is, it does not have absolute value for all times. These opinions were condemned. The Vatican Council [Vatican I, 1869-1870] renewed and gave more force to the decree of the Council of Trent in these words: "In all things of faith and morals belonging to the upbuilding of Christian doctrine, that sense must be regarded as the true sense of the Scriptures which our Holy Mother the Church held and holds, to whom belongs the right to judge of the true sense and interpretation of the Holy Scriptures. Hence, no one is allowed to interpret a Scriptural text against that sense, or also against the unanimous consent of the Fathers."[23] Such sense, or "Rule of Intelligence," formed by the "intellect" of our Holy Mother the Church, must simply be followed.

Neither the Council of Trent nor the [First] Vatican Council intends to forbid all interpretations, only those which amount to a denial and rejection of the sense which is already rendered by the Church or manifested in the unanimous consent of the Fathers. That sense belongs already to the Faith. The Church allows full liberty to the interpreters of Scripture in their efforts to improve the morality and knowledge of the Faithful, or to investigate the difficult and subtle passages without detriment to the Faith.

The Church is only solicitous that all the Faithful—learned and unlearned—accept and believe the sense which she has declared as the true sense of the Scriptures because her interpretation is the supreme "Rule of Intelligence."

---

23. Vatican Council, Sess. 3, C. I.

4

The Authentic Interpretation of the Church is a "Rule of Intelligence" in a *Negative* and an *Affirmative* Sense. If the Church has not Specifically Set Forth Any Authentic Interpretation, She is the "Supreme Canon of Interpretation" in a *Negative* Sense.

I. Whenever the Church declares the true sense of certain Scriptural texts, whether through her solemn definition or through the unanimous consent of her "pastors and doctors," her interpretation is not only in itself a "Rule of Intelligence," it is also a "Rule" which has both a *negative* and an *affirmative* sense.

By *negative* sense, we understand that *no one is allowed to give any Scriptural text a sense,* opposed to the one which the Church has announced.

By *affirmative* sense, we mean that *we must hold as true and revealed the sense* which the Church has given.

The definition not only declares a certain Scriptural text as true and revealed, and in what sense it must be taken, but also in what sense it must *not* be taken. It is for this reason that the Church is infallible—to keep us from error and to explain Tradition. And of this the Sacred Scriptures are the principal part.

The decree of Session IV of the Council of Trent (1545-1563) that "No one, confiding in his own prudence, should dare to bend to his own sense the Sacred Scriptures against the sense which our Holy Mother the Church always held and holds" contains in itself these two senses: one is *negative* and the other is *affirmative.* No one should dare to interpret the Scriptures in a sense repugnant to the sense declared by the Church—behold the *negative* sense. The sense which the Church gives to any Scriptural text must be accepted and believed as the sense which the Holy Ghost intended to convey through the inspired writers—behold the *affirmative* sense.

When the Church does not pronounce on a text, she is the supreme *"Canon of interpretation"* in a *"negative sense"*; that is, no interpretation of the Scriptures can be true when it gives a Scriptural text—declared by the inspired author—a sense repugnant to the proximate Rule of Faith. Truth cannot contradict truth; that is, again, when the Church has not yet defined or declared any determined *Scriptural text*—making *de fide* [of Faith] what is *proximum fidei,* [nearly of Faith]—the understanding or Intellect of the Church is the "Canon of interpretation" *in a negative* sense, from which it is dangerous to depart.

The Profession of Faith prescribed by Pius IV affirms: "I admit the Sacred Scripture, according to that sense which our Holy Mother the Church held and holds, to whom belongs the right to judge about the true sense and interpretation of the Holy Scriptures, nor will I ever accept or interpret it against the unanimous consent of the Fathers."

For this reason the Church proscribed [prohibited, denounced] the opinion of certain Modernists who asserted that the Church does not forbid us to give a different interpretation, nor to deny even the sense which she gives to any Scriptural texts, provided that we do not infer any doctrine contrary to the Catholic Faith. When the Church, they assert, interprets the text in (*James* 5:14-15) as proof for the institution of the Sacrament of Extreme Unction, we are free to deny that such sense is contained in that text, so long as we do not deny the above dogma, namely, that Extreme Unction is one of the Sacraments of the New Law. This view cannot be held.

5

In any Scriptural Doctrine the "Catholic Intellect" Helps and Leads to the Truth in a *Positive* Way.

Not every part of Sacred Scripture has been defined. There are many difficult places in Scripture—as well as many doctrines believed by the Faithful—on which the Roman Pontiffs and the General Councils of the Church have never pronounced. In these cases, we must always have recourse to the "Catholic Intellect," or the "Conscience of Faith" of the Universal Church, as the "Canon of Interpretation."

When a text is not clear, taken by itself, but we know that it refers to a special doctrine which is believed, professed or practiced in the Church, we must presume that, if the text is obscure to us, it was clear enough to the first Christians, to whom it was first addressed. The holy writer *presupposed* in his readers a fuller knowledge of the doctrine about which he wrote to them. The Scriptures of the New Testament were generally written to Christians who had already received the Faith *through the preaching* of the Apostles. Hence, what the Apostles wrote was intended to be only a help or a fuller explanation of what their hearers had learned through their preaching. Naturally, the Apostles added in their writings certain admonitions, councils and expositions which could not be rightly understood unless their readers were supposed to be already acquainted with certain doctrines which belonged to the Faith. This is evident from the warning of the Apostle to the Faithful to remain in that Faith which they had heard and received. "Now I beseech you . . . to mark them who make dissensions and offenses contrary *to the doctrine which you have learned,* and avoid them." (*Rom.* 16:17). "For *you know* what precepts I have given to you by the Lord Jesus." (1 *Thess.* 4:2).

This supposition on the part of the writers refers to that fuller knowledge which the first Christians possessed through the preaching of the Apostles—knowledge which *formed forever* the "Catholic Intellect" of the Church.

It was in view of this fuller knowledge that, speaking on the love which the husband owes his wife, the Apostle could exclaim: "This is a great sacrament, but I speak in Christ and in the church." (*Eph.* 5:32). The "Catholic Intellect" here understands the Apostle to speak of a true Sacrament. The same Apostle had already preached to the Ephesians that marriage among Christians is a Sacrament. Such an "understanding or intellect" remains in the Church to the present day.

It likewise perceives the indelible sacramental character in his words to the Corinthians: "He that confirmeth us with you in Christ, and that hath anointed us, is God: who also hath sealed us, and given the pledge of the Spirit in our hearts." (*2 Cor.* 1:21-22). We can hardly prove from Scripture the indelible character which three of the Sacraments produce in our souls. Led, however, by the "Catholic Intellect," we can demonstrate that the impression of an indelible character is sufficiently contained in these words. The "Catholic Intellect," imbued by the preaching of the Apostles, has always remained in the Church. It was always understood and believed, as it is today, that the Sacraments of Baptism, Confirmation, and Holy Orders produce this indelible character.

By the same reasoning, we prove the power of the Church to grant Indulgences and to forgive sins: "And I will give to thee the keys of the kingdom of heaven. And whatsoever thou shalt bind upon earth, it shall be bound also in heaven; and whatsoever thou shalt loose on earth, it shall be loosed also in heaven." (*Matt.* 16:19).

Who could ever prove from the Scriptures only that Extreme Unction is a Sacrament? The words of the Apostle James evidently have reference to that Sacrament. (*James* 5:14-15). But it is only through the "Catholic Intellect" that we believe Extreme Unction to be one of the Sacraments of the New Law.

One more example: "And the angel being come in, said unto her: Hail, full of grace, the Lord is with thee," (*Luke* 1:28), explains, proves and confirms God's privilege to Mary in her conception.

The authors, inspired by the Holy Ghost, taught truths in words which they afterwards mentioned in the Scriptures, though not in the same words as we use to explain Indulgences, Confession, Immaculate Conception, Confirmation, Ordination, Extreme Unction and so forth; nevertheless, they were intelligible to their hearers. They possessed a more intimate knowledge through the preaching of the Apostles. It was exactly this intimate knowledge of the first Christians which remains in the Church today. It forms that "Conscience of Faith," that "Catholic Intellect" which, under the assistance of the Holy Ghost, enables the Church to discern the true sense of the Scriptures.

For this same reason, Augustine, speaking on the validity of Baptism administered by heretics, declares: "We would never dare to assert such a thing were it not that we have for it the authority of the Church."[24] Sustained by this authority, he showed the fallacy of certain interpretations offered by St. Cyprian and other Catholics before the definition of the Church—and afterwards by the Donatists—against the validity of Baptism administered by heretics. He also proved from the Scriptures themselves its validity through the *help of Tradition.* The Church

24. August., *De Bapt.* L. II, C. IV.

never administered second Baptism to the same person, although the first was conferred by a heretic.

If, reading the Sacred Scriptures, we are inclined to think differently from the Church, we must rather confess our ignorance, because, as the same Augustine warns us on this point, "Not getting to know what the writer meant is one thing. To deviate from the Rule of piety is another."[25]

The "Catholic Intellect," therefore, helps and leads us in a *positive* way to the finding and the confirmation of truths contained in the Sacred Scriptures.

6

The "Catholic Intellect" is Not an Obstacle to a Progressive and Fuller Knowledge of the Scriptures.

It is impossible for everyone to be so familiar with Scripture as not only to read and study it, but also to be sure of its completeness, veracity and interpretation without an infallible authority.

This authority, however, is considered by our Separated Brethren as an obstacle to progress and to a fuller knowledge of the Scriptures. They say our reasoning is limited or restricted by such authority. By this they mean that there can be no room for exegesis, namely, for a scientific interpretation of the Scriptures.

This is a pitiable error. They fail to realize that, in any investigation, what counts is to find out the truth and nothing but the truth. That is the aim of our research. Hence, if for some reason or other we are not sure of the truth, we should never throw any doubt on the truth. Now the cause which can make us sure of the true sense of

25. August., *Genes. ad litt.,* I, C. XXI, N. 41

difficult texts of the Scriptures can only be an infallible authority. Such an authority may be compared to a safe and easy short-cut that leads unmistakably to our goal. All other expedients are only worthy of their origin, the human intellect, circling a long way in its frail efforts and losing itself in a labyrinth of systems and opinions. The result is doubt and more doubt.

Since Catholics believe in an infallible authority as an Article of Faith and have no doubt about it, the definitions of the Church cannot be but true, because truth cannot contradict truth. What is better than to believe in an infallible authority which cannot deceive nor be deceived? What is greater than to receive both Scripture and Tradition from a Church which—whether some like to hear it or not—saved both from oblivion and total destruction? What is safer than to accept from the same infallible authority the sense of the Scriptures, knowing well that any other sense opposed to it cannot be the true sense?

Faith and knowledge based on an infallible authority can never retard, obstruct or impede. Rather, they help immensely a scientific inquisition about the true sense of the Scriptures. In any scientific investigation, there is nothing more useful than to know *what cannot be true*—hence, what errors must be avoided in order to set out on the right way and consequently to strengthen the inquisition with the right arguments.

It is thus that the Catholic interpreter of the Scriptures is far superior, safer and more certain in his view than his Protestant adversary, who is hampered by a double error.

The *first error* is *dogmatic.* He does not believe in an infallible Church. He asserts that her solemn judgment is only an opinion, to be examined and judged by everyone. If it seems to him to harmonize with the doctrine of the

Scriptures, he accepts it. If not, he rejects it.

We have already shown how inconsistent and unhistorical is such a position. It will be enough to say here that, if only a human opinion is produced from a text of the Scriptures, and on the one hand, it is said that such an opinion must be examined and judged by the same Scriptures to find out if it is true or not, while on the other hand, that same opinion proposes the Scriptures as the only Rule, according to which everyone must interpret the Scriptures, it is an argument in a circle and leads nowhere. It is like the case of the poor fish that jumps out of the gridiron into the fire. Having rejected the divine authority of the Church as an unbearable yoke, they have assumed unto themselves a human authority, which slowly but surely is destroying those human churches which they built, not on the rock of Christ, but on the sand of human frailty.

On the contrary, admitting the infallible authority of the Church—which proclaims the Scriptures not only as the word of God, but also *in what sense that word must or must not be taken*—such authority cannot be an intolerable yoke. It is a natural, consequent obligation. It comes from the Constitution of the Church and is a happy guide to reject and refute falsehood, to embrace and defend the truth.

The *other error* is *scientific*. The non-Catholic interpreter fails to discern that, to know through an infallible authority *in what sense the Scriptures must or must not be taken* is one thing, and to perceive the reason *why* and *how* the sense given to the Scriptures is genuine and true, is entirely a different proposition. This latter is indeed the fruit of scientific interpretation, which the Church not only does not condemn, but approves, encourages and promotes in exegesis and in theology. The same principle evidently applies to all other subjects of Tradition.

There is still another opinion on this subject which has been condemned by the Church. It is the error of certain Catholic theologians who claimed that the interpreter of Sacred Scripture should begin his investigation with an unprejudiced mind, totally indifferent to all dogmas and losing all sight of what the Church might have pronounced on the subject under investigation. This means that the interpreter should not suppose any certitude of Faith, being entirely ignorant as to what conclusion his investigation may lead him. This opinion was rightly condemned because it amounts to nothing other than an examination of Revelation and of Faith with a positive doubt of the truth that is already a part of the Catholic Faith.

12

The Relation of Tradition To Scripture

1

In its Relation to Scripture, Tradition Comes First *Chronologically.*

THE Church, in certain respects, began with the first human family. And Tradition began with the Church. It is not, therefore, inaccurate to assert that Tradition had its beginning with the appearance of the first man and woman upon this earth.

In the first centuries, man's life was interwoven with so many vicissitudes and the material means of preserving history were so scant that it seems hardly possible that one, however inspired, could have ever related in writing even the principal facts of man's first relations with God.

But, as the Evangelist St. John at the end of his Gospel could say of Christ, the second Adam, "There are also many other things which Jesus did; which, if they were written every one, the world itself, I think, would not be able to contain the books that should be written," (*John* 21:25); so also Moses, the first inspired author, without any doubt could have related about the first Adam and his descendants many other things which he did not write. As the Evangelist, according to his testimony, wrote only the outlines of Christ's life and doings, in like manner

Moses merely gave the outlines of Creation and of man's first dealings with the Deity.

However, on account of the *long* but *few* generations of the Patriarchs, the world at the time of Moses was still fresh with the memories of the events which happened to the first man and his descendants. Hence, historically speaking, it could not be too difficult for him to give them to us. He wrote what God inspired him to write, as the Apostles wrote whatever God wanted them to write—not more and not less. Whatever he wrote, it was from Tradition. Tradition, considered in its strict sense, therefore, existed before the Old Law was ever written. Moses incorporated in the Law those traditions and promises, which God had made to Adam and the other Patriarchs. "He wrote them," as Suarez says, "not as new, but as ancient."[1]

After Moses came the Prophets, who in the course of time, augmented Revelation. The last inspired writer [of the Old Testament] was Malachias, who flourished four hundred years before Christ. They all explained the Law and delivered God's message to His people. Then came the Apostles who, after preaching the Religion of Christ, began to write the New Testament as the occasion demanded. They preached first and wrote the New Testament afterwards, because "all scripture, inspired of God, is profitable to teach, to reprove, to correct, to instruct in justice." (*2 Tim.* 3:16).

Therefore, we speak here of Tradition taken in its proper signification, compared to the written Revelation, that is, to the Scriptures. It is in this sense that the Fathers and the Theologians of the Church distinguish Revelation. Irenæus in the Second Century had this to say: "What then if the Apostles did not leave us the Scriptures? Had we

1. Suarez, *De Leg.*, L. IX, C. VI.

not then to follow the order of Tradition which they delivered to those to whom they committed the Churches? To such order assent many foreign peoples . . . without books and ink, having what belongs to salvation written in their hearts, and keeping faithfully the ancient Tradition."[2]

All this shows that Tradition, properly so-called, preceded the Scriptures in the order of time.

This, however, does not necessarily mean that Revelation was first completed and propagated by Tradition and afterwards consigned to the Scriptures. For before all Revelation came to an end, many parts of the Scriptures were already in existence, to which Christ and the Apostles appealed quite frequently. Nor does our proposition mean that every part of Tradition was preached before it was written, in order to become afterwards a part of the Scriptures. Many traditions never became a part of the Scriptures. On the other hand, we know that Revelation was sometimes consigned directly to the Scriptures. The *Psalms,* the moral and historical books, the *Apocalypse* and other parts of Scripture were written and made directly, only through the Scriptures.

The sense, therefore, is this: Revelation was made first to the Old Patriarchs without the help of the Scriptures. It was *kept only by Tradition* until the time of Moses, the first inspired writer. Tradition, therefore, preceded even the Books of the Old Testament in the order of time.

The same may be said of many parts of the writings of the Prophets, but especially of most of the New Testament. The Apostles preached first whatever they wrote afterwards, as a supplement to or explanation of their preaching.

There is more. The Revelation which God made to the

---

2. Iren. L. III, C. XIV.

Old Patriarchs and which was kept only by Tradition until Moses, contained *substantially* all the *subsequent* revelations, both through the Scriptures and without them. Whatever was in the course of time revealed to the Prophets and the Apostles was contained implicitly in the first revelations of God to the Patriarchs. Whatever the Prophets and the Apostles announced in both Testaments was an explanation, an enlargement and a completion of the Revelation made to the Patriarchs. Such was, for example, the revelation to the Patriarchs of a future Redeemer. It contained implicitly the faith in Christ's Incarnation, Passion, Death and Resurrection.[3] We may therefore say that all the articles of our Faith were kept for a long time substantially by Tradition only.

For more than two thousand years, Revelation was passed by word of mouth, from father to son, from one generation to the other. In the year 2369, after the creation of the first human family, Moses began to write the word of God, giving a brief account from Adam to his own times.

Later on, God called other men to be his ambassadors. Last but not least came the Apostles, who announced to the world that the Redeemer, promised to the Old Patriarchs, had already come, establishing a Religion which is the fulfillment of the Old Law. They preached for several years before they wrote any part of the New Testament. They wrote only as circumstances arose, to confirm and explain certain truths which they had already preached, in order to strengthen the faith of the followers of Christ.

For this reason, we may state that the Revelation to the Old Patriarchs—that is, Tradition in the strict sense of the word—was like a fundamental beginning, which the

3. See. St. Thomas II-II *ae* Q. I, A. 7.

Prophets developed and the Apostles enlarged, explained and completed.

2

According to the Order Established by Christ, No One Can Have a True Christian Knowledge of The Scriptures without Divine Tradition. Tradition thus Precedes the Scriptures Historically and Theologically.

Not only the average non-Catholic, but also the Protestant divines, fail to distinguish Tradition considered *historically* from Tradition considered *theologically.* Tradition considered historically is the foundation of critical and philosophical demonstration. Tradition considered theologically is a doctrine truly religious and divine. St. Peter, the Prince of the Apostles, is to the point: "Understanding this first, that no prophecy* of scripture is made by private interpretation. For prophecy came not by the will of man at any time, but the holy men of God spoke, inspired by the Holy Ghost." (*2 Ptr.* 1:20-21).

To this double distinction we must also add another distinction, namely, the *knowledge about the Scriptures* and the *knowledge contained in the Scriptures.* To the *knowledge about* the Scriptures belong their *genuineness, veracity, integrity* and *inspiration.* To the *knowledge contained in the Scriptures* belongs whatever doctrine or truth is contained in the Scriptures.

By *genuineness* we mean the origin of the writings from the authors to whom we attribute them.

By *veracity,* the conformity with the truth.

---

* "Prophecy," in the broad connotation of the word, means "interpretation or explanation of religious truth," rather than "prediction of future events," which is its narrow connotation. —*Publisher,* 2005.

By *integrity,* the completeness, if not of every text, at least of the work in general.

By *inspiration,* the supernatural, divine influence on the sacred writers by which they were enabled and qualified to communicate the truth without error.

Tradition, *historically* considered, comes before the Scriptures. Before one begins to study or meditate on the Scriptures, he must be sure of their genuineness, veracity and integrity.

Tradition, *theologically* considered, precedes the Scriptures. No one can know *with certitude* the doctrines *contained in Scripture* as truthful and divinely inspired without the institution established by Christ—[and no one can know] Divine Tradition, in other words, without the Church.

Here it will be well to repeat what Tertullian said eighteen hundred years ago: "The order of things requires in the first place [to know] to whom belongs the Faith itself. Whose are the Scriptures? By whom, and through whom, and when, and to whom was the authority to teach delivered, by whom men are made Christians? For where the true Christian discipline and doctrine are shown to be, there also will be the truths of the Scriptures and of their interpretation and of all Christian Traditions."[4]

I. With regard to the *knowledge about* the Scriptures, *historically* considered, strictly speaking, we can through human study and research find out the genuineness, veracity and integrity of the books of Scripture, just as we can prove with the same method the genuineness, veracity and integrity, for example, of the History of Livy or of Tacitus. This is a merely historical tradition. But a) this cannot be said of all the scriptural texts; b) nor can it be done by all the Faithful, because not all are able to learn or

4. Tertull., "Prescript.," C. XX.

investigate the truth; c) nor with that historical certainty and security which dispel all doubt whatsoever. Even granted such *historical knowledge,* we say that *inspiration* may also be proved from certain places of the same Scriptures, but with the above mentioned triple limitation, a) not of all the texts, because not every book of the Scriptures makes such mention; b) not by all the Faithful, because in the Church of Christ there will always be teachers and disciples; c) not with absolute certainty and security, as the history of the last few centuries unfortunately proves. All this may be granted, even by our adversaries. But such a concession is *only historical.* The testimony of Scriptures, historically considered, can only be historical. It is not the testimony of that Divine Tradition which Christ Himself instituted for the keeping and for the interpreting without error a) of all the Scriptural texts; b) for all the Faithful; c) in whatever condition or for any question which may arise about the Scriptures. In other words, the *historical testimony about* the Scriptures is not sufficient.

It [The historical Testimony] must also be *theological.* For though historical testimony may produce a scientific demonstration based on historical tradition that is useful and even necessary to defend the Faith, it is not in itself produced by Divine Tradition. It does not come from the infallible Church.

It is a fatal mistake to assume that Christ and the Holy Ghost intended to have Revelation preached by the Apostles and then simply placed in writing in the hands of every Christian, to be judged and interpreted at his own pleasure. "God is not mocked." Christ not only enriched the Apostles with the gift of Revelation, but He also established upon them His holy Church, "to the consummation of the world." (*Matt.* 28:20). He commissioned them and their successors in office to teach, preach, protect and keep her from error. Such a commission cannot be faithfully discharged unless the Apostles and their successors are also able to judge whatever is intimately connected with Revelation. Hence the Apostles and their successors in office are empowered by Christ and the Holy Ghost also to judge infallibly what belongs to the genuineness, veracity, integrity and inspiration of every single part of Sacred Scripture for the instruction of every member of the Faithful and for settling authoritatively every controversy for the good of the Church.

That Christ and the Holy Ghost established such an Apostolic Succession we have already shown. The first principles of knowledge about the Scriptures, then, may be acquired only from that institution.

The Church, or Divine Tradition, precedes the Scriptures. We must know what to think of the Scriptures before we commit ourselves to them, before we can use them prudently, safely and to our benefit.

II. The same is true of the doctrine *contained in the Scriptures.*

It is true that many things can be understood without Tradition. In our polemical discussions with some non-Catholics, the divine authority and the inspiration of *some Books* of Scripture are granted. Here the knowledge of doctrine comes first. And the Catholic controversialist—without begging the question and without subverting the priority of knowledge about the Scriptures—can prove the authority of the Church directly through the authority of the Scriptures.

But our contention is still true. Without Tradition, that is, without the Church, we cannot understand the doctrine *contained in Scripture.*

Whatever knowledge one may acquire without Tradition is more *historical* than *theological*. When our adversaries grant the inspiration of the Scriptures, it is only *hypothetical,* that is, *conjectural.* It is based on the will of the adversary; hence, *not theological.* Whenever there is controversy, or whenever Tradition is absent, there can be no *antecedent knowledge* of authority, much less of *inspiration of all the Sacred Books,* nor of the true sense *of all the doctrines contained in the Scriptures.* No such antecedent knowledge is granted by our adversaries. Their concession regards only the *inspiration of some, not of all* the Sacred Books. They grant the true sense of *only some texts or chapters* which are clear. Such historical demonstrations and hypothetical concessions are based only on private judgment, not on the Catholic Intellect of the Church.

Therefore, according to Christ's disposition, Tradition precedes the Scriptures *historically about their knowledge,* and *theologically about their doctrine.*

3

Tradition, Not the Scriptures, Was Intended by the Apostles to Rule the Church of Christ.

Time was when the books of the New Testament were not only unbound, but even unwritten.

The Catholic Church existed during this period. If the Church after the Ascension of Christ and the coming of the Holy Ghost, could have existed even for a day without the books of the New Testament, there is no reason, strictly speaking, why she could not similarly have existed until the present hour.

The New Testament began to appear gradually, several years after the Day of Pentecost, the Birth of the Church. The Gospel of St. Matthew was the first, and not before the year 40 A.D. The *Apocalypse* of St. John was the last

Book. It appeared about the year 94.

In the meantime, the Church was growing in the great centers of the Roman Empire by the *preaching* and *teaching of the Apostles,* without any, or with little of the New Testament being available.

Many of the first Christians lived virtuous lives and died martyrs and never saw a line of it. Practically more than one generation passed away before all the books were written. Not even *all* the Apostles themselves saw all of them. Some Books were written after the death of some of the Apostles.

The Faithful depended completely on the mere preaching and the Sacramental ministrations of the Apostles. Not unlike little children, without the help of a book which they could not read, the first Faithful learned from the Apostles the first elements of Religion.

It was only for the convenience of the Faithful that the Apostles wrote. Preaching Christ everywhere, they established congregations or parishes and ordained others to continue their work, only to go farther on and announce the Gospel to other nations.

It was in this way that many congregations sprang up among Jews and Gentiles. However, being too young and cosmopolitan to take care of themselves, the absence of the founders was soon felt. Disputes, troubles and even heresies began to break out among the members. The unconverted Jews and the sarcastic Gentile philosophers were another element to contend with.

The Apostles, anxious to keep the Unity of Faith and unable to be everywhere, wrote to their Churches on the most important questions of the day. Some wrote to settle controversies among the members; others explained certain doctrines not sufficiently understood; others, namely the majority of the Apostles, did not write at all, because there was no occasion for it.

The Gospel of St. Matthew, proving that Jesus was the Messias foretold by the Prophets, appeared first. The Church having been born among the Jews, who rejected the Messias, it was natural that the first call to embrace Christianity was made to the Jews. St. Matthew wrote his Gospel for the benefit of the Jews, rather than for the Gentile Faithful. He wrote what he had for years preached to the first Christians.

The Gospel of St. Mark may be called St. Peter's Gospel, and the Gospel of St. Luke, who also wrote the *Acts of the Apostles,* may be named St. Paul's Gospel. Both Mark and Luke, respectively, followed Peter and Paul's journeys, writing their preaching and adventures.

The last Gospel was written by St. John at the *request of his disciples* and against the heretics of his time.

In the meantime, the Apostles addressed many Epistles to the Churches they had founded, according to the particular nature of the controversy, trouble or heresy that afflicted them. St. Paul also wrote to different persons, not only for the spiritual welfare of the Churches with which they were connected, but also for their private and material advantage. Thus he writes to Timothy: "Do not still drink water, but use a little wine for thy stomach's sake, and thy frequent infirmities." (*1 Tim.* 5:23).

In this way were the Scriptures a great help to the newly established Churches, to the ancients and to the people. They became a guide and a direction for all Christians and were read every Sunday in their assemblies.

All this goes to show that the Apostles never intended to make a complete written work of the doctrine, discipline and worship of the Christian Religion. There is no method or order followed in their writings. What they wrote was simply prompted by the occasion.

If the Apostles did not intend to make such a complete work, how can the Scriptures be the rule and only rule of Faith? The Scriptures never anticipated, but followed the Apostles' preaching, according to St. Paul's words: "Faith cometh by hearing." (*Rom.* 10:17).

It is therefore illogical and unhistorical to assume that the Church was built on the authority of the Scriptures, or that the Faith should be maintained only through this channel.

4

In Comprehension, Tradition is Broader Than the Scriptures.

The object of Tradition is *what has been delivered.* It is *any* doctrine, object or institution, transmitted from the ancients in whatever manner or form. As St. Vincent of Lerin says: "It is the deposit which you have received, not what you have thought of; the object presented to you, not what you present."[5] This is the *material object* of Tradition—what must be believed—as distinguished from the *formal object*, the reason *for which we believe.*

As stated in a previous chapter, Revelation has been *partly written* and *partly unwritten.* When we affirm that Revelation is *partly unwritten,* we do not mean it was never written in any way. Rather, it was *first* propagated by inspired men only through word of mouth, and it was *afterwards* maintained or written by their disciples and successive generations. Unwritten doctrine is that part of Revelation which never formed part of the Scriptures. This is what, properly speaking, is called Tradition. We say *properly speaking* because Tradition can also be taken

5. *Commonit.,* N. 27.

to mean the whole of Revelation, whatever is or is not contained in the Scriptures.

It was in this sense that the Apostle, writing to the Thessalonians, says, "Therefore, brethren, stand fast; and hold the traditions which you have learned, whether by word, or by our epistle." (*2 Thess.* 2:14).

The Apostle evidently refers to his First Epistle to the same Thessalonians. He calls it "tradition," although it is evident that that Epistle is an important part of the Scriptures. The Apostle places on the same level the truths which he delivered, *"whether by word,"* that is, through his preaching to them, talking to them, instructing them, when for some time he dwelt among them; *or "by our epistle,"* that is, what he wrote them in his first Epistle. The Apostle, therefore, in his Second Epistle to the Thessalonians considers Tradition to mean whatever is Revelation, written or unwritten.

It is in this sense that we consider Tradition here. It embraces not only the Revelation which was made by God before the Scriptures began to be written, but also those truths which were preached after the Scriptures began to make their appearance, as well as the Scriptures themselves. This is particularly true with regard to the New Testament.

In the second place, it comprises *interpretation* or *intelligence* of the same Scriptures, as received and accepted from the ancients, which Clement of Alexandria, in the Third Century, called the *"non-written Tradition of the written Tradition."*[6]

Practically, all this is the definition of Tradition, considered in its broader signification.

In its *comprehension,* then, Tradition is *broader* than

6. Strom. VI, p. 679. Paris Edition 1641.

the Scriptures. It is the whole of Revelation. The Scriptures are only a part.

But observe that not everything in the Scriptures is also kept by Tradition, independently of the Scriptures. As Franzelin observes: "The Scriptures are maintained and explained through the Apostolic Succession, under the assistance of the Holy Ghost, in such a manner that, whatever is consigned to the Scriptures is preserved indirectly by Tradition. This is always true, although in many chapters of the revealed doctrine the immediate instrument of preservation for the teaching Church is the written letter. We must distinguish *theoretical* and *practical* dogmas. Some have been revealed in the Scriptures on account of themselves, that is, because of their dignity and necessity for our belief. Others [have been] incidentally revealed, that is, all those things which, under the inspiration of the Holy Ghost, have been consigned to the Scriptures, not really on account of themselves, but on account of other more important truths with which they are connected and to which they have reference."[7] For instance, the Mysteries of the Most Holy Trinity, the Incarnation of Christ, and the Holy Eucharist are dogmas revealed in the Scriptures on account of themselves. That Abraham had two sons, or that the Apostle was shipwrecked on the Island of Malta, and such other historical adventures, are merely mentioned in the Scriptures on account of other more important matters, to manifest Christ's divine majesty, His Mission, His Church and so forth.[8]

Those dogmas or Articles of Faith which have been revealed in the Scriptures on account of themselves and therefore must be believed explicitly by all are preserved

7. Franzelin, Trad., Th. XXI.
8. See St. Thomas II—*IIae.* Q. I, A. 6.

also by Tradition, independently of the Scriptures. It was in this sense that Irenæus declared: "What if the Apostles had not delivered to us the Scriptures? Had we not then to follow the order of Tradition?"[9] "However, in the present order of Providence, with regard to the written dogmas revealed on account of themselves, the Scriptures are a necessary element to the teaching body of the Church. On the other hand, what had been incidentally revealed cannot possibly be preserved by Tradition independently of the Scriptures, because [they are] not *absolutely* necessary to believe for salvation. They are preserved in the Scriptures, which Scriptures Tradition preserves."[10] Tradition, then, is broader than the Scriptures. Tradition is the whole material or quantity of Revelation. The Scriptures, as well as the doctrine about the Scriptures, are only a part of Tradition—the greatest and best part of it—but always a part.

5

The Nature Itself of the Scriptures is an Evidence That They are not the Principal, Nor the Only Means, Instituted by Christ for the Propagation and Preservation of the Church.

National constitutions are drawn up in such an elaborate, legal and solemn manner, but at the same time in such a plain way as to indicate the duties and privileges of the rulers, as well as the rights and obligations of the people. What would the citizens of the United States of America think of their government if the Constitution would contain things of very little importance which nat-

9. Iren. L. III, C. IV, N. 1.
10. Franzelin, Trad. note to Th. XXI.

urally do not work a great deal for the good of all the people? No national constitution which does not protect the material and civil welfare of the people, and is not solemnly and specifically proclaimed to be the "Law of the Land," will ever be able to safeguard the civil and religious liberties of a nation. Of what value would be the *Magna Charta* to the British, or the "Statute" to the Italian nation, if the rights of those peoples are not clearly defined and firmly established? It would certainly be ridiculous for the *Magna Charta* to describe profusely the harbor of Liverpool, or for the "Statute" to include greetings to the President of the United States and hardly to mention what is most important for the life of the Nation. Now, if the constitutions or fundamental laws of this world must speak plainly in order to safeguard the material welfare of the people, *how much more clearly should not the Scriptures be, if they were given by God to be our principal or only means to save one's soul?*

If the Scriptures were to become a substitute for all Church authority, namely, the Apostolic Succession, and to be the only Rule of Faith, why did not God Himself proclaim such a law in the Scriptures themselves? Why did not God make a solemn and plain statement to that effect? Such statement is nowhere to be found in the Scriptures, all assertions to the contrary notwithstanding. Rather, the Faithful are admonished to have recourse to the "Traditions which you have learned, whether by word, or by our Epistle." (*2 Thess.* 2:14).

The Scriptures do not even explain the principal articles of the Christian Religion. The Old Testament contains—for the most part—the history of the Jewish people and is full of figures and symbols concerning the future Messias. The Four Gospels are rather the history of the life and death of Christ and of His fragmentary sayings.

The "Acts" are the adventures of the Apostles. On the other hand, the rest of the Scriptures try to settle the difficulties which arose among the first Christians. They regard transitory facts which may never occur again. They contain greetings to some particular person or persons. They profusely extol and illustrate certain things which belong only to a few, such as the state of virginity, while the truths of the greatest importance and necessity, such as the Divinity of the Holy Ghost and the Dogma of the Most Blessed Trinity, are scarcely and indefinitely mentioned.

It cannot be said that, although the Apostles never intended to have the Scriptures be the only Rule of Faith, nevertheless God caused them to write in order that the Scriptures would providentially become the only Rule of Faith for the future generations. This hypothesis contradicts the dispositions and manner of acting of both Christ and the Apostles. Christ never commanded the Apostles to write—but to preach and teach! This explains why the majority of the Apostles never wrote a line of the Scriptures. And those who did, always emphasized the necessity of a living, constituted authority. Rather, it must be said that God, in His infinite Wisdom and Providence, wishing to aid our frail human nature, gave a special help to the living, constituted authority of the Church by placing in their hands a new instrument, which was not to destroy, but to edify, not to weaken, but to strengthen that Divine Economy which He established through Christ on the Apostles. That instrument He wanted to be the sole property of the Church. It was to keep for all generations the eternal truths which Christ and the Holy Ghost revealed to her first legislators. In the hands of the Church, it was to be the key that opens the way for the solution of difficulties in the course of the centuries. It was to be the beacon on the sea of life in care of the Church, to dispel the mists of darkness and error and of all human depravity.

The Scriptures, therefore, far from being independent of the Church, are the sole property of the Church. They are a donation, a gift, a boon to her, pure and simple, on the part of God. They are not a transaction between God and man. They do not constitute the *Do ut des,* * the "give and take," as it is among men in the affairs of this world. It will never be truly said that the Church received the Scriptures from God in order to give the people that authority which she received from Christ and the Apostles. By giving the Scriptures to the Church, God only wanted His children "to have plenty and more than plenty": *ut habeant et superabundantius habeant*—"that they may have, and have more abundantly." (cf. *John* 10:10). But if they are a gift, they are certainly a most precious gift, and one to be handled with care. Only the Church knows how to make the best use of them. Whoever uses them against her wishes is "a thief and a robber"—*est fur et latro.* Without the Church, they are of little value. Rather, they are a dangerous weapon placed in the hands of little children. They lead not to salvation, but to illusions, independence and pride.

Considering, therefore, the origin and the nature of the Scriptures; the causes that moved the Apostles to write, while most of them did not write; the matters of little value and consequence often contained in them; the *half omission* of what is most important and necessary to believe in order to be saved . . . *everything* points out that the Scriptures were never intended to be—neither by Christ nor by the Apostles—the principal, much less the exclusive means to propagate, preserve or rule the Church of God.

---

* *Do ut des*—literally, "I give that you may give," as in a contract, where one person does one thing, and the other person, another thing.
—*Publisher,* 2005.

13

Development of Tradition

Introduction

CHRISTIANITY is the universal Religion for all times and for every place. To influence the world, it must present its doctrines as much as possible according to its surroundings and the knowledge of the people. As one generation succeeds another and as circumstances vary, the principles of Christianity—while they remain steadfast and unchangeable as God Himself—require, not a new application, but a new presentation. Quite often—and this is the most important point—the progress of science and the attacks of heresy make a deeper study and discussion necessary. It was indeed such discussion and study which led men in the past and may lead them in the future to truths contained in the Scriptures that were hitherto unknown or obscurely contained therein. This is called *development of Christian truth.*

All Christians—Catholics and Protestants—appeal to the Scriptures. They argue from the Scriptures. But while the Catholic studies and interprets the Scriptures, he does so according to the Catholic Intellect of the Church. The Protestant, left to his private interpretation, deduces certain consequences and new doctrines quite frequently not warranted either by reason or by faith.

The whole of Revelation is written on the principle of development—from the promise by God of a Redeemer down to the last of the Apostles. "As the Revelation proceeds," writes Cardinal Newman, "it is ever new, yet ever old. St. John, who completes it, declares that he has 'no new commandment unto his brethren,' but an old commandment which they had from the beginning—and then he adds: 'A new commandment I write unto you.' The same test of development is suggested in Our Lord's words . . . 'Think not that I am come to destroy the Law and the Prophets; I am not come to destroy, but to fulfill.' He does not reverse, but perfects what has [been] done before."[1]

The more we delve into the mine of Christian truth, the more treasures we see, the more they sparkle, the more the wisdom of God shines forth.

Scripture is loosely constructed and figurative in style. As Cardinal Newman writes: "No one would presume at first sight to say what is in it and what is not. It cannot, as it were, be mapped or its contents catalogued; but after all our diligence, to the end of our lives and to the end of the Church, it must be an unexplored and unsubdued land, with heights and valleys, forests, and streams, on the right and left of our path and close about us full of concealed wonders and choice treasures."[2] And Butler, emphasizing this point, says: "Nor is it at all incredible that a book which has been so long in the possession of mankind should contain many truths as yet undiscovered. For all the same phenomena and the same faculties of investigation from which such great discoveries in natural knowledge have been made in the present and last age were equally in the possession of mankind several thousand years before."[3]

---

1. Newman, *Develop. of Christ. Doct.,* C. II, S. I, N. 10.
2. Newman, *Develop. of Christ. Doct.,* C. II, S. I, N. 14.
3. *Butler's Anal.,* II, 3.

Christian truth found in the Scriptures or in Tradition, may be compared to "a grain of mustard seed: which when it is sown in the earth, is less than all the seeds that are in the earth: And when it is sown, it groweth up, and becometh greater than all herbs, and shooteth out great branches, so that the birds of the air may dwell under the shadow thereof." (*Mark* 4:31-32). So does Christian truth develop in our mind. So did the salutation of the Angel to Mary, "Hail, full of grace," illumine the mind of Catholic Christianity. There is no greater or better argument to prove Mary's singular privilege of exemption from Original Sin than the above few words which the Angel addressed to Mary. Whole libraries have been written on the Immaculate Conception.

The Scriptures themselves, therefore, anticipated the development of Christian truth, which is not unlike the one which God Himself contemplated in the course of nature. Once more Butler: "The whole natural world and [the] government of it is a scheme or system; not a fixed, but a progressive one; a scheme in which the operation of various means takes up a great length of time before the ends they tend to can be attained. The change of seasons, the ripening of the fruits of the earth, the very history of a flower is an instance of this; and so is human life. Thus, vegetable bodies and those of animals, though possibly formed at once, yet grow up by degrees to a mature state. And thus rational agents, who animate these latter bodies, are naturally directed to form each his own manners and character by the gradual gaining of knowledge and experience, and by a long course of action. Our existence is not only successive, as it must be of necessity, but one state of our life and being is appointed by God to be a preparation for another; and that to be the means of attaining to another succeeding one; infancy to childhood, childhood to youth, youth to mature age. Men are impatient, and for precipitating things; but the Author of Nature appears deliberate throughout His operations, accomplishing His natural ends by slow successive steps. And there is a plan of things beforehand laid out, which from the nature of it, requires various systems of means, as well as length of time, in order to the carrying on its several parts into execution. Thus, in the daily course of natural providence, God operates in the very same manner as in the dispensation of Christianity, making one thing subservient to another; this, to somewhat farther, and so on, through a progressive series of means, which extend, both forward, beyond our utmost view. Of this manner of operation, everything we see in the course of nature is as much an instance as any part of the Christian dispensation."[4]

This is so certain that we may say *veritas crescit eundo*—"truth grows in time." It grows, not in itself, but in our mind and heart. Hence we may also say that there is scarcely a doctrine contained in the Scriptures, or in Tradition, which at first consideration is so complete in itself that afterwards does not gain anything from an investigation of faith, and even from the attacks of heresy.

1

All Catholic Revelation Must Be Believed,* If not *Explicitly,* at Least *Implicitly.

The word of God is good "because no word shall be impossible with God." (*Luke* 1:37). Christ also emphatically declares: "Heaven and earth shall pass away, but my words shall not pass away." (*Luke* 21:33).

---

4. *Butler's Anal.,* II:4.

All truths great and small which God has conveyed to man in one way or another must be accepted and believed. It is not the greater or lesser import of the truth that is the motive of our assent. Dignity, importance and necessity of truth are all good qualities of its material objcct, namely, of what must be believed. But they are not the cause nor the reason on account of which they must be believed.

The motive or reason of our belief is only one: the authority of God speaking to man. This is what the Church calls the *formal object of Faith,* distinguished from the material object—the matter that is to be believed.

From this it appears how absurd is the doctrine advanced by some Protestant theologians and later evolved by Calixt in Germany, Jurieu in France, Waterland in England and from time to time revived by many other Protestants in the United States: This is what they call the System of *Fundamental Articles.*

By this term, they understand "Certain general principles of the Christian Religion, a distinct faith and belief in which are necessary to salvation."[5] They classify the *essential* parts of the Christian faith which, as they say, must be believed and those *non-essential* doctrines which, as they declare, individual churches might accept or reject without forfeiting their claim to be parts of the Church Universal. One of the characteristic notes of this system is that not even its advocates have ever been able to enumerate and agree among themselves what is *fundamental* or *non-fundamental* in the Faith.

There seems to be no doubt that this "doctrine" of fundamentals and non-fundamentals was advanced by its authors to effect a reconciliation among all Christian denominations. But, however good their intentions, the

5. Jurieu, *Traitè,* p. 495.

Catholic Church can never accept that system. It conflicts with her dogma. The essential note of the Faith lies in the complete, willing, unhesitating acceptance of all Revelation. The *whole* Deposit of Revelation is all the "word of God." There is no reason whatever for which a part of the revealed truths contained in the Deposit should be accepted and believed and another part rejected. To any man who accepts and believes only part of Revelation we must quote the words of St. Augustine: "He believes himself, but not the Gospel."

For this reason, the conscious rejection of even one article of Revelation, according to St. Thomas Aquinas, is not only sufficient to render one guilty of heresy, but it also shows that one has not Faith. "In a heretic, who rejects a single article of Faith, there remains not the virtue of Faith. . . . The formal object of Faith is the Supreme Truth, in so far as revealed in the Holy Scriptures and in that doctrine of the Church which proceeds from the Supreme Truth. Hence, if any one does not hold to the doctrine of the Church, as to an *infallible and divine rule,* he does not possess the virtue of Faith.[6]

To this point Pope Pius XI said: "In matters of Faith it is not permissible to make a distinction between fundamental and so-called non-fundamental articles of Faith, as if the first ought to be held by all, and the second are free for the Faithful to accept or not. The supernatural virtue of Faith has as its formal cause the authority of God the Revealer, who does not make such a division."[7]

It cannot be denied that in the Deposit of Revelation there are certain truths which are of more vital moment than others. There are some which are so important to

6. St. Thomas, *Summa Theol.,* II—IIae Q. V, A. 3.
7. Pope Pius XI, *Encycl. on Religious Unity,* issued Jan. 6, 1928.

know and so necessary to believe that the Church requires explicit belief in them by all of her Faithful. These are the truths which, as the same St. Thomas Aquinas says, "conduct us directly to eternal life, such as are the three Persons of God and the Mystery of the Incarnation of Christ and such other truths."[8] These truths must be explicitly believed. On the other hand, there are truths which may not necessarily be known, and it is enough that they be *implicitly* believed.

This is evident from the universal practice of the Church, which did not and does not demand the same *explicit* faith in all of her truths from all of her Faithful. It is well known that, according to the times, conditions, environments or necessity, the Church was sometimes satisfied that some or most of her members professed only the Apostolic Creed. As to the rest of the Articles of Faith, she simply required the Faithful not to deny them, but to *implicitly believe* what she teaches.

By truth *implicitly believed* is meant that truth which one does not conceive, nor does he know as revealed; it is, however, contained in another truth, which *he knows* and *explicitly believes as revealed.* Thus, by the very fact that one declares, "I believe whatever God has revealed," or, "I believe whatever the Catholic Church believes and teaches," he at the same time elicits a general, though somewhat confused act of Faith.

The Church does not expect all her members to know everything that belongs to the Faith. She is satisfied that they know and believe what is necessary to know and believe. She does not even expect all her Faithful to know what they know in the same degree.

---

8. St. Thomas, *Summa Theol.,* II—II*ae* Q. I, A. 6.

2

It is *Possible* that not All Revelation Was at All Times and Everywhere *Explicitly* Declared and Believed In the Church.

The saying of the holy writer in the Old Testament, that "nothing under the sun is new" (*Eccles.* 1:10) may be applied to Revelation. Many truths which seem to be new or non-Scriptural were or are in reality contained in other universal truths or principles. The more we study and analyze Scriptural or traditional principles and truths, the more we perceive the beauty, the graces and gifts which the infinite wisdom of God prepared and donated to His Church.

When the last of the Apostles was called to his reward, there was nothing else which God wished to convey. His message was contained in the written and non-written Tradition, which the Apostles passed on.

But human infirmity or perversity caused the Church in every century to assert herself and vindicate her claims. This activity enabled her to uncover in the course of time—through human industry and the special assistance of the Holy Ghost—treasures which lay in the Deposit of Faith, her exclusive heritage.

What had to be known explicitly and believed by all was *explicitly* contained in the Scriptures or in Tradition and *clearly* and *abundantly* announced. But it was natural that, in defending herself against the many attacks of her enemies, the Church made clear what was hitherto obscure. She unfolded many revealed truths which were *implicitly* contained in *explicit* truths, delivered through the Scriptures or Tradition. It is therefore *possible* that, through human study and industry, through the many controversies and circumstances of times and places, and under the direction of the Holy Spirit, the Church may bring forth out of the *explicit,* throw more light upon what is obscure, and finally declare and define, if necessary, what seems less firm and certain.

This becomes more evident when we consider that the dogmas of our Faith are closely related to human needs, which are different at different times. It was unnecessary as well as impossible for the Apostles to announce explicitly each dogma to meet each error. Hence: 1) Certain universal truths or principals proposed by the Apostles may contain also some other particular truths. Once the Church proved from the Scriptures that grace is necessary for every salvific act, she could also declare against the Semi-Pelagians that grace is also necessary even for the beginning of the Faith *and* for final perseverance. 2) The Church might have proposed in parts what was composed of several elements. Christ was a true and perfect man; she could therefore attribute to Him now a human body and a rational soul, and now a human will and a human power. From the beginning, the Primacy of the Roman Pontiff was clear. Hence, in the course of time she affirmed its particular office and rights, implicitly contained in the Primacy. 3) Some truths were or are understood obscurely. This is particularly true of certain references about the future glorification of the Church contained in the *Apocalypse,* which perhaps may never be completely clear or understood before their completion. 4) To safeguard dogmas which are already believed or practiced, not through the Church teaching, but through the use and observance of the Faithful, the Church may judge it expedient to proclaim such belief or practice as an article of the Faith. In no other way could she keep intact in so many controversies and throughout so many centuries the Deposit of Faith.

There may be truths, then, contained in the Deposit of Faith which have not always nor everywhere been sufficiently known and proposed to the Faithful as a part of the Faith. We might expect this, especially in the beginning of the Church. Add the political turmoil of the times, the persecutions, the unrest, and it becomes evident that an *explicit* belief about all elements of the Faith in all times and in all places was a moral impossibility.

3

Many Truths Held Today as Revealed Were not Always so. They May Have Even Been Denied Without Shipwreck of the Faith.

What is possible may at any time become a fact. In the formation and structure of great deeds, when all difficulties are removed, when the material becomes available, when the genius of man is sufficiently developed and determined to succeed, there is nothing possible that in the course of time may not become a reality. What seemed difficult or impossible twenty or fifty years ago, today is a fact. And if from the material we pass to the spiritual, and what is most important, if we rely on the promises of Christ and the assistance of the Holy Ghost, the Church not only may come into possession of all her treasures, but will also triumph over all her enemies: ignorance, servitude and vice.

Theology is the science of sciences, and its noblest department is Revelation. Schools, seminaries, universities, the writings of the Fathers—nay, all General Councils and the definitions of the Supreme Pontiffs—all bear testimony to the solicitude of the Church for Revelation.

If the Church has always been the patron of all that is great in this world for the advancement of the human race, could she ever neglect her own field of labor, which Christ assigned her for the salvation of humanity? And what is more proper to the Church than the study and development of Christian philosophy, theology and the interpretation of the Scriptures and Tradition—all culminating in Revelation?

In the course of time, many questions had to arise. Men were always free to affirm or deny. But, though they followed different opinions, they agreed on one point. The doctrines about which the controversies centered did not yet belong to the Unity of Faith. When any doctrine became sufficiently clear, or was defined by the General Councils of the Church or by the Sovereign Pontiff, controversy ceased. It became *explicitly* part of the Deposit of Faith—not a new revelation, but a declaration of a truth. It had already been *implicitly* contained in another truth, revealed to the Patriarchs, the Prophets or the Apostles.

On this point Pope Pius XI writes: "In this extraordinary use of the teaching authority, nothing is invented, nor is anything new added to the sum of truths that are, at least implicitly, contained in the Deposit of Divine Revelation that was entrusted by God to the Church. Instead, points of faith are defined that could still seem obscure to some, or truths are established as matters of faith that for the first time were entering controversy."[9]

But the Church does not arbitrarily define what belongs to the Deposit of Faith. Circumstances are many times the motive that compels her to act. When the Protestants first admitted five, then four, then three, and at last, two Sacraments, the Church defined through the Council of Trent, that the Sacraments are seven—not more, and not less. For the same reason, the Council proclaimed which

9. Pope Pius XI, *Encyclical on Religious Unity,* issued Jan. 6, 1928.

are the inspired Books of the New Testament.

The Fathers of the Church foresaw, centuries before they were defined, many truths which are today a part of the Deposit of Faith. Irenæus writes that we must distinguish between the "substance of faith, which is admitted as one by all and . . . questions of deeper intelligence."[10] Origen remarks that there are "truths which are manifestly taught in the Church, which are described in the ecclesiastical preaching and of which one is the judgment of the whole Church; and also truths on other questions of Scripture which must yet be searched and thoroughly investigated, which cannot be easily discerned, which are not sufficiently distinguished in our doctrine and which are not evident in the ecclesiastical preaching."[11] Tertullian declares that there is a great difference between "the rule of faith on which there is no question among us, and that which may come under discussion without shipwreck of the faith."[12] "We must distinguish," says Augustine, "between the error which we may tolerate on questions not diligently examined and not yet defined by the full authority of the Church, and the error trying to upset the very foundations of the Church, which we cannot tolerate."[13] "What belongs to the foundation of the Faith is one thing, but it is a different proposition when, in good faith, the most learned and the best defenders of the Faith do not agree—with the result that one may say something better and truer than another."[14]

It is evident, then, not only that there *may be* truths contained in the Deposit of Faith which *may not always*

---

10. Iren. I, C. X, N. 2-3.
11. Origen, *De Principiis,* praef.
12. Tertull., "Prescript," C. XIII.
13. August., Serm. 294, N. 4.
14. August., *Contra Julian* I, C. VI, N. 22.

have been explicitly believed, but that *there are in reality* truths which were once implicitly contained in the Deposit of Faith and which must now be explicitly believed by all, under pain of eternal damnation. This follows from more recent definitions of the Sovereign Pontiffs and of the Councils. Those doctrines did not belong to the Faith because the Church had not yet passed judgment. They only became a part of the Faith after the Church had solemnly proclaimed that they must be explicitly believed by all. Such are the doctrines of the Immaculate Conception and the Infallibility of the Sovereign Pontiff.

This progress is still going on in the Church. There are questions still unsolved, which neither the General Councils nor the Supreme Pontiffs have thought expedient to define on account of no impending necessity. Such is the doctrine of the Assumption of Blessed Mary into Heaven.*

Hence, the distinction is made between *the Remote* and the *Proximate Rule of Faith.* The *Remote* Rule of Faith is the Objective Deposit. It contains revealed truths which—for some reason or other—were forgotten, obscure, or not sufficiently understood. Hence, they were brought into discussion, or denied without injury to faith until they became clear or were defined by the Church.

The *Proximate* Rule of Faith is the teaching of the Church sufficiently proposed and manifestly promulgated to the Faithful. If this Proximate Rule of Faith proclaims anything as belonging to the Remote Rule of Faith, it can no longer be challenged without shipwreck of the Faith. For unity of faith is whole and entire only while there is

---

* The Assumption of Mary body and soul into Heaven was solemnly declared a doctrine of the Faith by Pope Pius XII in 1950. This fact reinforces what the author is saying in this paragraph, and the reader should keep in mind that *Tradition and the Church* was first published in 1928. —*Publisher,* 2005.

no dissent with the Proximate Rule of Faith. On this point Gregory of Valentia declares: "The Church has from darkness brought to light with her infallible authority some doctrines which, through human negligence or malice or perversity of mind, remained concealed. And mayhap there are some still hidden in the Church."[15]

4

Those Truths Which Were not Always Explicitly Believed as Revealed Could Never Have Been so Obscure That An Opposite and Negative Consent Could Ever Have Prevailed Against Them.

The Catholic Church never disdains the study of her divine truths. She welcomes it. Careful inquiry, close research, watchful investigation into the Deposit of the Faith cannot but bring forth the truth more resplendent than ever. The Church cannot be afraid of the truth. Is not her Divine Bridegroom "the way, the truth and the life?" (*John* 14:6). Ignorance, rather, is one of her greatest enemies. Could the Church be given full liberty to make her doctrines known to friend and foe, were she not handicapped by the many obstacles which so-called Christian States set in her way, the world would be happier, more enlightened, more Christian. The whole world would be Catholic, and heathenism at an end. Study must be made, however, in a good spirit. It must not be prejudiced; it must not proceed with the view of combating the Church. It always was the pretense of knowing more than the Church that brought schism and heresy. Too many errors have been proclaimed, too many crimes committed in the name of religious liberty. And what is more

15. *Comment. Theol.* T. 3, Disp. I.

astonishing, the greater the man, the greater sometimes is his error. But only the truly great man acknowledges his error. By retracting it, he becomes greater before the eyes of his fellow men. For this reason, it may be said that no heresiarch, born and reared in the bosom of the Church, but who died outside of her communion, has been truly great. Such was Martin Luther. Were it not that he found a corrupted society, the ground ready for a fruitful dissemination of his errors, and the sword of the civil authorities ready to protect him, the great rebellion of the 16th Century would not have succeeded. Luther betrayed his own weakness when he allowed bigamy to the Elector Philip, his protector and defender. It was different with poor Tertullian. He was born a pagan, embraced the Catholic Faith only in his manhood, and did not fall into heresy before he became too old a man to recognize his errors. But Tertullian testified so beautifully to the Catholic Faith, fought so valiantly for it, and wrote so brilliantly about it in his manhood that he is hailed to this day—although improperly—as one of the early Fathers of the Church. God permits errors in order that truth may be made manifest. But He never did nor ever will permit that, on account of any obscurity or circumstances, error should supersede truth in His Church.

It may take long, but in the end truth will triumph. *Magna est veritas et prævalebit*—"Truth is great and it shall prevail!" The Catholic Church alone has the truth. Other religions sooner or later will disappear.

Truth in its fight with error is like oil on water. It comes to the surface. No matter how troubled may be the sea of human depravity, the oil of truth overpowers it, brings calmness and renders more visible the magnitude of the shipwreck of the Faith. Heresy is darkness. It brings certain death. But truth, the sister of light, points the way to salvation.

In the course of time, where the truth was obscure, it became clear; where it was doubtful, it became certain; where it seemed certain, it became evident. This process shall continue to the End of Time.

This process corresponds to what we call the three periods of progressive growth in the attainment of the full knowledge of divine truth.

First period: A doctrine is well-known and explicitly believed. There is no question about it. It contains implicitly some other doctrine, tacitly believed. The Church always explicitly held that Mary is the Mother of Christ. At the same time, she implicitly believed that, on account of such a Motherhood, Mary must have been Immaculate from the first instant of her Conception.

Another instance: a doctrine explicitly believed by all contains implicitly another doctrine which is admitted by all rather through its *use and practice* than through explicit teaching. The Church always explicitly believed in the necessity of Baptism. At the same time it believed implicitly in its validity—even when conferred by a heretic.

Second period: A doctrine implicitly contained in another doctrine and believed by all begins to be questioned or doubted; it is then more diligently examined and discussed.

Third period: The controversy is brought to an end. Either the doctrine appears so clearly and evidently revealed that it is believed by the Faithful without any explicit decision, or it is decided by the infallible authority of the Church. In either case, it passes to the *explicit* Catholic Intellect and is seen clearly as a part of the Deposit of Faith. It is not a new doctrine, but one which was already contained in a doctrine better known and revealed. It passes from the *implicit* to the *explicit,* from the Remote to the Proximate "Rule of Faith."

These three periods are remarkably indicated by St. Augustine: "Do not take exception to us by the authority of Cyprian with regard to the repetition of Baptism . . . for that question had not yet been diligently discussed; the Church kept the most salutary rule concerning even schismatics and heretics: to correct what is wicked, not to repeat what has been given. That custom is, I believe, an Apostolic Tradition, like so many others which are not found in the Epistles of the Apostles."[16] This is the first period: when a tradition, not having yet been questioned, is more in the custom or practice of the Faithful than in the doctrine and preaching of the Church.

The holy Doctor continues: "St. Cyprian says that this most salutary custom began to be almost corrected by Agrippinus, his predecessor. . . . Once a question so vital began to be debated . . . backed with little reason, but strengthened with the authority of Agrippinus and of a few more men who agreed with him on this question, reasons were brought forth which had only the appearance of truth, but which quickly blinded their eyes and shut the way to an investigation of the truth. . . . Exhausted, Cyprian, under the influence of the previous Council, which was called by Agrippinus, preferred to defend what seemed to be established by his predecessors in the See of Carthage since Agrippinus, rather than to work harder in search of the truth."[17] This second stage shows some obscurity. The question is involved in controversy. Soon, however, we come to the *third* stage. "Afterwards, however, having been dealt with and thoroughly scrutinized, the truth was not only found out, but also strengthened

16. August., *De Bapt.* II, 12-14
17. Idem.

by the authority and power of the Plenary Council, after the martyrdom of Cyprian, it is true (Year 258), but before we were born (Year 353)."[18] It is at an end with the full consent of the Catholic Church. Whoever dissents from it becomes a schismatic and heretic. Such became the Donatists, who did not submit to the decree of the Plenary Council against the repetition of Baptism.

These three stages indicate the progressive knowledge of revealed truths. The first period constitutes the shadow of the truth; the second, the transition period; the third, its full light and the consent of the Church.

The transition, or shifting from the second to the third period, shows the ever-living alertness and vigilance of the Church in preventing error from prevailing over *revealed truth.* This consent of the Church is a sure and infallible test of Divine Tradition.[19]

Not all the truths of the Deposit of Revelation have reached the third period. Progressive knowledge on our part is still going on. The Church, however, does not without necessity announce her infallible decision; only when there is danger or perversion of the revealed truth. Such is the revealed truth of the Assumption of the Blessed Virgin Mary, which some day may be proclaimed by the Church, to the comfort and joy of all the Faithful. [This infallible proclamation was in fact made by Pope Pius XII in 1950. See the footnote on page 287.—*Publisher,* 2005].

5

The Definitions of the Church on Any Revealed Truth Contain not *only Some of the Truth,* But the Truth Pure and Simple.

18. Idem.
19. See Franzelin, *Trad.,* Th. XXIII.

When the Church explains or defines any revealed truth, we must accept her explanation or definition according to the definite sense which she intends to convey. That sense must not be distorted, perverted or diminished by any so-called science or philosophy.

The Church cannot allow any false science or any human intellect to divert her solemn definition to any other sense which she never intended, under the pretext that the Church—especially the Church of the first centuries—lacked the philosophy and the sciences of our times. This is the error of Günther, who, writing in the middle of the 19th Century, claimed that the definitions of the Church, although infallible, contain *only a part of the truth,* but not all the truth. His theory may be summed up as follows: The Church, lacking modern philosophy and the knowledge of modern sciences, did not understand her own definitions. She did not possess a definite manner of expressing dogmatic truths; hence, her definitions, although infallible, were only the best *adaptation* of understanding and expressing revealed truths according to the knowledge and the circumstances of the times. They contained a *part of the truth,* but *not the whole truth,* nor that perfect and true intelligence which really belongs to revealed truths. For this reason, the "doctrinal intelligence," or the "conscience of the Church" on revealed truths, was less perfect in the Apostles than in the Fathers, and less perfect in the Fathers than in the Theologians of modern times. Through the help, however, of a perfect—Güntherian—philosophy, the "doctrinal intelligence" or "conscience of the Church" has now so developed to the point that it cannot go any further. Thus, and always according to Günther, when the Council of Ephesus in the Fifth Century defined that Christ is one Divine Person, the Church was infallible in her definition. But that definition contained only a part of the truth. The real truth is that Christ having two distinct persons—the human and the divine persons—they remain two persons, being joined together in one composite person. We, Günther continues, could not expect the Church to understand the supreme intelligence of that dogmatic truth. She had not yet a perfect philosophy, nor could she know the sciences of the 19th Century. The Holy Ghost did not think it expedient to supply that defect in the Church according to His all-wise judgment. He did not reveal to Moses in the Old Dispensation the Mystery of the Most Holy Trinity, just as Christ told the Apostles: "You cannot bear them now."

This approach does away with the true idea of Divine Tradition and with the infallibility of the Church. Were we to accept Günther's opinion, the Church would have to review the whole work of her General Councils, while the sublime writings of the Fathers would be consigned to a pitiful oblivion as old-fashioned scribblings. Instead of leaving philosophy to be the humble servant of theology, Günther and his school constitute philosophy as the queen of theology; they proclaim reason superior to Faith; and in practice they try to increase Revelation through the help of science and modern philosophy. But the Church declares: "If any one says that in the dogma once proposed by the Church it is possible through the progress of science to give a different sense from the one which the Church understood and understands, let him be anathema."[20] "The doctrine of the Faith which God revealed is not proposed to human intellects to be perfected as some philosophical theory, but being delivered as a Divine Deposit to the Spouse of Christ, it must be faithfully kept and infallibly declared. For this reason, the sense of the

---

20. Vatican Council, C. III.

sacred dogmas—to be retained forever—is that one which holy Mother Church once declared, nor is it to be diverted from that sense under the specious name of higher intelligence."[21]

The definitions of the Church arc to be believed by an unchangeable and immovable faith in those formal words and in that understanding which are proposed to the Faithful. This is done principally by the assistance of the Holy Ghost, who directs the legislators of the Church rightly to understand Revelation and to choose the right words in expressing, explaining and declaring it to the Faithful.

The enlightenment of the Holy Ghost, therefore, *comes first.* It causes the human element of philosophy, science and philology to take the right course, to declare what is right and to use the right terms in the declaration of the truth. In all this there can be no contradiction, no ambiguity, no place for retraction—even where the Church defines a dogma which is connected with another dogma as a further declaration of the truth. For instance, when the Church defined against the Nestorians that Christ is one Divine Person and afterwards declared against the Monophosites that the same Christ has two natures—the human and the divine nature—it will always remain infallibly true that Christ has not two persons, although He has two natures. For this reason, neither modern philosophy nor any science can ever effect that Christ, having two natures, must also be two persons, but only One Divine Person.

Finally, the comparison of the knowledge of the Apostles with the knowledge of modern theologians is meaningless. The Apostles had nothing to learn from any human philosophy or science. They knew intimately the myster-

21. Vatican Council I, C. IV.

ies of the Faith and all Revelation by that supernatural gift with which the Holy Ghost filled them on the day of Pentecost. They acquired their knowledge directly from God by an infused science, which no human effort can ever reach or even approximate. It is true that the Apostles did not propose every dogma in all possible forms in order to overcome all kinds of errors and heresies. They did not even use certain terms to express the revealed truths with the precision, clearness and distinctness which the Councils of the Church later employed to crush heresy. But such forms and terms are only *contingent* and *secondary*. They are not inspirations. They are simply the work of man under the assistance of the Holy Ghost. It is the human element which, according to times or circumstances, has first of all the promise of Christ and of the Holy Ghost "that it may not go into error," as Augustine says. Secondly, that same human element which forms the common consent of the Church, or the true definition of the revealed truth, is led and guided by the Holy Ghost's assistance, which does not destroy, but elevates man's nature.

Whatever may be the human element in the definitions of the Church, that human element can never come from philosophy left to itself, but only from the assistance of the Holy Ghost. As St. Athanasius says: "The word of Faith remains forever and ever."[22] This point was understood by the Fathers. They always considered the "Sciences to be founded on Faith." "Faith comes first in order that the science of the things of the Faith may follow."

No human philosophy of the 19th Century, or of any other century, can add more truth to the definitions of the Church. Any attempt is a perversion of truth. To the

22. Athanas., *Ep. ad Afros,* N. 2.

point Vincent of Lerin says: "Intelligence, science and wisdom must therefore grow and abundantly benefit the people, the individual and the Church in every age and in all stages of life, but in their own class, that is, in the samc dogma, in the same sense and in the same proposition. . . . Whatever has been sown by the Faith of the Fathers in this field of the Church of God, it behooves the children to cultivate and care for; it must flourish and come to maturity. It must benefit others and become more perfect in itself. For it is permissible to attend to, to lime, to polish in the course of time the ancient dogmas of heavenly philosophy, but they are not allowed to be changed, to be dissected, to be mutilated. Let them receive more evidence, more light, more renown, but they must retain their fullness, their integrity, their propriety."[23]

If, therefore, in the definitions of the Church there may be any progress, it is "the progress of the faithful in the Faith, rather than of the Faith in the faithful," as St. Albert the Great remarks.[24]

The definitions of the Church, therefore, contain in themselves, *not only a part of the truth, but all the truth, simple and pure.*

---

23. *Commonit.,* NN. 27-32.
24. *Albert the Great,* 3 Dist., 25A. I.

14

Completeness of Revelation

1

Catholic Revelation Must Not Be Confounded With Private Revelation.

CATHOLIC Revelation—that is, what God revealed to us to be universally believed under pain of eternal damnation—came to an end at the death of the Apostles.

We say *Catholic,* to distinguish it from *private* revelation, which God in His infinite mercy and wisdom, condescends from time to time to make known to His servants upon this earth. This private revelation is designed by God to make manifest the sense of some truths contained in the Catholic Revelation which has not yet been defined by the Church nor sufficiently understood by the Faithful. Sometimes private revelation refers to things which do not concern the sense of Scripture. Witness the revelations to St. Catherine of Genoa and to St. Teresa of Avila and others.

It is also possible that God may disclose privately to the Supreme Pontiff or to some Fathers assembled in a General Council the true sense of a dogmatic truth. But this private manifestation of the true sense of a divine doctrine in which is involved, not only the doctrine proposed to the Faithful, but also the infallibility of the Pontiff and of the Church, is not really private revelation. It is the assistance of the Holy Ghost promised by God to His Church. A revelation or, as the case may be, a prophecy declared after the death of the Apostles does not belong to the *Deposit of Faith.* It is simply a *private revelation* or a *private prophecy* directed to private individuals. These persons—unlike the Apostles, the Prophets and the other inspired writers of the Scriptures—are not commissioned by God to be His legates to the Church. They may receive certain revelations, either for their own benefit, or for the direction of others. On the contrary, what the Apostles and all the other inspired writers left us in the Scriptures were intended for the whole Church, for her own general direction, edification and belief. Their writings constitute *Catholic Revelation,* or what we usually call the *Deposit of Faith.* Therefore, private revelations and prophecies—strictly speaking—do not even belong to the promotion or explanation of the Deposit of Faith. To do this, Christ instituted an ordinary ministry: a Head of the Church and an Apostolic Succession united with that visible Head, with a promise of infallible assistance. Hence, according to Benedict XIV, when a private revelation is suspected, the Holy See declares "if it is revealed, which is yet under the judgment of the Church."[1] Private revelations and prophecies may be made by God, because nothing is impossible to Him, but they do not belong to the Deposit of Faith. Hence, they are not *Catholic* revelations or *Catholic prophecies.* They may belong to what theologians call *divine faith,* as distinguished from *Catholic Faith.*

Divine faith embraces whatever God has been and will be pleased to reveal in the course of the centuries. *Catholic Faith* contains what must be believed by all.

---

1. De Canoniz., SS. III, C. LIII, N. 8.

If there are motives for credibility, new revelations must be believed by divine faith by him to whom God has made them known. This is the most common opinion among theologians. Such faith is not called Catholic or universal.

If the Church has passed judgment on them and approved of their veracity, they are not proposed to the faithful to be believed either by divine faith or Catholic Faith. The Church simply declares: 1) That there is nothing in them against the Catholic Faith or Christian morality and discipline; 2) That there are sufficient indications for which such revelations may be believed in human faith piously, prudently and without superstition, or as Cardinal de Turrecremata (quoted and approved by Pope Benedict XIV) says, that "they may be read in the Church of God in the same manner in which the Faithful are allowed to read the books of many doctors, or the accounts and history of the Saints";[2] 3) That private revelations should not be despised after the approval of the Church—or if the Church has not yet passed judgment but there are, however, sufficient reasons for their genuineness.[3]

Therefore, the conclusion is that, when we declare that Catholic Revelation came to an end with the death of the Apostles, we do not mean that private revelations or prophecies cannot be made any more by God, but that they are not to be confounded with Catholic Faith, which must be accepted by all.

---

2. De Canoniz., SS. L, I-III, C. LIII.
3. See Franzelin, *De Trad.,* Th. XXII.

2

Catholic Revelation Has So Come to an End that It Excludes the Formation of a New Church, or of Another Testament of a More Perfect Order, or with A More Abundant Divine Communication of Truth.

Man's intellect, when not influenced by noble and unselfish motives, left to itself, always seeks new theories and systems to subvert the present order of society, civil or divine. Heresy has appeared many times and in many ways in the Church of God. Innumerable sects, both ancient and modern, not satisfied with Christ and His Church, expect another Dispensation, or another Testament, with a new and more abundant effusion of the Holy Spirit. The ancient sect of the Montanists, with some heretics of the Middle Ages and the more recent Anabaptists, Irwingites and the followers of the *"Future Church,"* hoped or hope for a more perfect Third Dispensation, viz., the future "Church of the Holy Ghost." As there are Three Persons in the Holy Trinity, they declare that there must also be three Dispensations. The first, or the Old Testament, they ascribe to the Father. The second, or the New Testament, they assign to Christ. The third, or "Future Testament," they attribute to the Holy Ghost. According to them, as the second or present New Testament is more perfect than the first or Old Testament, so also will the Last or "Future Testament" be more perfect than the other two Dispensations. This "Last Testament," or "Church of the Holy Ghost," will have the same relation to the Church of Christ, as this same "Church of Christ" has to the Synagogue, the "Church of the Father."

That all Revelation has been completed by the Son of God while "He dwelt amongst us," and then by the Holy Ghost through the Apostles, is evident from the fact that the Scriptures show the establishment through the Apostles of a new, Last and Perfect Dispensation, that is finally to give place only to the Beatific Vision in Heaven.

The Scriptures indicate how the New Testament—the Testament of Jesus Christ—is an institution that is throughout firm and immovable, while the Old Testament, on account of its imperfection, inefficiency and instability, must soon be transferred into a better and more perfect state. The Scriptures point out how the Old Law is only an inception and an imperfection, which is to be made so perfect by the New Dispensation that no other will be required, because it will be full, permanent and unchangeable. The Old Testament marks the sighs of the Patriarchs and the predictions of the Prophets—sighs that are to be fully satisfied and prophecies that will be fulfilled in the ever-glorious Kingdom of Christ.

The characteristic note of the Old Testament is hope and expectation that is to be realized only and forever through the advent of the Messias, the Saviour of mankind.

All this is wonderfully illustrated by the Apostle in his Epistle to the Hebrews. Interpreting the words of the Prophet Aggeus, "*Yet once more,* and I will move not only the earth, but heaven also," (*Aggeus* 2:7), he declares, "And in that he saith, '*Yet once more,*' he signifieth the translation of the moveable things as made, that those things may remain which are immovable. Therefore, receiving an immovable kingdom, we have grace." (*Heb.* 12:27-28). The "moveable things" are nothing else but the Old Testament; the "immovable Kingdom" is the New Testament. This he confirms by comparing both Testaments: "If that which is done away (the Old Testament) was glorious, much more that which remaineth (the New Testament) is in glory." (*2 Cor.* 3:11).

According to the Apostle, the New Testament

"remaineth" because Christ is "a priest forever, according to the order of Melchisedech." (*Ps.* 109:4). The priesthood is the heart of religion. Take out that heart, and nothing remains of religion: it is the pulsation of life. If, therefore, a priesthood is imperfect, imperfect must also be its religion. If imperfect, it must be "translated" (abolished) and a "translation" (abolition) must be made also of its religion. For this reason, as the Levitical priesthood was imperfect, Christ's eternal priesthood put an end both to the Levitical priesthood and to Jewish Religion. Hence, the Apostle argues: "If then perfection was by the Levitical priesthood . . . what further need was there that another priest should rise according to the order of Melchisedech? . . . For the Priesthood being translated, it is necessary that a translation also be made of the law. . . . There is indeed a setting aside of the former commandment, because of the weakness and unprofitableness thereof. (For the law brought nothing to perfection) but a bringing in of a better hope, by which we draw nigh to God. . . . But this (Christ) for that he continueth forever, hath an everlasting priesthood, whereby he is able also to save forever them that come to God by him." (*Heb.* 7:11-25).

This Doctrine of the Apostle does not stop here; it goes much further. Having compared the imperfection of the Old Testament with the perfection of the New Testament, the Apostle declares that the state of the New Testament is in itself imperfect, compared with the Beatific Vision. While in the Epistle to the Hebrews, (Chapter 10, Verse 1) he calls the Law only "a *shadow* of the good things to come, not the *very image* of the things," viz., of the New Testament; in the First Epistle to the Corinthians, he designates this present order as only a part, hence as imperfect, when compared to the one that is to come. "We know in part, and we prophesy in part. But when that which is perfect is come, that which is in part shall be done away. . . . We can see now through a glass in a dark manner; but then face to face. Now I know in part; but then I shall know even as I am known." (*1 Cor.* 13:9-12).

This description is of the Beatific Vision, compared to which the New Testament is imperfect, just as the Old Testament compared to the New is imperfect. No intermediary state to succeed the present order is given by the Apostle; he only designates the Beatific Vision.

Hence, there are three States enumerated by the Apostle which God in His Divine Providence successively established with regard to humanity. They are the three stations which conducted or conduct the children of God to the possession of their eternal heritage. Not unlike the steps of Jacob's ladder, one succeeds another and is co-ordinated with the other, as the low to the higher and the higher to the highest. The Old Testament was the *shadow;* the New Testament is the *reality;* the Beatific Vision is the *consummation.* The Church of Jesus Christ is midway between the shadow of the Old Testament and the consummation of the promises of Christ. She bears relation, on the one hand, to the Old Testament, and on the other, to the Beatific Vision. On this point St. Bruno beautifully writes: "The first Tabernacle is the Synagogue, the second is the Church, the third is Heaven. . . . The first was in shadow and in figure, the second in figure and in truth, the third only in truth."[4]

After the present Dispensation, Testament or Church, no other State must be expected but the *Beatific Vision* for the children of light and "the exterior darkness" (*Matt.* 22:13) for the children of the world. "And they that have done good things shall come forth unto the resurrection

4.. *St. Bruno of Asti.,* 34 Hom.

of life; but they that have done evil, unto the resurrection of judgment." (*John* 5:29).

3

Catholic Revelation was Completed by the Holy Ghost Through the Apostles. No Other Is To Be Expected.

Like a father among his children, whose hour is fast approaching to be unjustly delivered to the executioners, Christ Jesus Our Lord, "having loved his own who were in the world, he loved them unto the end." (*John* 13:1). The very night before He died, He instructed His Disciples for the last time. Most earnestly and affectionately He spoke to the Apostles: "I have yet many things to say to you, but you cannot bear them now. But when he, the Spirit of truth, is come, he will teach you all truth. For he shall not speak of himself; but what things soever he shall hear, he shall speak; and the things that are to come he shall show you. He shall glorify me because he shall receive of mine and shall show it to you. All things whatsoever the Father hath are mine. Therefore, I said that he shall receive of mine and show it to you." (*John* 16:12-15).

These words of Christ concern *directly* the *persons* of the Apostles. They affected them in that present condition *when* addressed by Christ, namely, as weak and ignorant: "You cannot bear them now." They also refer to the Apostles, as Apostles, that is, as Ambassadors of Christ who not only know and believe, but must also preach, teach and testify. In other words, those who on account of weakness and ignorance could "not bear them now," are the same ones who, after the Descent of the Holy Ghost, are to be taught "all truth." They are therefore to be taught "all truth," not only on account of themselves, but more so on account of the Church of Jesus Christ.

The *ultimate* purpose for which they are to be taught "all truth" is the whole Church. Ultimately, therefore, Christ's words concern His Church. Hence, the Church is also taught "all truth." No other truths are to be expected because whatever Christ and the Holy Ghost wanted the Church to know was to be made known by the Apostles, who were taught "all truths." That this "all truth" is to be made known to the Church appears from the aim of Revelation, from the office of the Apostleship, and from the command of Christ to the Apostles, "Go ye into the whole world and preach the gospel to every creature." (*Mark* 16:15). Truly, the Apostles were sent by Christ to the whole world to give testimony of Him, just as the Holy Ghost was to give testimony of Christ. "I will send you from the Father, the Spirit of truth . . . he shall give testimony of me. And you shall give testimony because you are with me from the beginning." (*John* 15:26-27).

These words of Christ were delivered in the course of His last sermon to the Apostles. He concluded it with a most beautiful and sublime prayer for the sanctification of all those who were to believe in Him in all truth: "Holy Father . . . sanctify them in truth. Thy word is truth. As thou hast sent me into the world, I also have sent them into the world. And for them do I sanctify myself, that they also may be sanctified in truth. And not for them only do I pray, but for them also who through their word shall believe in me." (*John* 17:11, 17-20).

Christ therefore prayed for all those who were to believe in Him in all truth, without any distinction of *time or place.* They were to believe in Him through the teaching of those same Apostles who were taught "all truth," even if the Faithful were to belong to all ages and to all nations.

Hence, they must observe all things "whatsoever" Christ commanded to the Apostles—*visibly,* when He taught them Himself and *invisibly* through the sending of the Holy Ghost. This is the Gospel of Jesus Christ, besides which there is no other. All Truth, therefore, has been proclaimed by the Apostles because, according to the promise of Christ, they were to be taught all truth. "He (the Holy Ghost) will teach you all truth." (*John* 16:13). That the Apostles taught "all truth" to the world is evident from the commission Christ gave them after His Resurrection to "go and teach all nations." The Apostles, faithful to the command of the Master, preached everywhere. *"Their sound hath gone forth into all the earth, and their words unto the ends of the whole world."* (*Ps.* 18; *Rom.* 10:18).

All those who change, mutilate or add to the Gospel incur the anathema of the Apostle: "But though we, or an angel from heaven, preach a gospel to you besides that which we have preached to you, let him be anathema [excommunicated]. As we said before, so now I say again: If any one preach to you a gospel, besides that which you have received, let him be anathema." (*Gal.* 1:8-9).

Catholic Revelation, therefore, came to an end at the death of the Apostles. Whoever expects an increase of this Revelation places himself outside the pale of the Church of Christ.

4

The Catholic Church Has Always Considered Revelation, Both in Doctrine and in Practice, as Closed Forever.

The essential doctrine of the true Church must be unchangeable, because truth is unchangeable. The Church has always believed that what is new is heresy and not the Faith of Christ.

While novelty and mutability have always been the two characteristic notes of every heresy, the substantial doctrine of the Catholic Church has been the same in every century, both in *theory* and in *practice.*

I. *In Theory:* St. Vincent of Lerin says, "In almost every heresy it is always correct and lawful to introduce profane novelties, reject old doctrines, and by giving a false name to science, wreck the Faith. On the contrary, it is proper for Catholics to keep the Deposit of Faith and the directions of the ancients and to condemn profane novelties."[5]

Hence the injunction of Pope Stephen I (254-257) in the Third Century: *"Nothing must be introduced but what has been delivered."* This is also what St. Augustine expresses in other words: "Antiquity is retained, novelty repudiated."

Since these two famous "dicta" were first laid down, they have always been quoted in the proving of "Apostolicity," or antiquity from the time of the Apostles, as a necessary Mark of the True Church. It is for this reason that Clement of Alexandria says that the "Apostolic Faith" and the "Faith of the Church"[6] mean the same thing. And Irenæus: "Through nobody else we knew what we must do for our salvation than through those by whom the Gospel came to us."[7] "Neither he who may say much about the Faith should amplify, nor he who does not know much should diminish it."[8] For this reason, everywhere and in every century there prevailed the principle laid down in a certain Epistle—n. 19—attributed by some to St. Barnabas, companion of St. Paul, but probably writ-

5. *Commonit.,* C. XXIV.
6. *In Strom., VII,* p. 763.
7. Iren. III, 1.
8. Iren. I. 10, N. 2.

ten by some other Christian at the end of the First or at the beginning of the Second Century: "The Rule of light is this: keep what thou hast received, neither adding to nor subtracting from it."

Hence, St. Basil of Cappadocia enjoins "those who believe in Christ, not to be so curious as to inquire about what does not belong to the old Faith."[9] St. Jerome interpreting the words: "The Lord shall tell in His writings of peoples, and of princes, of them that have been in her," writes: *"Of them that have been,* not of them *that are in her,* in order to show that, with the exception of the Apostles, whatever may be said afterwards, is of no authority. For, no matter how holy and learned a Saint may be, after the death of the Apostles, he has no authority."[10]

What Vincent of Lerin wrote and proclaimed 1,500 years ago may be said in very truth of our own days: "I cannot understand why many men like to follow so many errors. They are not satisfied with the rule which was once delivered and accepted from antiquity; they rather look every day for new things and always try to add, change, detract from religion, as if the heavenly dogma which was once revealed is not good enough."[11]

Therefore, as the rule of the Church is always to believe only what was delivered from the Apostles, without diminution, corruption or addition, the expectation of new Revelations to be believed by all is nothing but a dream.

II. *In Practice:* What the Church believed in theory she also *practiced,* in the way of expressing herself, as well as in her actions.

Whenever the Church defined a doctrine to belong to the Deposit of Faith, she always proclaimed that doctrine,

9. *Basil,* Ep. 175.
10. Jerome in *Ps.* 86.
11. *Commonit.,* C. XXVI.

not as a new Catholic revelation, nor as a new doctrine, but as coming to us from the Apostles, because contained either in Scripture or in Tradition. Thus, Athanasius, speaking of the Nicene Council, testifies: "When they (the Fathers of the Council) defined anything about the Faith, they never said, *'It is herewith decreed,'* but, *'So believes the Catholic Church,'* in order to make manifest that their sentence is not recent, but Apostolic."[12]

In the same way, the Fathers of the Council of Trent expressed themselves in the Fourth Session.

It was thus also that Pope Pius IX solemnly defined the doctrine of Mary's Immaculate Conception: "The Divine (Scriptural) statements, the venerable Tradition, the perpetual understanding of the Church, the sentiment of the bishops and of the Faithful," as he says, induced him to declare that "the doctrine, which declares [that] Mary, the Mother of God, was in the first instant of her Conception . . . preserved immune from Original Sin, *is revealed by God* and consequently to be constantly and firmly believed by all."[13]

Hence, the *History of Definitions* and the Acts of all the Councils of the Church teach us that whenever there was a question about an article of Faith to be believed by all, it was always asked "whether or not was such a doctrine contained in the Scriptures or in the Apostolic Tradition."

The Church never expected a new Revelation to be believed by all, nor does she expect any in the future.

Certain revelations, supposed to have taken place in the past, or expected to take place in the future, are only fraud or fanaticism.

---

12. Athanas., *De Syn.*, N. 6.
13. *Bulla Dogm., Pii Papae IX.*

5

The Deposit of Faith is Greater and More Complete the Closer It Is to the Plenitude of Time, That Is, to Christ.

Faith was always necessary to salvation—in the beginning, today and to the end. It consists in a belief in God and in the Redemption of Christ. This is the *substance of Faith,* without which the Church never did nor could exist. The Church, in a sense, did not begin with Christ nor with Moses. It began with the solemn and consoling words of God to Adam and Eve after their Fall: "I will put enmities between thee (the serpent) and the woman (Mary, the Mother of the Redeemer), and thy seed (the enemies of God and of Christ's Church) and her seed (Christ and all those who will believe in Him): she shall crush thy head (*i.e.,* on account of Christ's merits, Mary will break the scepter of the dominion of the devil; she will be Immaculate), and thou shalt lie in wait for her heel (thou, O devil, shalt be defeated by her). (*Gen.* 3:15). Since that fatal day, belief in a future Redeemer became necessary for the fallen race of Adam and Eve, "For there is no other name (Jesus) under heaven given to men, whereby we must be saved." (*Acts.* 4:12). "This is eternal life: That they may know thee, the only true God, and Jesus Christ, whom thou hast sent." (*John* 17:3).

However, this faith made known through Revelation in the institutions and the "sacraments" *before* Christ is not of the same import as the faith manifested in the institutions and the Sacraments *after* the coming of the Redeemer.

The former were only the shadow, the preparation, the promise; the latter are the reality, the completion, the fulfillment. Hence, the two separate Dispensations: the Old and the New Law. The central point of both is Christ. The Old Law believed in a future Redeemer—in a reconciliation to come through Christ. The New Law believes in such a reconciliation as already accomplished. Still, the Ancient Law, running from Adam to Christ, is characterized by what we call the Natural Law. It embraced all the peoples of the earth before the coming of Christ, with the exception of the Israelite Nation, whom God selected to Himself and to whom He gave written laws through Moses and the Prophets. Hence, the Old Law or Economy is further distinguished as the Patriarchal and the Mosaic Economies.

To a certain degree we may say that the Patriarchal Economy, or the Natural Law, is still in existence in our own days. Innumerable tribes of human beings have not yet been evangelized.* Many of them have not yet even heard the name of Christ. All these people have scarcely any vestige left of the Patriarchal Revelations, but they have the moral law written in their hearts. Strictly speaking, however, the Patriarchal Law came to an end with the Revelation of God to Moses, who gathered together the children of Israel, wrote all Patriarchal Revelations from Adam down to Abraham, Isaac and Jacob, and all those truths which God revealed to him, entering with him and with his people into a certain pact, which we call the Mosaic Economy or Dispensation, or as it is more commonly called, the Old Testament. This Testament, however, comprises not only the truths which God revealed to Moses, but also the revelations and the prophecies of messengers

---

* This was still true at the publication of the First Edition of this Book in 1928. But with the improved transportation and communications of our times, especially since World War II (ended 1945), most of the peoples of the world have been reached with the message of Christ's Gospel. —*Publisher,* 2005.

whom God from time to time sent to His people Israel. They regard [i.e., comprise] the doctrine on God and the moral law, which is a development of the Patriarchal Revelations and the prophecies, as morally following and supplementing one another. They all had reference to the future Messias, in whom they found their fulfillment. From this, the following consequences are evident.

I. The Deposit of Revelation was greater in the Written Law, that is, in the Old Testament, than in the Patriarchal Economy, for more truths on moral law were proclaimed; more direct understanding of God became known; more prophecies about Christ and His Church were announced. Such truths, knowledge and prophecies are all new revelations which could not be known without God's special intervention. They are all the word of God, which continually, successively and objectively increased the Deposit of Revelation.

Besides the sublime manner in which God spoke to Moses "mouth to mouth," (*Num.* 12:8), the Jews distinguish four grades through which God may speak to His creatures. The first is by *Prophecy,* joined with some vision; the second is by the *Holy Spirit,* through a divine internal inspiration; the third is by Urim and Tummim, namely, by *showing and believing,* through which God used to reveal Himself to the priests; the fourth is by *"the daughter of the Voice,"* which is a certain indirect revelation granted to some learned and pious souls after the time of Malachias [c. 420 B.C, the last Old Testament prophet before Christ] during the Second Temple.

This shows that the Jews did not deny a certain continuation of supernatural revelation, even during the time of the Second Temple, that is, from the last of the Prophets [Malachias, c. 420 B.C.] to the time of Christ.

II. The increase of Revelation made by God Himself

from time to time came to an end and reached, so to speak, its culminating point with the announcement by Christ Himself of the Mystery of the Most Holy Trinity. Hence, if we compare the three Laws, or Economies, with one another, viz., the Patriarchal, the Mosaic and the Christian, we cannot fail to see, *first of all,* that the closer they are to Christ, the more complete and the more excellent they are. For this reason, the Mosaic is more complete and more excellent than the Patriarchal, as the Christian is more complete and more excellent than the Mosaic Economy. "Our Faith," says St. Thomas, "consists principally in two things: first, in the knowledge of God . . . secondly, in the mystery of the Incarnation. . . . If, therefore, we speak of prophecy, inasmuch, as it has reference to the faith of the Deity, it increased according to the three distinctions of time, viz., before the Law [Patriarchal Dispensation], under the Law [Old Testament], and under Grace [New Testament]. For before the Law, Abraham and other Fathers were instructed prophetically about those things which belong to the faith of the Deity. Hence, they are also called prophets. (*Ps.* 4:15). . . . Under the Law, prophetic Revelation was made of those things which belong to the faith of the Deity more excellently than before, because it was then necessary to institute about it, not only special persons or certain families, but the whole people. (*Ex.* 6:2). . . . Lastly, however, in the time of Grace, the mystery of the Trinity was revealed by Christ Himself."[14]

In the *second place,* comparing the status of the three Dispensations with one another—but not the persons to whom Revelation was made—we must conclude that the first Revelation made in *each* Dispensation is more excellent than any other subsequent revelation made *in the*

14. *St. Thomas,* II-II*ae*, Q. 174, A. 6.

same Dispensation. "Thus," the Angelic Doctor continues, *"in each state* the first Revelation was more excellent. The first Revelation *before* the Law [Patriarchal Dispensation] was made to Abraham (the same may be said of Adam, for St. Thomas here considers the human race as renewed after the Deluge); to Isaac, however, was made an inferior Revelation, because founded on the revelation made to Abraham; hence God said, 'I am the God of Abraham thy father' (*Gen.* 26:24); likewise, God said to Jacob, 'I am the Lord God of Abraham thy father, and the God of Isaac.' (*Gen.* 28:12). Likewise, in the state of Law [Old Testament], the first Revelation—made to Moses—was more excellent, because every Revelation of the Prophets is founded on it. So it is also in the time of Grace [New Testament], that the whole faith of the Church is founded upon the Revelation made to the Apostles, that is, the faith of the Unity and Trinity of God. With regard to the faith in the Incarnation of Christ, it is evident that those who were nearer to Christ, either before or after, were generally more fully informed: more fully after than before, according to the Apostle, 'As you reading, may understand my knowledge in the mystery of Christ, which in other generations was not known to the sons of men as it is now revealed to his holy apostles and prophets in the spirit.'" (*Eph.* 3:4-5). See St. Thomas.[15]

The Revelation made to the Apostles by Christ and the Holy Ghost is the completion of all previous Revelation, the fulfillment of the Prophecies, the plenitude of time. It is the New Testament, which is equally near to Christ today as it was in the time of the Apostles: "Behold I am with you all days, even to the consummation of the world." (*Matt.* 28:20).

---

15. *St. Thomas,* II-II*ae*, Q. 174, A. 6.

Analytical Index

(The First number refers to the Chapter; the Second to the Article)

D

E

The 33 Doctors of the Church

1. St. Athanasius c. 297-373
   The Father of Orthodoxy
2. St. Ephrem c. 306-c. 373
   Harp of the Holy Ghost
   Mary's Own Singer
   Father of Hymnody
3. St. Cyril of Jerusalem c. 315-386
   Doctor of Catechesis
4. St. Hilary of Poitiers c. 315-c. 368
   The Athanasius of the West
5. St. Gregory Nazianzen c. 329-c. 389
   The Theologian
   The Christian Demosthenes
6. St. Basil the Great c. 329-379
   Father of Eastern Monasticism
7. St. Ambrose c. 340-397
   Patron of the Veneration of Mary
8. St. Jerome c. 342-c. 420
   Father of Biblical Science
9. St. John Chrysostom c. 347-407
   The Golden-Mouthed
   Doctor of the Eucharist
10. St. Augustine 354-430
    Doctor of Grace
    Doctor of Doctors

11. St. Cyril of Alexandria c. 376-444
    Doctor of the Incarnation
    Seal of the Fathers
12. Pope St. Leo the Great c. 400-461
    Doctor of the Unity of the Church
13. St. Peter Chrysologus c. 406-c. 450
    The Golden-Worded
14. Pope St. Gregory the Great c. 540-604
    The Greatest of the Great
15. St. Isidore of Seville c. 560-636
    Schoolmaster of the Middle Ages
16. St. Bede the Venerable c. 673-735
    Father of English History
17. St. John Damascene c. 676-c. 749
    Doctor of Christian Art
    Doctor of the Assumption
18. St. Peter Damian c. 1007-1072
    Monitor of the Popes
19. St. Anselm 1033-1109
    Father of Scholasticism
    Defender of the Rights of the Church
20. St. Bernard of Clairvaux c. 1090-1153
    The Mellifluous Doctor
    Oracle of the Twelfth Century
    Thaumaturgus of the West
    Arbiter of Christendom
    The Last of the Fathers
21. St. Anthony of Padua 1195-1231
    Doctor of the Gospel
    Hammer of Heretics
    Ark of Both Covenants
22. St. Albert the Great c. 1206-1280
    (*Albertus Magnus*)
    The Universal Doctor

23. St. Bonaventure c. 1221-1274
    The Seraphic Doctor
24. St. Thomas Aquinas c. 1225-1274
    The Angelic Doctor
    The Common Doctor
25. St. Catherine of Siena 1347-1380
    The Seraphic Virgin
    Mystic of the Incarnate Word
    Mystic of the Mystical Body of Christ
26. St. Teresa of Avila 1515-1582
    Doctor of Prayer
27. St. Peter Canisius 1521-1597
    Doctor of the Catechism
28. St. Robert Bellarmine 1542-1621
    Prince of Apologists
    Gentle Doctor of *The Controversies*
29. St. John of the Cross 1542-1591
    Doctor of Mystical Theology
30. St. Lawrence of Brindisi 1559-1619
    The Apostolic Doctor
31. St. Francis de Sales 1567-1622
    The Gentleman Doctor
    Patron of the Catholic Press
    Everyman's Spiritual Director
32. St. Alphonsus Liguori 1696-1787
    Prince of Moralists
    Most Zealous Doctor
    Patron of Confessors and Moral Theologians
33. St. Therese of Lisieux 1873-1897
    Doctor of The Little Way of Spiritual Childhood
    Doctor of Merciful Love

If you have enjoyed this book, consider making your next selection from among the following . . .

Christian Perfection and Contemplation. *Garrigou-Lagrange, O.P.* 21.00
Practical Commentary on Holy Scripture. *Bishop Knecht.* (Reg. 40.00) . .30.00
The Ways of Mental Prayer. *Dom Vitalis Lehodey* 16.50
The 33 Doctors of the Church. *Fr. Christopher Rengers, O.F.M. Cap.* . . 33.00
Pope Pius VII. *Prof. Robin Anderson* 16.50
Life Everlasting. *Garrigou-Lagrange, O.P.* 16.50
Mother of the Saviour/Our Int. Life. *Garrigou-Lagrange, O.P.* 16.50
Three Ages/Int. Life. *Garrigou-Lagrange, O.P. 2 vol.* 48.00
Ven. Francisco Marto of Fatima. *Cirrincione,* comp. 2.50
Ven. Jacinta Marto of Fatima. *Cirrincione* 3.00
St. Philomena—The Wonder-Worker. *O'Sullivan* 9.00
The Facts About Luther. *Msgr. Patrick O'Hare* 18.50
Little Catechism of the Curé of Ars. *St. John Vianney.* 8.00
The Curé of Ars—Patron Saint of Parish Priests. *Fr. B. O'Brien* 7.50
Saint Teresa of Avila. *William Thomas Walsh* 24.00
Isabella of Spain: The Last Crusader. *William Thomas Walsh* 24.00
Characters of the Inquisition. *William Thomas Walsh* 16.50
Blood-Drenched Altars—Cath. Comment. on Hist. Mexico. *Kelley* 21.50
The Four Last Things—Death, Judgment, Hell, Heaven. *Fr. von Cochem* 9.00
Confession of a Roman Catholic. *Paul Whitcomb* 2.50
The Catholic Church Has the Answer. *Paul Whitcomb* 2.50
The Sinner's Guide. *Ven. Louis of Granada* .15.00
True Devotion to Mary. *St. Louis De Montfort* 9.00
Life of St. Anthony Mary Claret. *Fanchón Royer* 16.50
Autobiography of St. Anthony Mary Claret 13.00
I Wait for You. *Sr. Josefa Menendez* 1.50
Words of Love. *Menendez, Betrone, Mary of the Trinity* 8.00
Little Lives of the Great Saints. *John O'Kane Murray* 20.00
Prayer—The Key to Salvation. *Fr. Michael Müller.* 9.00
Passion of Jesus and Its Hidden Meaning. *Fr. Groenings, S.J.* 15.00
The Victories of the Martyrs. *St. Alphonsus Liguori* 13.50
Canons and Decrees of the Council of Trent. *Transl. Schroeder* 16.50
Sermons of St. Alphonsus Liguori for Every Sunday 18.50
A Catechism of Modernism. *Fr. J. B. Lemius* 7.50
Alexandrina—The Agony and the Glory. *Johnston* 7.00
Life of Blessed Margaret of Castello. *Fr. William Bonniwell* 9.00
Catechism of Mental Prayer. *Simler* 3.00
St. Francis of Paola. *Simi and Segreti* 9.00
St. Martin de Porres. *Giuliana Cavallini.* 15.00
The Story of the Church. *Johnson, Hannan, Dominica* 22.50
Hell Quizzes. *Radio Replies Press* 2.50
Purgatory Quizzes. *Radio Replies Press* 2.50
Virgin and Statue Worship Quizzes. *Radio Replies Press* 2.50
Meditation Prayer on Mary Immaculate. *Padre Pio* 2.50
Little Book of the Work of Infinite Love. *de la Touche* 3.50
Textual Concordance of The Holy Scriptures. *Williams. pb.* 35.00
Which Bible Should You Read? *Thomas A. Nelson* 4.00
The Way of Divine Love. *Sister Josefa Menendez* 21.00
The Way of Divine Love. (pocket, unabr.). *Menendez* 12.50
Mystical City of God—Abridged. *Ven. Mary of Agreda* 21.00

Prices subject to change.

Visits to the Blessed Sacrament. *St. Alphonsus* 5.00
Moments Divine—Before the Blessed Sacrament. *Reuter* 10.00
Miraculous Images of Our Lady. *Cruz* 21.50
Miraculous Images of Our Lord. *Cruz* 16.50
Saints Who Raised the Dead. *Fr. Hebert* 18.50
Love and Service of God, Infinite Love. *Mother Louise Margaret* 15.00
Life and Work of Mother Louise Margaret. *Fr. O'Connell* 15.00
Autobiography of St. Margaret Mary. 7.50
Thoughts and Sayings of St. Margaret Mary 6.00
The Voice of the Saints. *Comp. by Francis Johnston* 8.00
The 12 Steps to Holiness and Salvation. *St. Alphonsus* 9.00
The Rosary and the Crisis of Faith. *Cirrincione & Nelson* 2.00
Sin and Its Consequences. *Cardinal Manning* 9.00
St. Francis of Paola. *Simi & Segreti* 9.00
Dialogue of St. Catherine of Siena. *Transl. Algar Thorold* 12.50
Catholic Answer to Jehovah's Witnesses. *D'Angelo* 13.50
Twelve Promises of the Sacred Heart. (100 cards) 5.00
Life of St. Aloysius Gonzaga. *Fr. Meschler* .13.00
The Love of Mary. *D. Roberto* 9.00
Begone Satan. *Fr. Vogl* 4.00
The Prophets and Our Times. *Fr. R. G. Culleton* 15.00
St. Therese, The Little Flower. *John Beevers* 7.50
St. Joseph of Copertino. *Fr. Angelo Pastrovicchi* 8.00
Mary, The Second Eve. *Cardinal Newman* 4.00
Devotion to Infant Jesus of Prague. *Booklet* 1.50
Reign of Christ the King in Public & Private Life. *Davies* 2.00
The Wonder of Guadalupe. *Francis Johnston* 9.00
Apologetics. *Msgr. Paul Glenn* 12.50
Baltimore Catechism No. 1 . . . . 5.00
Baltimore Catechism No. 2 . . . . 7.00
Baltimore Catechism No. 3 . . . . .11.00
An Explanation of the Baltimore Catechism. *Fr. Kinkead* 18.00
Bethlehem. *Fr. Faber* 20.00
Bible History. *Schuster* 16.50
Blessed Eucharist. *Fr. Mueller* 10.00
Catholic Catechism. *Fr. Faerber* 9.00
The Devil. *Fr. Delaporte* 8.50
Dogmatic Theology for the Laity. *Fr. Premm* .21.50
Evidence of Satan in the Modern World. *Cristiani* 14.00
Fifteen Promises of Mary. (100 cards) 5.00
Life of Anne Catherine Emmerich. 2 vols. *Schmoeger.* (Reg. 48.00) 40.00
Life of the Blessed Virgin Mary. *Emmerich* 18.00
Manual of Practical Devotion to St. Joseph. *Patrignani* 17.50
Prayer to St. Michael. (100 leaflets) 5.00
Prayerbook of Favorite Litanies. *Fr. Hebert* .12.50
Preparation for Death. (Abridged). *St. Alphonsus* 12.00
Purgatory. (From *All for Jesus*). *Fr. Faber* 6.00
Bible History. *Johnson, Hannan, Dominica* 24.00
Fundamentals of Catholic Dogma. *Ludwig Ott* 27.50
Spiritual Conferences. *Faber* 18.00
Trustful Surrender to Divine Providence. *Bl. Claude* 7.00
Wife, Mother and Mystic. *Bessieres* 10.00
The Agony of Jesus. *Padre Pio* 3.00

Prices subject to change.

Seven Capital Sins. *Benedictine Sisters* 3.00
Confession—Its Fruitful Practice. *Ben. Srs.* 3.00
Sermons of the Curé of Ars. *Vianney* 15.00
St. Antony of the Desert. *St. Athanasius* 7.00
Is It a Saint's Name? *Fr. William Dunne* 3.00
St. Pius V—His Life, Times, Miracles. *Anderson* 7.00
Who Is Therese Neumann? *Fr. Charles Carty.* 3.50
Martyrs of the Coliseum. *Fr. O'Reilly.* 21.00
Way of the Cross. *St. Alphonsus Liguori* 1.50
Way of the Cross. *Franciscan version* 1.50
How Christ Said the First Mass. *Fr. Meagher* 21.00
Too Busy for God? Think Again! *D'Angelo* 7.00
St. Bernadette Soubirous. *Trochu* 21.00
Pope Pius VII. *Anderson* 16.50
Treatise on the Love of God. 1 Vol. *de Sales. Mackey, Trans.* 27.50
Confession Quizzes. *Radio Replies Press* 2.50
St. Philip Neri. *Fr. V. J. Matthews.* 7.50
St. Louise de Marillac. *Sr. Vincent Regnault* 7.50
The Old World and America. *Rev. Philip Furlong* 21.00
Prophecy for Today. *Edward Connor* 7.50
The Book of Infinite Love. *Mother de la Touche* 7.50
Chats with Converts. *Fr. M. D. Forrest.* .13.50
The Church Teaches. *Church Documents* .18.00
Conversation with Christ. *Peter T. Rohrbach* 12.50
Purgatory and Heaven. *J. P. Arendzen* 6.00
Liberalism Is a Sin. *Sarda y Salvany* 9.00
Spiritual Legacy of Sr. Mary of the Trinity. *van den Broek* 13.00
The Creator and the Creature. *Fr. Frederick Faber* 17.50
Radio Replies. 3 Vols. *Frs. Rumble and Carty* 48.00
Convert's Catechism of Catholic Doctrine. *Fr. Geiermann* 5.00
Incarnation, Birth, Infancy of Jesus Christ. *St. Alphonsus* 13.50
Light and Peace. *Fr. R. P. Quadrupani* 8.00
Dogmatic Canons & Decrees of Trent, Vat. I. *Documents* 11.00
The Evolution Hoax Exposed. *A. N. Field* 9.00
The Primitive Church. *Fr. D. I. Lanslots.* 12.50
The Priest, the Man of God. *St. Joseph Cafasso* 16.00
Blessed Sacrament. *Fr. Frederick Faber* .20.00
Christ Denied. *Fr. Paul Wickens* 3.50
New Regulations on Indulgences. *Fr. Winfrid Herbst* 3.00
A Tour of the Summa. *Msgr. Paul Glenn* .22.50
Latin Grammar. *Scanlon and Scanlon* 18.00
A Brief Life of Christ. *Fr. Rumble* 3.50
Marriage Quizzes. *Radio Replies Press* 2.50
True Church Quizzes. *Radio Replies Press* 2.50
The Secret of the Rosary. *St. Louis De Montfort* 5.00
Mary, Mother of the Church. *Church Documents* 5.00
The Sacred Heart and the Priesthood. *de la Touche* 10.00
Revelations of St. Bridget. *St. Bridget of Sweden* 4.50
Magnificent Prayers. *St. Bridget of Sweden* 2.00
The Happiness of Heaven. *Fr. J. Boudreau* 10.00
St. Catherine Labouré of the Miraculous Medal. *Dirvin* 16.50
The Glories of Mary. *St. Alphonsus Liguori* 21.00
Three Conversions/Spiritual Life. *Garrigou-Lagrange, O.P.* 7.00

Prices subject to change.

Spiritual Life. *Fr. Adolphe Tanquerey* . . . 32.50
Freemasonry: Mankind's Hidden Enemy. *Bro. C. Madden* . . . 8.00
Fourteen Holy Helpers. *Hammer* . . . 7.50
All About the Angels. *Fr. Paul O'Sullivan* . . . 7.50
AA-1025: Memoirs of an Anti-Apostle. *Marie Carré.* . . . 7.50
All for Jesus. *Fr. Frederick Faber.* . . . 16.50
Growth in Holiness. *Fr. Frederick Faber.* . . . 18.00
Behind the Lodge Door. *Paul Fisher.* . . . 21.00
Chief Truths of the Faith. (Book I). *Fr. John Laux* . . . 12.50
Mass and the Sacraments. (Book II). *Fr. John Laux* . . . 12.50
Catholic Morality. (Book III). *Fr. John Laux.* . . . 12.50
Catholic Apologetics. (Book IV). *Fr. John Laux* . . . 12.50
Introduction to the Bible. *Fr. John Laux* . . . 18.00
Church History. *Fr. John Laux* . . . 27.50
Devotion for the Dying. *Mother Mary Potter* . . . 12.00
Devotion to the Sacred Heart. *Fr. Jean Croiset* . . . 16.50
An Easy Way to Become a Saint. *Fr. Paul O'Sullivan* . . . 7.00
The Golden Arrow. *Sr. Mary of St. Peter.* . . . 15.00
The Holy Man of Tours. *Dorothy Scallan* . . . 15.00
Hell—Plus How to Avoid Hell. *Fr. Schouppe/Nelson* . . . 15.00
History of Protestant Ref. in England & Ireland. *Cobbett* . . . 21.00
Holy Will of God. *Fr. Leo Pyzalski* . . . 7.50
How Christ Changed the World. *Msgr. Luigi Civardi* . . . 9.00
How to Be Happy, How to Be Holy. *Fr. Paul O'Sullivan* . . . 9.00
Imitation of Christ. *Thomas à Kempis. (Challoner transl.)* . . . 15.00
Life & Message of Sr. Mary of the Trinity. *Rev. Dubois* . . . 12.00
Life Everlasting. *Fr. Garrigou-Lagrange, O.P.* . . . 16.50
Life of Mary as Seen by the Mystics. *Compiled by Raphael Brown* . . . 15.00
Life of St. Dominic. *Mother Augusta Drane* . . . 15.00
Life of St. Francis of Assisi. *St. Bonaventure* . . . 12.50
Life of St. Ignatius Loyola. *Fr. Genelli* . . . 18.50
Life of St. Margaret Mary Alacoque. *Rt. Rev. Emile Bougaud* . . . 15.00
Mexican Martyrdom. *Fr. Wilfrid Parsons* . . . 12.50
Children of Fatima. *Windeatt.* (Age 10 & up) . . . 11.00
Cure of Ars. *Windeatt.* (Age 10 & up) . . . 13.00
The Little Flower. *Windeatt.* (Age 10 & up) . . . 11.00
Patron of First Communicants. (Bl. Imelda). *Windeatt.* (Age 10 & up) . . . 8.00
Miraculous Medal. *Windeatt.* (Age 10 & up) . . . 9.00
St. Louis De Montfort. *Windeatt.* (Age 10 & up) . . . 13.00
St. Thomas Aquinas. *Windeatt.* (Age 10 & up) . . . 8.00
St. Catherine of Siena. *Windeatt.* (Age 10 & up) . . . 7.00
St. Rose of Lima. *Windeatt.* (Age 10 & up) . . . 10.00
St. Hyacinth of Poland. *Windeatt.* (Age 10 & up) . . . 13.00
St. Martin de Porres. *Windeatt.* (Age 10 & up) . . . 10.00
Pauline Jaricot. *Windeatt.* (Age 10 & up) . . . 15.00
Douay-Rheims New Testament. *Paperbound* . . . 16.50
Prayers and Heavenly Promises. *Compiled by Joan Carroll Cruz* . . . 6.00
Preparation for Death. (Unabr., pocket). *St. Alphonsus* . . . 13.50
Rebuilding a Lost Faith. *John Stoddard* . . . 16.50
The Spiritual Combat. *Dom Lorenzo Scupoli* . . . 12.00
Retreat Companion for Priests. *Fr. Francis Havey* . . . 9.00
Spiritual Doctrine of St. Cath. of Genoa. *Marabotto/St. Catherine* . . . 12.50
The Soul of the Apostolate. *Dom Chautard* . . . 12.50

Prices subject to change.

St. Margaret Clitherow—"The Pearl of York." *Monro* 6.00
St. Vincent Ferrer. *Fr. Pradel, O.P.* 9.00
The Life of Father De Smet. *Fr. Laveille, S.J.* 18.00
Glories of Divine Grace. *Fr. Matthias Scheeben* 18.00
Holy Eucharist—Our All. *Fr. Lukas Etlin* 3.00
Hail Holy Queen (from *Glories of Mary*). *St. Alphonsus* 9.00
Novena of Holy Communions. *Lovasik* 2.50
Brief Catechism for Adults. *Cogan* 12.50
The Cath. Religion—Illus./Expl. for Child, Adult, Convert. *Burbach* . . .12.50
Eucharistic Miracles. *Joan Carroll Cruz* .16.50
The Incorruptibles. *Joan Carroll Cruz* 16.50
Secular Saints: 250 Lay Men, Women & Children. PB. *Cruz*. 35.00
Pope St. Pius X. *F. A. Forbes* 11.00
St. Alphonsus Liguori. *Frs. Miller and Aubin* 18.00
Self-Abandonment to Divine Providence. *Fr. de Caussade, S.J.* 22.50
The Song of Songs—A Mystical Exposition. *Fr. Arintero, O.P.* 21.50
Prophecy for Today. *Edward Connor* 7.50
Saint Michael and the Angels. *Approved Sources* 9.00
Dolorous Passion of Our Lord. *Anne C. Emmerich* 18.00
Modern Saints—Their Lives & Faces, Book I. *Ann Ball* 21.00
Modern Saints—Their Lives & Faces, Book II. *Ann Ball* 23.00
Our Lady of Fatima's Peace Plan from Heaven. *Booklet* 1.00
Divine Favors Granted to St. Joseph. *Père Binet* 7.50
St. Joseph Cafasso—Priest of the Gallows. *St. John Bosco* 6.00
Catechism of the Council of Trent. *McHugh/Callan* 27.50
The Foot of the Cross. *Fr. Faber*. 18.00
The Rosary in Action. *John Johnson* 12.00
Padre Pio—The Stigmatist. *Fr. Charles Carty* 16.50
Why Squander Illness? *Frs. Rumble & Carty* 4.00
Fatima—The Great Sign. *Francis Johnston* 12.00
Heliotropium—Conformity of Human Will to Divine. *Drexelius* 15.00
Charity for the Suffering Souls. *Fr. John Nageleisen* 18.00
Devotion to the Sacred Heart of Jesus. *Verheylezoon* 16.50
Who Is Padre Pio? *Radio Replies Press* 3.00
The Stigmata and Modern Science. *Fr. Charles Carty* 2.50
St. Anthony—The Wonder Worker of Padua. *Stoddard* 7.00
The Precious Blood. *Fr. Faber* 16.50
The Holy Shroud & Four Visions. *Fr. O'Connell* 3.50
Clean Love in Courtship. *Fr. Lawrence Lovasik* 4.50
The Secret of the Rosary. *St. Louis De Montfort* 5.00
The History of Antichrist. *Rev. P. Huchede* 4.00
Where We Got the Bible. *Fr. Henry Graham* 8.00
Hidden Treasure—Holy Mass. *St. Leonard* 7.50
Imitation of the Sacred Heart of Jesus. *Fr. Arnoudt* 18.50
The Life & Glories of St. Joseph. *Edward Thompson* 16.50
Père Lamy. *Biver*. 15.00
Humility of Heart. *Fr. Cajetan da Bergamo* 9.00
The Curé D'Ars. *Abbé Francis Trochu* 24.00
Love, Peace and Joy. (St. Gertrude). *Prévot* 8.00

At your Bookdealer or direct from the Publisher.

Toll-Free 1-800-437-5876 ***Fax 815-226-7770***
Tel. 815-226-7777 ***www.tanbooks.com***

Prices subject to change.